EDITOR & PUBLISHER: VEFA ALEXIADOU, ATHENS
RECIPES, PREPARATION & STYLING: VEFA & ALEXIA ALEXIADOU
ENGLISH LANGUAGE EDITOR: LINDA MAKRIS, ATHENS
INTRODUCTIONS: LINDA MAKRIS, ATHENS
ART DIRECTOR: KOSTIS KOLIOS
            MARY MOURTIKA
PHOTOGRAPHER: GEORGE DRAKOPOULOS, ATHENS
STYLIST: MAKIS GEORGIADIS, ATHENS
TYPESETTING: COM•AD, ATHENS
COLOR SEPARATION & MONTAGE: ADAM HELLENIC
                        REPRODUCTION ABEE, ATHENS
PRINTING: PERGAMOS SAIC, ATHENS
BINDING: KOSTAS PAPADAKIS, ATHENS

ISBN 960-90137-3-2 COPYRIGHT © 2001 VEFA ALEXIADOU
LEONIDOU 4, METAMORPHOSIS, ATHENS, TEL. +301 2848086

VEFA ALEXIADOU

This book is dedicated with gratitude to all those in Greece and elsewhere who inspired me not only to create the dishes herein but also to preserve the ancient canons of a wholesome diet which govern the quality of life.

sunny
mediterranean
cuisine

VEGETARIAN & SEAFOOD RECIPES

The Author

Vefa Alexiadou, a gifted cook from Volos, is the leading culinary authority in Greece today. With a degree in chemistry from the Aristotle University in Thessaloniki, she combined her culinary talents with scientific principles to modernize Greek cooking without sacrificing authentic character and flavor of the traditional cuisine. During her frequent trips and extended studies abroad, she furthered her knowledge of culinary arts, food styling, table decoration, nutrition and dietetics.

In 1980 Mrs. Alexiadou self-published "Invitation to Diner," fulfilling a life-long dream of creating a "user-friendly" cookbook. An immediate success, it firmly established Vefa Alexiadou Editions in the competitive world of cookbook publishing. After three more cookbooks in the "invitation" series, she revitalized interest in traditional Greek cookery for a whole new generation of urban cooks with her 2-volume premier work, "Greek Cuisine" and "Greek Pastries and Desserts," published in 1989-91 in both Greek and English. To date she has published a total of 11 cookbooks, of which three are available in English. During the past 5 years 3 titles at least, have appeared monthly on the Greek best sellers list. Also her books "Greek Cuisine" and "Greek Pastries and Desserts" as reported in the Hellenic Literature Society's Newsletter, "Greece in Print," are listed as best sellers among Greeks of the Diaspora in 36 countries.

Since 1990 she has appeared daily on Greek Antenna TV's most popular morning coffee show (viewed via satellite in North America, Europe and Australia) where she continues to pass the Greek food traditions to hundreds of thousands of households, making her the First Lady of Greek Cuisine. By popular request from Greek readers and viewers eager to acquire her books and products and utensils mentioned in them, she conceived in 1994 the idea of "Vefa's House" franchise which counts today 20 stores around Greece.

In 1995, her recipes began appearing in Greece's top-circulating family magazine, "7 Days TV". With its publisher, Liberis Publications, she and her daughter Alexia wrote and edited a series of recipe booklets "20 Best Recipes for..." which won the 1998 Diplome d' Honneur at the Perigueux World Cookbook Fair as the most successful commercial cookbook series.

Mrs. Alexiadou has served on the Board of Archestratos: the Center for the Preservation & Advancement of Traditional Greek Gastronomy. She attended both the 1997 and 1999 "Tasting Australia" events, invited by the Australian Government as a special guest and is an active member of the International Association of the Culinary Professionals. Also a member of the Greek Publishers' Association, she is an active participant in Greek and International book fairs. Her articles and recipes frequently appear in Greek and international magazines and she travels frequently to other areas of Greece and abroad to lecture and give demonstrations on Greek gastronomical traditions. At the 2000 World Cookbook Awards in the "Salon International Livre Gourmand of Perigueux" Vefa Alexiadou won the award for the "best Mediterranean cookbook in Greek" and also the special prize for "Best Culinary Business Professional."

Married to Constantine Alexiades, Professor of Chemistry, Aristotle University, they have two married daughters, Angela and Alexia and one granddaughter. They divide their time between their home in Halkidiki and Athens, where their business activities are based.

Preface

Dear Friends and Fellow Cooks,

The Greek edition of Sunny Mediterranean Cuisine was originally meant to be utilized by Orthodox Christians who observe the age-old custom of the religious fast which excludes most animal-derived foods. However, it is above all a collection of wholesome tasty dishes from the timeless Greek and Mediterranean gastronomic tradition which has always taken into consideration the relevance of the diet to the quality of life.

In recent decades people the world over have become more and more concerned with this relationship. Recent published results of nutritional studies have confirmed that old cliche, we are, literally, what we eat! A proper diet is one of the most important factors in the improvement and maintenance of good health throughout our lives, the very key, perhaps, to longevity itself. The idea of what exactly constitutes a healthy diet has, however, been drastically altered in recent years. Fifty or sixty years ago low-fat foods containing plant fiber and protein were considered "foods of the poor". Today they are at the top of the shopping lists of a more health-conscious public.

Ingredients containing saturated fats such as margarine, butter, meat, bacon, lard, and cream which traditionally characterized Northern European cuisine are being replaced in the modern kitchen with the traditional foods of the Southern European region. The traditional gastronomic practices of the Mediterranean peoples are gaining new respect with doctors, scientists, and nutritionists who are urging the mass adoption of the principles of what has come to be known as "The Mediterranean Diet."

The recipes in this book utilize the bountiful ingredients found in the sunny Mediterranean of today. Most of the dishes are in a traditional vein while others represent either modern adaptations or completely new ways of using "old" foods. Vegans will appreciate the easy-to-prepare vegetable, legume, pasta, and soya dishes. For those who believe a healthy diet should also contain some animal-derived protein, I have included a large number of fish and seafood recipes. In an effort to make this book as user-friendly as possible, you will find at the beginning of each chapter an introduction with historical and nutritional information as well as advice for using the ingredients focused on in that section. Besides the complete index at the end of the book, you will also find a glossary, weight and temperature conversion tables.

It is my wish that this cookbook will pave the way to more wholesome and enjoyable eating for those who read it and cook from it.

Vefa Alexiadou

This landscape is as harsh as silence,

It hugs to its breast the scorching stones,

Clasps in its light the orphaned olive trees and

Vineyards. There is no water. Light.

Y. Ritsos, *Romiosini* *

In this passage, Greece's beloved poet has succeeded in distilling the very essence of the Aegean. Olive, vine, and light – elements that describe so eloquently the place where Western culture was born, are the very same that characterize the Mediterranean in a wider context. According to Greek mythology, the olive was the Goddess Athena's gift to the first inhabitants of the Eastern Mediterranean, the source of life and sustenance. The Wine God, Dionysos arrived somewhat later with the vine. The olive and the vine that came to characterize the life and civilization of the Mediterranean, together with the other foods that took root in the sparse soil, all flourished in the unrelenting light of the region. These were the source of everything that followed, the basis of a "biological experiment" that has been evolving for thousands of years. The fruits of that experiment are only now being "discovered," studied, and put into practice. The result of man's interaction with Mother Nature has only recently been given a name: The Mediterranean Diet.

Fifty years ago, the foods of the Mediterranean were viewed as the foods of poverty and deprivation. In the aftermath of World War II, the Rockefeller Foundation dispatched, in 1947, a team of scientists to the island of Crete on a fact-finding mission with a view to improve the life of the inhabitants who had suffered so grievously during the German occupation. To their amazement, the Cretans proved to be infinitely healthier and longer-living than the average citizen of the USA! For Americans brought up on bacon and eggs for breakfast, meat at nearly every meal, liberally buttered white bread, all washed down with tall glasses of rich whole milk, their initial findings must have come as a shock. How could these "under-developed" islanders who survived on beans, barley rusks, wild greens, snails, olive oil, and red wine not only have fought off the German invaders longer than any European army, but also exhibit so little of the disease and mortality that increasingly plagued the more "developed" societies of the West?

It took the researchers 10 years to overcome their shock. But when they did, they decided to learn more about the source of the vitality of that mountainous island. Thus, a study that compared the eating habits of the men living in 7 countries – Holland, Finland, Yugoslavia, the US, Japan, Italy, and Greece was carried out during the late 50's and early 60's. The results, which confirmed that the Cretans did indeed live longer and healthier than any other group (besides the Japanese), actually gave rise to more questions than answers. One area that puzzled them was the fact that Cretans consumed from 10-15% more fat than the 30% "recommended allowance." Initial interest was focused on fat consumption - i.e. animal-derived saturated fats as opposed to unsaturated fats in olive oil. Clinical studies have shown that

THE ELEMENTAL MEDITERRANEAN: OLIVE, VINE AND LIGHT

by Linda Makris

olive oil's high mono-unsaturated (72%) oleic acid (omega-9) and 8% linoleic acid (omega-6) content has a positive effect on the cardiovascular system. Some researchers now believe that the poly-unsaturated fats in seed oils (olives are fruits) are too easily metabolized, giving rise to too many toxic free-radicals in the blood, a good reason to prefer olive oil over other oils. Perhaps this explains why women in Spain, Italy, and Greece have the lowest rates of breast cancer in Europe.

In the ensuing decades, comparative studies began to include other areas in the Mediterranean such as France, where large quantities of goose-liver pate, butter, and cream are consumed, people were still living long and healthy lives. Attention began to be focused on other elements of the diet such as the popularity of red dry wines of the Mediterranean countries, consumed in moderate amounts and always accompanied by food. These findings led to the conclusion that the tannins in these wines also play a role in protecting the cardiovascular system even in the presence of saturated fats. Research is presently focused on the anti-oxidant properties of the herbs of the Northern coastal region, the spices of the African coast, as well as the vitamins and trace elements contained in the fresh vegetables, pulses, dried fruits and nuts, and whole grains which make up the bulk of the Mediterranean diet. Thus, the effort to uncover Mother Nature's secrets which began over half a century ago in Crete continues into the third millenium.

The National Center for Nutrition in Athens has identified the basic features of the Mediterranean Diet as: (1) A high ratio of mono-unsaturated fat intake to saturated fat; (2) High consumption of legumes, cereals and bread, fresh vegetables and fruit. (3) Low consumption of red meat (compared to a higher intake of fish, poultry, and seafood); (4) Moderate alcohol consumption in the form of wine; (5) Moderate consumption of dairy products (including eggs). It should be pointed out that the geographical factors and climate of the region assure that a large variety of these foodstuffs are (in general) readily available the year round, and that the time and distance between producer/consumer (garden/kitchen) are at a minimum compared to that in areas outside the Mediterranean. These advantages of the Mediterranean diet are just as important as the foods themselves.

Parallel to these findings at the molecular or nutritional level, many interpretations of the term "Mediterranean diet" have arisen in recent years. Perhaps the modern usage of the word "diet" as a means of controlling calorie intake is the problem. The ancient Greek word "diet(a)" referred to the way of man's life, a philosophy which took into consideration the social nature of eating and drinking, always in close harmony with the seasonal cycle of Mediterranean life. Herein lies the heart of the entire matter. One can make drastic changes in his diet, eating beans and seafood instead of meat, olive oil instead of butter, wine instead of beer or whiskey. But if he does not consider what he eats in relation to his life as a whole, if he is unable to see himself as part of the entire scheme

of things, all the benefits of the Mediterranean diet are for nothing! It isn't enough to "eat Mediterranean," one must live it!

One example of "the Mediterranean way" is the Greek habit of beginning any meal large or small, with the words Kali Orexi ("Good Appetite"). Likewise the French have their Bon Appetit. Most of us have failed to appreciate the wisdom of these words, perhaps because "good appetite" isn't used in English. In order for the body to get the full advantage of the nutrients, one must have an appetite for what is eaten. It is the appetite that promotes the proper hormonal conditions for the body to receive and absorb the nutrients. And the appetite is stimulated by the five senses: vision and smell are stimulated by the appearance and aroma of the food; next comes the feel of its texture in our mouths, the crunching sounds in our ears as we chew, and finally, the taste on our palates. If all our senses are positively stimulated when we eat something, then we can be said to have enjoyed it and will derive the most benefit from the food. Appetite is just one aspect of the complex manner of eating in the Mediterranean which is also enhanced by the presence of good company and pleasant conversation in a relaxed atmosphere, the merry clinking of glasses, music and dancing, etc. It is this whole-life concept which draws so many visitors from the far reaches of the earth to the shores of the Sunny Mediterranean!

The ultimate irony is, however, that even as the eating habits and life-style of the Mediterranean peoples are under scrutiny, the hi-tech food industry is making every effort to market and promote fast food, snacks, and other highly processed convenience foods which everyone agrees are "empty" calories rather than viable sources of nutrition. Children and young people who are the most vulnerable to relentless advertising campaigns for these foods and drinks, are turning away from the traditional eating patterns of their grandparents and parents. The unfortunate results are obvious in the increase of obesity, bulimia, alcoholism, etc. in today's youth. Other developments on the current food scene with which we absolutely must take exception include genetic "tinkering" with plants and animals and increased pollution of the air, soil, and waters of the Mediterranean basin (and not only) by high quantities of chemical and organic waste. To reap the full benefits of the wholesome Mediterranean diet, we must seek out organically produced ingredients, those grown (as much as possible) by traditional, sustainable agricultural techniques. And if we find them difficult to procure, we must insist that the grocers, super-markets, and restaurants in our neighborhoods make them available. We must urge local authorities to sponsor educational seminars and courses in our schools to enable adults and young people to make the right food choices for their health and well-being. Only then will the elemental wisdom that flowered in the timeless Mediterranean with the olive, vine, and light be preserved for future generations.

*Translation: Kimon Friar, *Modern Greek Poetry*, Efstathiadis, 1999

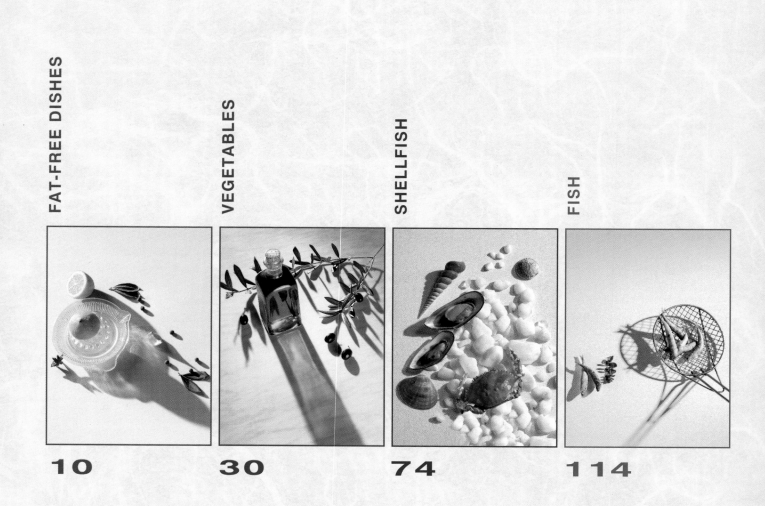

CONTENTS

*Why do you weaken your body
with luxury and the love of pleasure
and wither it?
Why do you destroy bodily vitality
with fatty greasy foods?
Fatness is weakness for the body and not
strength. That which nourishes man
is to eat as much as is needed.
Superfluous (food) not only
does not nourish, but destroys.
Therefore let us not load our body with
fat. Cut out the unnecessary,
give it (the body) whatever is necessary.
To eat as much as is needed
is nothing but nourishment,
contentment, and health.*

FAT-FREE DISHES

On Fasting, by St. John Chrysostom, Patriarch of
Constantinople, c. 400 AD
*(in "The Festive Fast", By Kokkinou & Kofinas,
Akritas P. Athens 1994)*

One of the most confusing issues of modern nutrition is that of lipids (the fats and oils) in our diet. The mysterious lingo with words like saturated fat, cholesterol, tri-glycerides, LDL's (bad fats) versus unsaturated fats, HDL's, EFA's (essential fatty acids) the omegas 3, 6, and 9 (good fats) sounds more like the final showdown in an athletic contest than a discussion of dietetics. Most people end up tuning out on the issue of fat or blaming it for every malady and disease of the modern world. The reality is, however, that fat is as necessary to life as air and water. Fat, together with glycogen (animal starch), constitutes the immediate food reserve of our cells. Without fat, we have dry skin, hormonal unbalances, nervous disorders, and even reduction or loss of brain function. Without it our bodies cannot absorb vitamins nor does our food have much taste.

The evolutionary process is what has made fat biologically necessary for it fueled the very existence of our primitive hunter-gatherer ancestors. Without it, they were doomed to death. The most important source of fat for primitive man was the meat of wild animals, and, if he lived near water, fish. Although early homo sapiens collected wild plants, fruits, and herbs (limited sources of fat), he continued to prefer meat simply because it provided more energy than any other food available before the advent of agriculture. Thus, meat and fat played a central role in prehistoric ritual as revealed in the Greek myth of Prometheus.

First recorded in Hesiod's Theogony, the story of Prometheus is thought to have explained the origin of the ancient practice of dedicating the inedible parts (bones and fat) of the sacrificial animal to the immortal deities while reserving the edible portions (meat with some fat) for mortal men. This occurred, Hesiod relates, as the result of a trick Prometheus played on the Father of Gods and Men, the great Zeus: For him (Zeus), Prometheus

Mt. Olympus, returning it to men on earth in a stalk of fennel.

Thus ritual sacrifice and the eating of meat and fat (not just fat itself, it will be noticed) was an incumbent feature of the ancient Greek religious and social system from the Homeric era onward. Individuals who refused to participate in the sacrifice and meat/fat-eating ritual were considered "misanthropes" not worthy of even citizenship in the ancient democratic system. It should not, however, be construed that the diet of the ancient Greeks consisted only of meat. On the contrary, most of the ancients led a virtual vegetarian existence for much of the year, the consumption of meat confined to the celebration following the sacrifice. Supplements of animal protein and fat were derived from small game, seafood (for those who lived near the sea), cheese, and an occasional egg from wild birds. The ancient Greeks, especially Athenians and Spartans, were known for their frugal eating habits. Meat and most fish were considered luxury items in those days.

In ancient Greece, a *diet(a)* was "a way of life" rather than a means of losing weight. The science of dietetics was "invented" by Hippocrates who believed that regulation of food intake along with digestion, exercise, climate, seasons, cooking methods, comprised a complex system by which "the balance of the humors" (i.e. good health) could be attained. Hippocrates and his followers succeeded in incorporating centuries of observation and practical experience into a unique system of dietetics and medicine. Despite their lack of knowledge of chemistry, food groups, etc., the Hippocratic writers amazingly achieved what we consider today a proper "balanced diet" containing protein (pulses, fish, cheese, very little meat), carbohydrates (grains, honey), unsaturated fats (mostly from olive oil), and minerals and vitamins (wild plants, fruits, and nuts). The Hippocratic writers, also aware of the dangers of excess, preached the Greek

FAT-FREE DISHES

put in a hide meat and the inner parts rich in fat, wrapped in the ox's stomach. For men, he arranged with cunning the white bones and wrapped them in glistening fat. Prometheus then asked Zeus to choose, knowing full well which one he would choose. With both hands, Zeus took up the white fat and when he saw the bones, he grew angry at Prometheus' cunning. As a result, tribes of men burn white bones and fat at aromatic altars. In his wrath, Zeus withheld fire from mortal men on earth. But clever Prometheus had the last word. He stole back the fire from

philosophy of "moderation in all things," a basic tenet applied to every facet of life in the ancient world. The ancient Greco-Roman system of dietetics/medicine, preserved and transmitted by Arab scholars, held sway in Europe even into the modern era.

The philosophy of "moderation" of food intake included periods of complete abstinence or fasting (the Greek *nistia*). Originally related to the necessary rationing of dwindling food supplies until new crops were harvested or other sources of food could be found, fasting was practiced as an act of religious purification in many parts of the Mediterranean Basin and the Near East. Greek participants in the Orphic and Eleusinian Mysteries fasted in remembrance of Demeter's (Goddess of Crain and Agriculture) mourning over the loss of Persephone, the period during which she caused the earth to be barren.

If the precepts of the ancient dietary tradition were already inherent in the culture of the early Christians, the Fathers of the Church sought to bring new life and spiritual meaning to the old ways. Their canons were based on the prophets of the Old Testament as well as the teachings of Christ and the Apostles. The original prohibition against eating was imposed by the Creator who forbade Adam and Eve to eat the fruit of the Tree of Knowledge. They disobeyed and were condemned to "eat the herbs of the field and toil for their daily bread." The Fathers also cited the 40 days Moses spent on Mt. Sinai without bread or water before receiving the Ten Commandments and the similar fast of Christ in the desert. The re-instatement of man (Adam) in the spiritual Garden of Eden was for Christians the ultimate reward of fasting.

In the early days of the Orthodox Church, Christians fasted for a few hours or days just prior to the Pascha or Easter. They also fasted two days of every week symbolic of mourning: Wednesday, the Day of Christ's Betrayal, and Friday, the Day of Crucifixion. As time went by, the number of fast days increased, the manner of fasting gradually changed and instead of complete abstention, the consumption/exclusion of particular foods was instituted. At first only flesh containing blood – meat and fish – was forbidden. This stricture was eventually extended to include all animal products, including cheese, milk, and eggs. It is interesting to note that the Lenten and Advent fasts occurring in early Spring and early Winter, assured the abundance of meat

complex systems of ritualistic food-behavior, however, is still actively practiced in the modern world by millions of Orthodox Christians. Throughout the nearly 2000 years that Orthodoxy has preserved the fast, modifications continue to be made. What is surprising is that there have been so few, given the length of time and difficult circumstances that Hellenism has faced throughout its history. It remains, along with the language, a unifying force among people of Greek origin the world over. The consumer-oriented way of life we carry into the 3rd millenium has become the cause of much concern not only about the foods we eat, but also for the future of mankind and life as we know it on this planet. It would be well to re-examine and imitate these sagacious traditions which have proved so effective in preserving the integrity of both human health and the environment.

The recipes in this section were originally designed to uphold the strictest rules of the modern Orthodox fast which continues to exclude all meat and dairy products for periods up to 7 weeks (i.e. the Great Lenten Fast) as well as olive oil and wine on Wednesdays and Fridays throughout the year. If this rigorous regime appears extreme to the point of being detrimental to health, we must remember that the Church Fathers wisely allow, indeed they even require the consumption of oil (and wine) on Saturdays and Sundays, even during the Great Lent. Likewise wine and oil are permitted and fish dishes consumed on any feast day that falls during Lent and on Palm Sunday. Although olive oil is restricted for strict fasting, quantities of olives are eaten regularly and small amounts of tahini or sesame oil can be substituted.

The recipes that follow have been termed "fat-free" in the sense that they can be prepared without the addition of "extra" fats or oils. It goes without saying that any lipids (fat or oil) of your choice can be utilized. But even without the addition of lipids, their tastiness

and diary products during the remainder of the year. In other words, the Church Calendar was neatly juxtaposed onto the ancient cycle of Mediterranean agricultural life, taking into account the Hippocratic system of balance and moderation.

By the time of the French Revolution, the Western Church had abandoned the age-old institution of religious fasting. Today fasting in every sense of the word is considered by most "a mere historical or culinary curiosity." The Orthodox fast, one of the most

and healthfulness is guaranteed by use of olives, avocados, tahini, garlic, vinegar, lemon juice, aromatic herbs, and spices, mustard, sun-dried tomatoes, mushrooms, etc. Frying and sauteeing is replaced by steaming or broiling. These methods, in keeping with both the canons of the Church as well as modern principles of dietetics, can be used not only for the recipes in this section but also for all others in this book. Not only do they promise viable alternatives to your daily menu, but will surely widen the horizons of your diet for more healthy, if not more interesting eating.

FAT-FREE DISHES

Broiled Sweet Prawns

Serves 5-6
Preparation time 1 hour
Cooking time 20 minutes

2 lb (1 kg) prawns
1/4 cup balsamic vinegar
1/2 cup cornstarch
salt and pepper
1/2 teaspoon powdered ginger
1/3 cup honey dissolved in
1/4 cup water
1/2 cup sesame seeds
2 tablespoons tahini
2 cloves garlic, minced
2 teaspoons grated fresh ginger
2 large onions, cubed/chopped
1 carrot, thinly sliced
1 red or green bell pepper, in small squares
14 oz (400 g) canned pineapple,
strained and cut into pieces

for the sauce
1 tablespoon cornstarch dissolved in
2 tablespoons water
2 tablespoons balsamic vinegar
1/2 cup pineapple juice
1/3 cup ketchup
1/4 cup corn syrup

Peel and devein the prawns, leaving the tails intact. Rinse, and put them in a bowl. Sprinkle with the balsamic vinegar and stir to coat. Refrigerate for 30 minutes. Combine the cornstarch, salt, powdered ginger, and pepper in a large plastic bag. Drain the prawns and shake them in the bag until well-coated with the cornstarch mixture. Empty into a colander and shake to remove the excess cornstarch. Dip each one in the dissolved honey and roll in the sesame seeds. Line a baking sheet with waxed paper and arrange the prawns on top. Refrigerate for about 30 minutes until the coating sets. Broil the prawns 6 inches (15 cm) away from the grill or broiler for about 3 minutes on each side. Combine the tahini, garlic, fresh ginger, onions, carrot, bell pepper, and pineapple in a heavy-bottomed pan and cook over medium heat for 5-6 minutes. Add salt and

pepper. Combine the ingredients for the sauce and stir into the tahini mixture. Simmer until clear and thick. Remove from the heat. Serve the prawns immediately after broiling accompanied by basmati rice and the sauce.

Pasta Salad with Spinach

Serves 4
Preparation time 30 minutes

10 oz (300 g) farfalle pasta
3 green onions, finely chopped
3 oz (100 g) spinach leaves,
coarsely chopped
3 oz (100 g) rocket leaves
3 sun-dried tomatoes
1/3 cup pine nuts
for the dressing
1 teaspoon red pepper flakes
1 clove garlic, minced
1 teaspoon oregano
1/4 cup balsamic vinegar
1 tablespoon assorted peppercorns,
coarsely crushed salt

Soak the sun-dried tomatoes in warm water several hours to plump them up. Drain, squeeze out the excess water, and chop. Stir the pine-nuts in a non-stick pan over medium heat until lightly browned. Cook the pasta in salted boiling water until tender and rinse briefly under cold water. Combine the pasta with the onions, spinach, rocket, tomatoes, and pine nuts. Turn out onto a deep serving platter. Combine the ingredients for the dressing in a well-sealed jar and shake until blended. Pour on the pasta salad and toss lightly. This salad is even more filling if you add thin slices of pickled octopus. To prepare, see recipe on page 100.

BROILED SWEET PRAWNS

Tomatoes Stuffed with Prawns

Serves 4
Preparation time 25 minutes

4 medium tomatoes
8 prawns, cooked, peeled and deveined
2 octopus tentacles, cooked as for
pickled octopus, page 100
1 large potato, cooked and cubed
8 green olives, quartered
1/4 cup finely chopped pickles
2 tablespoons capers
2 tablespoons finely chopped parsley
2 tablespoons balsamic vinegar or
2 tablespoons lemon juice

salt and freshly ground pepper
1/4 cup tahini sauce (optional)

Wash and wipe the tomatoes thoroughly. Slice off the tops and scoop out most of the pulp with a spoon, taking care not to break through the skin and spoil their shape. Sprinkle the inside lightly with salt and turn upside down on a rack to drain. Cut the larger and firmer pieces of the tomato pulp into small pieces and combine with the remaining ingredients. Slice the octopus and the prawns into bite-sized pieces and add to the tomato mixture. Stuff the tomatoes with the salad and cover with plastic wrap. Refrigerate until ready to serve. If desired, the prawn salad may be served with tahini sauce (see basic recipes).

Shrimp and Avocado Cocktail

Serves 4
Preparation time 20 minutes
Cooking time 7 minutes

2 lb (1 kg) shrimp
1 teaspoon seafood seasoning or
1 teaspoon paprika and a pinch of cayenne
1 head of lettuce
2 avocados
1/4 cup lemon juice
2 tablespoons finely chopped green onions
2 tablespoons finely chopped parsley

for the cocktail sauce
1/2 cup vegetarian cream (optional)
1/4 cup ketchup
10 drops Tabasco sauce
1/2 teaspoon chili powder
1/2 teaspoon horseradish
salt and freshly ground pepper

Peel and devein the shrimp, leaving the heads and tails intact. Cook the shrimp in salted water with the seafood seasoning or the paprika and cayenne for about 7 minutes, until they turn pink. Wash, drain, and separate the lettuce leaves. To prepare the cocktail sauce, beat the cream until slightly thickened and combine with the remaining ingredients. Alternatively, the sauce can be made omitting the cream. Peel the avocado and remove the pit. Cut into eighths and sprinkle with the lemon juice to prevent discoloration. Arrange the shrimp and the avocado slices on the lettuce leaves and serve accompanied by the cocktail sauce. Garnish with the finely chopped onion and parsley.

Shrimp Soup

Serves 4
Preparation time 35 minutes
Cooking time 8 minutes

2 lb (1 kg) shrimp
1 cup water
1 tiny hot pepper, in rings
1 small carrot, sliced
1 stalk of celery, sliced
1 teaspoon paprika
1/2 teaspoon garlic powder (optional)
salt and freshly ground pepper
1/3 cup lemon juice
2 tablespoons finely chopped parsley or dill
2-3 tablespoons finely chopped green onion

Peel the shrimp, leaving the heads and tails intact. Devein, rinse, and drain well in a colander. Put the water in a heavy-bottomed pan with the hot pepper, carrot, celery, paprika, salt, and pepper and bring to a boil. Cook 5 minutes on high heat. Add the shrimp and garlic powder (if used), cover the pan and cook on high heat for 7-8 minutes, stirring occasionally. Do not overcook or the shrimp will dry out. Remove from the heat, stir in the lemon juice, and serve the soup in deep plates sprinkled with the parsley or dill and the green onions.

Jellied Crab Salad

Serves 5
Preparation time 30 minutes

1 envelope unflavored or aspic gelatin
1 cup cold water
2½ cups chopped frozen cooked crab or shrimp
2 green onions, finely chopped
1/4 cup finely chopped celery
2 tablespoons mustard-pickle relish
2 tablespoons lemon juice
1 tablespoon finely chopped dill
1 tablespoon finely chopped onion
salt and freshly ground pepper
1/2 cup vegetarian cream, whipped (optional)

Sprinkle the gelatin on the water in a pan and stir over low heat until completely dissolved. Cool slightly. Combine the shrimp or the crab with the green onions, celery, pickle relish, lemon juice, dill, chopped onion, salt, and the pepper. Stir in the dissolved gelatin and the whipped cream (if used). Pour the

mixture into 5 small round molds and refrigerate. When the aspic has set, unmold onto tender spinach or lettuce leaves. Serve with sliced tomato and crackers.

Marinated Squid

Serves 4
Preparation time 30 minutes
Cooking time 40-60 minutes
Marinating time 12 hours

1 lb (500 g) fresh squid
2 tablespoons lemon juice
4 green onions, finely chopped
1 tablespoons finely chopped parsley
1 tablespoon finely chopped basil
1/2 cup finely chopped red pepper
1/4 cup balsamic vinegar
1 teaspoon oregano
1 bunch rocket (arugula) leaves
Bibb or curly lettuce leaves
2 tablespoons sesame oil (optional)

Prepare the squid according to the general directions on page 78. Cut into rings and cook in a small amount of water for about 40 minutes or until tender. Drain and place in a bowl with the remaining ingredients except for the rocket and lettuce. Cover and refrigerate for at least 12 hours or overnight. Serve the marinated squid on a bed of rocket and lettuce leaves. If desired, dribble sesame oil on top.

1/2 teaspoon hot pepper flakes
14 oz (400 g) fusilli pasta
2 oz (60 g) pine nuts

Prepare the avocado sauce omitting the cream and stir in the pepper flakes. Put the pine nuts in a small frying pan and stir over medium heat until lightly browned. Cook the pasta in salted water for about 8 minutes and drain. Toss the hot pasta with the pine nuts and as much avocado sauce as desired, until well-coated. Serve the dish accompanied by cucumber strips sprinkled with salt and balsamic vinegar.

Pasta Salad with Avocado Sauce

Serves 4
Preparation time 30 minutes

10 oz (300 g) tri-color fusilli pasta, cooked
1 red bell pepper, julienne
1 large carrot, julienne
2 green onions, finely chopped
1/4 cup pickle relish
1/4 cup finely chopped canned jalapeno peppers
1 cup avocado sauce (see basic recipes)

Combine the cooked pasta with the peppers, carrot, onions, pickles, and jalapenos in a salad bowl and mix well. Prepare the avocado sauce with or without the cream and pour on top or serve separately with the salad.

Fusilli with Olive Sauce

Serves 4
Preparation time 30 minutes
Cooking time 8 minutes

1 cup olive sauce (see basic recipes)
14 oz (400 g) fusilli pasta
2 oz (60 g) pine nuts
salt and freshly ground pepper

Prepare the olive sauce omitting the olive oil. Cook the pasta in boiling salted water for about 8 minutes. Meanwhile, stir the pine nuts in a small frying pan over medium heat until lightly browned. Drain the pasta and toss with the pine nuts and as much olive sauce as desired. Serve immediately on warmed plates accompanied by rocket leaves sprinkled with balsamic vinegar.

Piquant Roast Nuts

Preparation time 6 minutes

2 teaspoons Worcestershire sauce
1/4 teaspoon garlic powder
1/2 teaspoon mustard powder
1 teaspoon salt
1/4 teaspoon chili sauce
2 cups unsalted pistachios, almonds, or hazelnuts

Combine the Worcestershire sauce with the garlic powder, mustard powder, salt, and chili sauce in a bowl. Add the nuts and toss until well-coated with the mixture. Spread out in one layer on a baking sheet and roast in a 350°F (175°C) oven until dry and crisp. Remove from the oven and cool. Store in an air-tight jar.

Hot Pasta with Avocado Sauce

Serves 4
Preparation time 30 minutes
Cooking time 8 minutes

1 cup avocado sauce (see basic recipes)

PASTA SALAD WITH AVOCADO SAUCE

Avocados Stuffed with Shellfish

Serves 6
Preparation time 30 minutes
Marinating time 12 hours

8 oz (250 g) frozen shrimp, cooked
8 oz (250 g) frozen crabmeat, cooked and diced
1 clove garlic, minced
2 tablespoons lemon juice
2 tablespoons balsamic vinegar
1 teaspoon prepared mustard
salt and freshly ground pepper
3 ripe avocados
1/4 cup lemon juice
1 red bell pepper, finely chopped
1 firm tomato, finely chopped
4 green onions, finely chopped
1/4 cup stuffed green olives, sliced
1/4 cup finely chopped pickles
6 tablespoons brik (red caviar) (optional)

Combine the shrimp and crabmeat in a bowl. Combine the garlic, lemon juice, vinegar, salt, and pepper in a jar and shake until well-blended. Pour over the shellfish. Refrigerate at least 12 hours or overnight to marinate. Shortly before serving, cut the avocados in half lengthwise, and twist to separate. Carefully remove the pits, and brush with lemon juice to prevent discoloration. Slice a bit off the bottoms so they will sit without tipping. Scoop some of the pulp out with a spoon to make the indentations larger. Chop the pulp and add to the shellfish mixture along with the red pepper, chopped tomato, onions, olives and pickles. Fill the prepared avocados immediately with the mixture. Sprinkle with salt and freshly ground pepper. If desired, garnish each stuffed avocado with finely chopped fresh dill or mint and a spoonful of brik. Arrange on a platter surrounded by parboiled broccoli florets or rocket leaves and cucumber strips sprinkled with balsamic vinegar. Although no oil is used, this salad is tasty and filling.

Vegetable Soup

Serves 4
Preparation time 20 minutes
Cooking time 40 minutes

1 leek, white part only, finely chopped
1/2 cup thinly sliced celery
1/4 cup finely chopped onion
1 small clove of garlic, minced
4 cups vegetable stock
(see basic recipes) or
water and 1 vegetable bouillon cube
1/2 cup finely chopped carrot
1 cup finely diced potato
5 oz (150 g) orzo or vermicelli pasta
1 1/4 teaspoons saffron
2 tablespoons lemon juice
salt and freshly ground pepper
paprika for garnish

Cook the leek, celery, onions, and garlic in 1/2 cup of water, stirring over high heat continuously until all the liquid evaporates and the vegetables wilt. Add the vegetable stock or water and the bouillon cube. Add the carrots and the potato. Taste and adjust the seasoning, adding salt and freshly ground pepper, if needed. Cover, lower the heat, and simmer until the vegetables are tender. Stir in the orzo or pasta and simmer 8-10 minutes until tender. The soup should be thick. Remove from the heat and stir in the lemon juice. Serve immediately in deep soup plates or bowls sprinkled with a little paprika and freshly ground pepper.

Shellfish Platter

Serves 6
Preparation time 30 minutes
Cooking time 7- 10 minutes

12 prawns, peeled and deveined
12 hard shell clams
12 cockles
12 oysters or mussels
5 small cucumbers, cut into strips
10 oz (300 g) fresh green beans or snow peas, steamed
10 oz (300 g) broccoli florets, steamed

for the dressing
1/4 cup sesame oil (optional)
1/4 cup lemon juice
1 small clove of garlic, minced
1/4 teaspoon salt
1/4 teaspoon pepper
1 teaspoon prepared mustard
15 drops Tabasco sauce

Put 2 cups of water and 1 teaspoon of seafood seasoning in a large pan and bring to boil. Add the shrimp and cook for 7 minutes. Scrub the shellfish and refrigerate until ready to cook. During this time they will open slightly. To test freshness, insert a knife into each open shell which should close immediately if the shellfish is still alive. If this does not happen, discard that particular one. Pull the flat of the knife toward the muscle holding the two shells together and turn the blade upright to open the shells. Arrange the fresh raw shellfish with the steamed vegetables on a large platter and serve with lemon quarters. If desired, the shellfish can be steamed briefly before serving. Shake the ingredients for the dressing in a well-sealed jar and pour on top of the shellfish. Alternatively, serve with sesame sauce (see basic recipes).

Spaghetti with Vegetables

Serves 4
Preparation time 30 minutes
Cooking time 15 minutes

10 oz (300 g) spaghetti
1/4 cup lemon juice
2 teaspoons prepared mustard
3 medium carrots, julienne
14 oz (400 g) canned artichokes
2-3 green onions, finely chopped
1 small finocchio bulb, chopped
1 stalk of celery, sliced
salt and freshly ground pepper
2 tablespoons sesame oil (optional)

Drain the artichokes, rinse with cold water, drain again, and cut in half. Put the lemon juice in a heavy-bottomed pan with the mustard dissolved in 1/3 cup water, carrots, artichokes, celery, onions, finocchio, salt, and pepper, cover, and simmer for about 15 minutes. Meanwhile, cook the spaghetti in salted boiling water al dente and drain. Empty into the pan with the vegetables, sprinkle with the sesame oil (if used), and toss gently until mixed. Serve immediately sprinkled with freshly ground pepper.

Broiled Lobster Tails

Serves 4
Preparation time 45 minutes
Cooking time 12 minutes

4 lobster tails, fresh or frozen, about 1 lb (500 g) each
salt and freshly ground pepper
4 cups water or vegetable broth (see basic recipes)
2 tablespoons lemon juice
2 tablespoons sesame oil (optional)
2 tablespoons capers
12 basil or mint leaves, finely chopped
red or green lettuce leaves
1 cup of tahini or avocado sauce
(see basic recipes)

Cook the lobster tails 10 minutes in boiling salted water or the vegetable broth with 2 tablespoons lemon juice. Drain, devein, and remove lungs and sac with a knife. Slice and brush each piece with sesame oil (if used). Sprinkle with salt and pepper and broil about 2 minutes. Rinse the prettiest lettuce leaves, drain well, and arrange on a platter. Place the lobster medallions on the bed of lettuce and sprinkle with the capers and chopped basil or mint leaves. Garnish with lemon slices. Serve accompanied by either tahini or avocado sauce (see basic recipes).

Spaghetti with Olives and Cherry Tomatoes

Serves 4
Preparation time 15 minutes
Cooking time 8 minutes

10 oz (300 g) spaghetti
1/2 cup finely chopped basil or mint leaves
5-6 cherry tomatoes, quartered
1 clove garlic, minced
1/2 cup chopped Calamata olives
3 tablespoons balsamic vinegar
salt and freshly ground pepper
1 teaspoon thyme
2 tablespoons sesame oil (optional)

Cook the pasta, drain, and rinse with cold water. Empty into a deep serving dish and toss with the remaining ingredients. Sprinkle freshly ground black pepper and thyme on top. Serve as a first course, salad or main course.

BROILED LOBSTER TAILS

Bean Soup

Serves 6
Preparation time 1 hour
Cooking time 1 hour

8 oz (250 g) medium dried white beans
8 oz (250 g) dried pinto or kidney beans
1 large onion, grated
2 large carrots, sliced
1/2 cup chopped celery with the leaves
1 small hot pepper (optional)
1 large green bell pepper, chopped
14 oz (400 g) canned chopped tomato or
2 lb (1 kg) fresh ripe tomatoes chopped
2 tablespoons ketchup
1/4 cup finely chopped parsley
salt and freshly ground pepper

Soak both kinds of beans 8 hours or overnight in water to cover. Discard soaking water, and put them in a large pan with 8 cups (2 liters) of fresh water. Simmer until half-cooked, about 30 minutes. Meanwhile, steam the onions in a saucepan on medium heat, stirring occasionally to prevent sticking. Add the carrot, celery, and peppers, and continue stirring until the vegetables wilt. Stir in the tomatoes, ketchup, parsley, salt, pepper, and 4 cups (1 liter) of hot water. Drain the half-cooked beans and add to the pan with the vegetables. Cover and simmer the soup until the beans are tender and the soup reaches the desired consistency. Add more water, if needed. The cooking time and the amount of additional water required depends on the quality of the beans. Serve the soup hot with olives and pickled vegetables.

Bean Salad with Olives

Serves 4
Preparation time 15 minutes
Cooking time 1 hour

10 oz (300 g) small white dried beans
2 medium tomatoes, seeded and finely chopped
1 medium onion, thinly sliced
1/2 cup finely chopped pickles
1 cup pitted, sliced black olives
1 red and 1 green bell pepper, julienne
several pieces of baby corn

for the dressing
4 tablespoons balsamic vinegar
2 tablespoons finely chopped cilantro or
1 teaspoon ground coriander
1 teaspoon chili powder
1/2 teaspoon garlic powder
1/4 teaspoon sugar
1/2 teaspoon salt
1/4 teaspoon freshly ground pepper

Cook the beans in salted water until tender, about 1 hour. Drain, rinse in cold water, and empty into a large bowl. Add the remaining salad ingredients. Combine the dressing ingredients in a well-sealed jar and shake until blended. Pour on the salad and toss. Refrigerate several hours to develop flavor. Serve chilled. This salad is even better the next day.

Noodles with Octopus

Serves 4
Preparation time 1 hour
Cooking time 15 minutes

4 lb (2 kg) octopus cooked as for pickled
octopus, page **100**

for the sauce
3 oz (100 g) blanched almonds
2 tablespoons sesame oil
2 cloves garlic, minced
2 tablespoons grated fresh ginger
2 tablespoons ketchup
13 oz (400 gr) tomato juice
1 teaspoon red pepper flakes
10 oz (300 g) noodles or vermicelli
3 green onions, finely chopped

Cut the octopus into bite-sized pieces. In a heavy-bottomed pan, saute the almonds in the sesame oil over medium heat for several minutes. Remove with a slotted spoon and set aside. In the same oil saute the garlic and ginger for 2-3 minutes. Add the octopus along with the ketchup, tomato juice, and pepper flakes. Cover and simmer until tender, about 30 minutes. Meanwhile, cook the noodles, drain, and transfer to a warm serving dish. Pour the octopus and on top. Sprinkle with the chopped onions and serve immediately.

Lentil Soup

Serves 4
Preparation time 15 minutes
Cooking time 30 - 60 minutes

1 lb (500 g) lentils
1 lb (500 g) ripe tomatoes or
14 oz (400 g) canned tomatoes
2 tablespoons ketchup
1 small onion, finely chopped
2 cloves garlic, sliced
2 bay leaves
2 tablespoons vinegar
salt and freshly ground pepper
1 teaspoon oregano

Rinse the lentils and drain. Put in a pan with water to cover and bring to a boil. Cook 5 minutes and drain. This prevents the lentils from darkening during cooking. Puree the tomatoes in a food processor. Steam the onions and the garlic with a little water in a large pan until the water evaporates and the onion and garlic wilt. Add 4 cups (1 liter) of water, the pureed tomatoes, ketchup, bay leaf, salt, and pepper and bring to a boil. Add the parboiled lentils and simmer covered for 30 minutes to 1 hour (depending on the quality of the lentils), until they are tender. Stir in the vinegar and the oregano and cook 5 minutes. Take off the heat and remove the bay leaf. Sprinkle the soup with freshly ground pepper and extra oregano and vinegar, if desired. Serve with olives and pickled vegetables. The soup may be served hot or cold.

Minestrone Soup

Serves 6
Preparation time 15 minutes
Cooking time 30 minutes

2 green onions, finely chopped
1 small leek, white part only, finely chopped
5 cups vegetable broth (see basic recipes)
1/2 cup finely chopped red bell pepper
8 oz (250 g) chopped mixed vegetables, frozen
1/2 cup star-shaped pasta
salt and freshly ground pepper
1 teaspoon paprika
1/4 teaspoon cayenne
lemon juice

Steam the chopped onions and leeks with a little water in a pan until the liquid evaporates and the vegetables wilt. Pour in the vegetable broth and add the other vegetables, bring to a boil, and simmer 15 minutes. Add the pasta, salt, pepper, paprika, and cayenne. Continue cooking until the vegetables and pasta are tender, about 15 minutes more. Remove from the heat, stir in the lemon juice, and serve immediately sprinkled with freshly ground pepper. The soup may be served hot or cold.

Seafood and Onion Stew

Serves 6
Preparation time 40 minutes
Cooking time 2 hours

2 lb (1 kg) octopus, pickled (see page 100)
1 lb (500 g) shrimp
1 teaspoons paprika
7 oz (200 g) shelled mussels
7 oz (200 g) shelled scallops (optional)
3 tablespoons sesame oil
3 large onions, sliced
6 cloves garlic, thinly sliced
2/3 cup finely chopped red bell pepper

1/4 cup finely chopped hot red pepper
14 oz (400 g) finely chopped canned tomatoes
2 tablespoons tomato paste
1/4 cup ketchup
2 tablespoons mixed peppercorns
10 whole allspice berries
2 bay leaves
1/4 cup balsamic vinegar
salt and freshly ground pepper

Prepare the octopus as in the recipe and cut into 1-inch (2.5-cm) pieces. Peel and devein the shrimp, leaving the heads and tails intact. Put in a pan with 1/2 cup water and the paprika. Cook for 4 minutes, drain, and reserve the liquid. Remove heads and tails, and cut into pieces. Set aside. Put the mussels in a pan and cook over high heat for 5 minutes to release some of their juices. Do not overcook as they turn tough. Drain and reserve the liquid. Heat the sesame oil in a pan and saute the onions and garlic until transparent. Add the peppers, tomatoes, tomato paste, bay leaves, shrimp, and mussel liquids. Stir to mix, cover, and simmer until the sauce thickens. Add the scallops, octopus, and vinegar, lower the heat and simmer for another 20 minutes, until the sauce thickens again. Add the mussels, shrimp, salt, and pepper and simmer for 5-7 minutes. Serve the stew with aromatic rice.

Raisin Pilaf Arabia

Serves 4
Preparation time 15 minutes
Cooking time 20 minutes

1½ cup basmati rice
1 green onion, finely chopped
2 tablespoons white raisins
salt and black pepper
3 tablespoons toasted pine nuts
1 teaspoons saffron stigmas
2 tablespoon lemon juice
2 tablespoons sesame oil (optional)
1 tablespoon sugar (optional)

Soak the rice in water to cover for 30 minutes. Drain and rinse with cold water. Bring to a boil with 3 cups of water and cook for 3 minutes, uncovered. Stir in the onion, raisins, salt, and pepper. Cover and bring again to a boil. Turn off the heat and leave the pan for 20 minutes on the hot element, until all the water is absorbed. Add the pine nuts, sprinkle with the saffron, lemon juice, and the sesame oil and sugar, if used. Fluff up with a fork and serve hot.

Pickled Vegetable Salad

Serves 4
Preparation time 30 minutes

2 cups mixed pickled vegetables such as carrot,
cauliflower, onions, peppers, cucumbers
1 small fresh carrot, thinly sliced
7 oz (200 g) Italian endive or spinach
1 bunch rocket leaves
1 recipe of tahini sauce (see basic recipes)

Taste the pickled vegetables and if necessary, soak in cold water to remove the excess salt. Drain and cut into pieces. Wash the fresh vegetables thoroughly and drain well. Cut into bite-sized pieces and mix with the pickled vegetables. Put the salad on a deep platter and sprinkle with a little tahini sauce and plenty of freshly ground pepper. Serve accompanied by extra tahini sauce.

Greek Fava

Serves 4
Preparation time 10 minutes
Cooking time 1 hour

1 lb (500 g) green or yellow split peas or
dried broad beans
5 cups water
1 small onion, grated
salt and freshly ground pepper
oregano (optional)
3 tablespoons finely chopped parsley or dill
4 green onions, finely chopped
a few spoonfuls of sesame oil (optional)
lemon juice

Rinse the split peas in a colander and drain well. If using dried broad beans, they must be soaked in cold water overnight, drained, and skinned. Bring the water to a boil and add the peas or broad beans. Cover and simmer until half-cooked, about 35 minutes. Skim off the scum with a spoon from time to time as it rises to the surface. Steam the onion in a saucepan until wilted. Stir the onion, salt, pepper, and, if desired, a little oregano into the fava and continue simmering until it thickens, about 30 minutes. Remove from the heat and whip vigorously with a wooden spoon until smooth (as for mashed potatoes). Distribute into 6 bowls or deep plates and sprinkle with the chopped parsley, chopped green onions, and lemon juice. Serve hot or cold. Sprinkle with sesame oil, if you wish. Fava is traditionally served with olives.

Rice with Shellfish-Tomato Sauce

Serves 6
Preparation time 20 minutes
Cooking time 35 minutes

2 lb (1 kg) shrimp
1 lb (500 g) shelled mussels
1 teaspoon seafood seasoning or
1 tablespoon paprika
2 cups basmati rice

for the sauce
1 large onion, sliced
2 leeks, white part only, finely chopped
3 cloves garlic, minced
1 green bell pepper, julienne
1 red bell pepper, julienne
4 medium ripe tomatoes, peeled,
seeded, and chopped
1/4 cup ketchup
1/2 cup finely chopped dill or parsley
2 teaspoons paprika
1/2 teaspoon cayenne
salt and freshly ground pepper
1 teaspoon cornstarch dissolved in
2 tablespoons water

Peel and devein the shrimp leaving the heads intact. Bring 3 cups of water with the seafood seasoning (or the paprika) to a boil, add the shrimp and the mussels and cook for 5 minutes. Remove with a slotted spoon to a bowl. Remove the heads from the shrimp and discard. Cut the cooked shrimp into pieces. Strain the shellfish liquid through a fine sieve or cheesecloth. Measure and, if needed, add enough water to make 3 cups. Pour in a pan and bring to a boil. Add the rice and simmer until all the liquid is absorbed and the rice is fluffy. Meanwhile, prepare the sauce. Steam the onions, leeks, garlic, and peppers in a saucepan until wilted. Add the tomatoes, ketchup, dill, paprika, cayenne, salt, and freshly ground pepper. Cover and simmer the sauce for 30 minutes. Add the dissolved cornstarch. Continue simmering while stirring until the sauce thickens slightly. Remove from the heat, add the cooked shrimp, mussels, and freshly ground pepper. Put the rice on a platter and pour the shellfish-tomato sauce on top. Serve hot or cold.

SOCRATES: *First let us consider
how they will live.
They will produce grain and wine,
cloaks and shoes. They will prepare their
flours from barley and wheat... They
will have appetizers, salt, olives
and cheese, and they will boil up
bulbs and other vegetables
as they do now in the country.
And perhaps we will serve them desserts,
figs, chickpeas and beans and they will
drink moderately with their meals.
And with a peaceful
and healthy life of this kind,
they will no doubt reach old age
and pass on a similar style of life
to their offspring.*

V E G E T A B L E S

Book II of Plato's *Republic* (372-3)

Vegetables, whether cultivated in field and garden or gathered wild, are an unlimited source of nutrients necessary not only for elementary sustenance but for the maintenance and enhancement of good health. Vegetables play a major role in the Mediterranean diet, where they are featured – raw or cooked – as the main course, not just as side dishes to accompany the meat or fish course. More often that not, vegetables are cooked or combined with meat, poultry, or seafood dishes rather than served separately. The virtual kaleidoscope of colors and flavors represented by the vegetables available to the modern cook has inspired these "wizards of the kitchen" to create visually attractive yet healthy "taste sensations", sophisticated enough to please the most demanding gourmet.

The Greeks who traveled widely and established colonies, the armies of Rome, and later, the Arabs, who conquered wide areas of the Mediterranean Basin, were responsible for introducing new vegetables and their use to its inhabitants. Likewise, the Spanish after discovering and conquering the New World in the 16th century in their search for gold and spice, returned instead with the seeds and roots of corn, tomatoes, beans, sweet peppers, and potatoes, treasures that proved infinitely more valuable than gold.

The botanical experiments of the Austrian monk, Gregor

V E G E T A B L E S

Mendel, revolutionized the cultivation of vegetables. The laws he formulated in the early 19th century based on his observations of peas, enabled botanists to improve the existing varieties of vegetables and predict the characteristics of new ones. The continued improvement of cultivation techniques combined with Mendel's laws permitted botanists to develop larger pest-resistant vegetable varieties as well as more productive crop-yields needed to feed the expanding populations of Europe. As the world awaits the outcome of present-day genetic experimentation, we can expect even more amazing specimens from the food technologists' laboratories.

Thanks to modern-day cultivation, shipping and storage techniques, most vegetables are available the year around. Some 2500 years ago Hippocrates, the Father of Medicine, made the following observation: "All fresh foods provide more strength than the alternatives..." Just as in ancient Greece, it is still preferable to use fresh vegetables in their appropriate season. Not only are they tastier and cheaper, they are ultimately more nourishing. It is also wise to buy fresh vegetables from farmers' markets and green grocers which are more likely to procure their produce locally in contrast with large supermarket chains which tend to rely on having their produce shipped in from long distances under refrigeration. Consumers concerned about the excessive use of pesticides and artificial fertilizers should seek out sources of organically grown produce, a movement which is, fortunately, slowly but surely gaining ground in many parts of the world.

Vegetables are a primary source of vitamins A and C as well as other vitamins and minerals such as potassium, sodium, calcium, magnesium and iron, all vital to metabolism and

necessary to aid absorption of nutrients from the digestive tract as well as lower blood cholesterol and stabilize blood sugar levels. A fiber-rich diet low in animal protein and fat assures the proper action of the intestinal tract which many researchers believe helps prevent colon cancer and other disorders.

Most vegetables contain limited amounts of protein with the exception of legumes like soya, beans, and peas, all excellent sources of plant protein. Amino acids, the basic components of plant protein, are, however, not sufficient to cover the biological needs of our bodies. It is, therefore, a good idea to consume vegetables with seafood, fish, eggs, or other products of animal origin. Thus we provide our bodies with all the necessary amino acids which, together with the other nutritional elements found in vegetables make up a balanced healthy dietary regime. These basic precepts for good health were first understood by the ancient Greeks.

We are fortunate to be living in an era in which all the products imperative to good health and longevity are readily available. The traditional Mediterranean diet, based on vegetables and fruits, pulses, grains, nuts, aromatic herbs, and seafood in combination with olive oil, the precious liquid gold of old, has been recognized and is being promoted by nutrition experts as one of the most healthful in the world, one that assures not

other functions of the human organism. Vegetables are also rich in trace elements such as cobalt, copper, manganese, iodine, zinc, selenium, and phosphorus which act as catalysts in the biochemical reactions carried out in our cells. Vegetables contain large amounts of fiber which are indigestible carbohydrates called cellulose. Although not metabolized by the body, fibrous elements in the diet are

only a longer life, but one of quality and vitality. The recipes in this book were developed with the idea that healthful nourishment need not be lacking in taste or imagination but gastronomically satisfying as well as beneficial to our health and well-being.

VEGETABLES

Eggplant Timbale

Serves 6
Preparation time 1 hour 40 minutes
Cooking time 50 minutes

7 oz (200 g) penne macaroni
4 lb (2 kg) long eggplant
1 medium zucchini, grated
1/2 cup olive oil
1 medium onion, grated
1 clove garlic, minced
1 medium carrot, grated
1/2 cup pulped ripe tomatoes
1/8 teaspoon cinnamon
1/4 teaspoon ground allspice
1/3 cup finely chopped parsley
salt and freshly ground pepper
2 tablespoons cornstarch
1 cup soybean milk or
1 cup vegetarian cream
1/8 teaspoon nutmeg

Cut 3-4 round slices from one of the eggplants, and slice the remaining ones lengthwise into long thick pieces. Sprinkle generously with salt and let them drain in a colander for 1 hour. Rinse well and squeeze out the excess water. Lightly fry in olive oil and drain on absorbent paper. Sprinkle the grated zucchini with a little salt and allow to drain in a colander. Rinse and squeeze out excess water. To prepare the sauce, saute the onions and garlic in the oil until wilted. Add the carrots and zucchini and stir over the heat until wilted. Add the tomatoes, spices, parsley, salt, and pepper. Simmer the sauce for 20 minutes or until thick. Brush a round oven-proof glass or metal dish 8 inches (20 cm) in diameter and 3 inches (8 cm) deep with oil. Place the eggplant rounds in the center of the dish and cover the remaining surface of the bottom and sides, arranging the long slices around the dish so they overlap like the flower petals. Dissolve the cornstarch in a small amount of water and stir into the soybean milk or cream. Cook, stirring continuously over medium heat until thick. Stir in the nutmeg, salt, and pepper. Cook the pasta in salted water with 2 tablespoons olive oil and drain. Combine the tomato and cream sauce with the cooked, drained pasta. Carefully pour half of the pasta mixture into the eggplant-lined dish. Cover the surface with a layer of eggplant slices. Spread the remaining pasta mixture on top and cover with the remaining eggplant slices. Bring the ends of the outer layer of eggplant towards the center. Bake the timbale in a 400°F (200°C) oven for 45-50 minutes. Allow to stand 10 minutes before unmolding. Serve immediately.

Stuffed Red Peppers

Serves 4
Preparation time 30 minutes
Cooking time 1 hour 30 minutes

12 large pointed red Italian or Florina peppers
2 lb (1 kg) eggplant
2 large onions, grated
1 cup olive oil
1/3 cup short-grain rice
1/2 cup parsley, finely chopped
2 lb (1 kg) ripe tomatoes, pulped and strained
1 oz (30 g) pine nuts
salt and freshly ground pepper

Slice the unpeeled eggplant lengthwise, cut the slices lengthwise into strips, and then crosswise into small square pieces. Immediately put into salted water and allow to stand 1 hour. Drain well, and squeeze out the excess water. Saute the eggplant in half the oil until lightly browned. Remove with a slotted spoon and set aside. Briefly saute the onions in the rest of the oil, add the tomatoes and simmer until onions are soft. Add the parsley, rice, sauteed eggplant, pine nuts, salt, and pepper. Cut the caps off the peppers and remove the seeds. Fry lightly in olive oil, fill with the prepared rice mixture, and arrange in a baking dish. Add 1/3 cup water and bake in a 350°F (180°C) oven until the peppers are soft and lightly browned. Serve hot or at room temperature.

EGGPLANT TIMBALE

Saffron Rice with Peas

Serves 4-5
Preparation time 30 minutes
Cooking time 1 hour

2 cups basmati rice
5-6 saffron stamens, crushed
3 lb (1½ kg) fresh or
1 lb (500 g) frozen peas
2/3 cups olive oil
1 cup finely chopped green onions
25 oz (750 g) ripe tomatoes or
14 oz (400 g) canned chopped tomatoes
1/2 cup finely chopped dill
salt and pepper

Cook the rice with the saffron according to package directions. Shell the peas, rinse, and drain. Heat the oil on high heat and saute the onions. Add the peas with the remaining ingredientsand 1 cup hot water. Cover and simmer until the peas are tender and the sauce has cooked down almost to the oil. Depending on the size and condition of the peas, it may be necessary to add a little more water. Serve the rice with the peas, hot or cold.

Tomato Pilaf

Serves 4
Preparation time 30 minutes
Cooking time 1 hour

1/3 cup olive oil
2 lb (1 kg) ripe tomatoes, chopped
2 cloves garlic, minced
3 tablespoons finely chopped parsley
1 teaspoon sugar
1½ cup vegetable stock (see basic recipes)
1½ cup long-grain rice
salt and freshly ground pepper

Heat the oil in a pan on high heat and saute the garlic. Add the tomatoes, cover, and simmer 30 minutes. Add the parsley, sugar, stock, salt, and pepper. Increase the heat and when the sauce comes to a boil, add the rice, lower the heat, cover and simmer until the rice is just tender, but not all the liquid has been absorbed. Remove from the heat, put absorbent paper towels between the lid and the pan and allow the rice to swell. Serve hot or cold, accompanied by olives.

Mushroom Moussaka

Serves 6
Preparation time 1 hour
Cooking time 45-50 minutes

1 large onion, grated
2 cloves garlic, finely chopped
1/2 cup olive oil
28 oz (800 g) canned mushrooms, drained and finely chopped or ground like meat
1½ lb (800 g) fresh ripe tomatoes, finely chopped or 14 oz (400 g) canned tomato pulp
2 tablespoons ketchup
salt and pepper
1/3 cup finely chopped parsley
2 tablespoons dry bread crumbs
4 lb (2 kg) eggplant, sliced, and fried in olive oil

for the topping
1 lb (500 g) potatoes, peeled and chopped
salt and freshly ground pepper
1/8 teaspoon nutmeg
1/2 cup vegetarian cream
1/4 cup corn oil

Saute the onions and garlic in the oil. Add the mushrooms and saute several minutes. Add the tomatoes, ketchup, salt, and pepper, cover, and simmer until the mushrooms are wilted and the sauce is thick. Stir in the chopped parsley. Brush a baking

dish 8 x 12 inches (20 x 30 cm) with oil and sprinkle with the breadcrumbs. Lay half the eggplant slices on the bottom and spread the mushroom mixture on top. Sprinkle with a little freshly ground pepper. Lay the remaining eggplant slices on top. Put the potatoes in a pan with a little water and simmer until all the water has been absorbed and the potatoes are soft. Mash the potatoes with the salt, pepper, nutmeg, cream, and corn oil. Spread on top of the eggplant. Bake the moussakas in a 400°F(200°C) oven for about 45 minutes until lightly browned. Serve warm.

Vegetable Giouvetsi

Serves 6
Preparation time 30 minutes
Cooking time 1 hour 30 minutes

2 medium eggplants, diced
3 zucchini, cut in half-rounds
1/2 cup olive oil
2 cloves garlic, minced
1 large onion, grated
16 oz (500 g) orzo-type pasta
4 large ripe tomatoes, chopped
3 cups water
1 stalk of celery, sliced
2 medium carrots, sliced
1 cup grated vegetarian cheese (optional)

Salt the eggplant and zucchini and allow to stand in a colander for 1 hour. Heat the olive oil in a large pan on high heat and saute the onion and the garlic until wilted. Add the orzo and stir in the oil several minutes. Add the tomatoes, water, celery, and carrots, mix and pour into a giouvetsi dish or any ceramic or oven-proof baking dish. Bake in a 425°F (220°C) oven for 1 hour and 30 minutes until the pasta is tender. It may be necessary to add some additional hot water. Meanwhile, rinse and squeeze excess water from the eggplant and zucchini. Fry lightly in olive oil and stir into the orzo 15 minutes before removing from the oven. Sprinkle with the grated cheese and continue baking until done. Serve immediately.

Baked Vegetables-Briami

Serves 6
Preparation time 1 hour
Cooking time 2 hours

2 medium eggplants

2 medium zucchini
2 small carrots
1 green and 1 red bell pepper
2 large ripe tomatoes
1 large onion
10 large fresh white mushrooms
1 cup olive oil
1 1/2 cup tomato juice
20 drops Tabasco sauce
2-3 cloves garlic, minced
1/2 cup finely chopped parsley

Peel the eggplant and zucchini and cut into bite-size pieces. Salt and allow to stand in a colander for 1 hour. Rinse and squeeze out excess water with your hands. Peel the carrot, deseed the peppers, and cut into bite-size pieces. Chop the tomatoes and the onion and slice the mushrooms into thick pieces. Put all the vegetables in a baking dish, pour in the olive oil, tomato juice, and Tabasco sauce. Add the garlic and parsley, mix lightly, and bake in a 400°F (200°C) oven for about 2 hours or until the vegetables are tender and the juices have cooked down almost to the oil. Serve the dish hot or cold.

Piquant Rice with Tomatoes

Serves 6
Preparation time 30 minutes
Cooking time 30 minutes

1/3 cup margarine
1/4 cup finely chopped onions
3 cloves garlic, minced
2 cups long-grain rice
1½ teaspoons salt
1 teaspoon sugar
1/4 teaspoon white pepper
1/4 teaspoon ground cumin
1/2 teaspoon cayenne
1/2 teaspoon ground coriander
2 lb (1 kg) ripe tomatoes, finely chopped or
27 oz (800 g) canned tomatoes
1 tablespoon tomato paste
20 drops Tabasco sauce
1 cup vegetable stock (see basic recipes)
1 cup finely chopped red bell pepper

Melt the margarine in a large pan and saute the onion and garlic. Stir in the rice and saute 2 minutes. Add the salt, sugar, spices, tomatoes, tomato paste, Tabasco sauce, and stock. Mix well, cover and bring to a boil on high heat. Lower the heat and simmer for 20 minutes. Stir in the finely chopped peppers and simmer for another 5 minutes. Serve hot or at room temperature accompanied by olives and taramosalata.

Tri-Color Rice Ring

Serves 6
Preparation time 20 minutes
Cooking time 20 minutes

1½ cups long-grain rice
3 tablespoons margarine
2 teaspoons salt
1 cup cooked peas
2 tablespoons finely chopped parsley
1/4 cup vegetarian cream
2 tablespoons tomato paste
1 tablespoon ketchup
1 teaspoon turmeric (optional)

Bring 3 cups of water to a boil in a large pan. Stir in the rice, margarine, and salt. Cover, lower the heat, and simmer about 20 minutes, until all the water has been absorbed and the rice is fluffy. Remove from the heat and divide the rice into three

equal portions. Process the peas and the parsley with half the cream in the food processor on low speed until just blended. Stir the mixture into the first portion of rice and mix. In a bowl combine the tomato paste and ketchup with the remaining cream. Stir into the second portion of rice and mix well. If desired, stir the turmeric into the third portion of rice, or leave it white. Grease a 9½-inch (24 cm-) tube pan with corn oil and pat the three portions of colored rice firmly inside. Unmold the rice ring on a round platter and serve with the preceding baked vegetable dish (briami). The rice can be steamed while still in the pan or heated in a 220°F (100°C) oven.

Risotto with Pumpkin

Serves 6-8
Preparation time 20 minutes
Cooking time 10-20 minutes

1/4 cup olive oil
1/3 cup finely chopped onion
2 cloves garlic, minced
2 tablespoons fresh rosemary
1 lb (500 g) peeled seeded yellow squash, cubed
1/4 cup vegetable stock (see basic recipes)

for the risotto
1/4 cup finely chopped onion
1/3 cup margarine
1²/3 cup short-grain rice
1½ liters vegetable stock,
salt and freshly ground pepper
1/4 cup fresh rosemary for garnish

Heat the oil on high heat and saute the onions and the garlic until wilted. Add the rosemary, squash, and stock. Cover and simmer 10-20 minutes until the squash is very tender. Melt half the margarine in a large pan and saute the onions until wilted. Add the rice and stir over the heat 1-2 minutes. Add the stock in small amounts (up to a cup each time) continually stirring until it has been absorbed by the rice. Add as much stock as needed to soften the outer part of the rice which should appear translucent while the whitish centers should be "chewy." After about 8 -10 minutes, when the rice is half-cooked, add the squash and continue simmering until the rice is creamy and tender and the sauce has cooked down. Remove from the heat and stir in the remaining margarine. Taste and correct the seasonings, adding as much salt and pepper as desired. Serve in deep heated plates, sprinkled with rosemary.

Stewed Okra

Serves 4
Preparation time 30-40 minutes
Cooking time 15 minutes

1 lb (500 g) fresh or frozen okra
14 oz (400 g) finely chopped canned tomatoes
3/4 cup olive oil
1 medium onion, thinly sliced
1/3 cup finely chopped parsley
1/8 teaspoon sugar
salt and pepper
3 round slices of lemon without rind
1 ripe tomato, thinly sliced

If using fresh okra, carefully remove the stems with a sharp knife without cutting into the caps. Dip cut ends into a plate of salt and allow to stand 30 minutes. Rinse well in water and a little vinegar or lemon juice. If using frozen okra, simply rinse in water and vinegar or lemon juice. Heat the oil in a shallow pan on high heat and saute the onions lightly. Add the tomatoes, parsley, sugar, pepper, lemon slices, and simmer 10 minutes. Add the prepared okra and toss in the sauce to coat. Arrange the tomato slices on top and sprinkle with a little salt and pepper. Cover, lower heat to medium, and simmer 15 minutes. Do not stir the okra. If necessary, gently shake the pan in a circular motion. Also avoid overcooking. Okra easily lose their shape and become mushy. Add water only if the sauce cooks down to the oil and the okra are not thoroughly cooked. Taste and correct seasoning only at the end. Serve hot or at room temperature. Alternatively, okra can be baked in the oven, but it will take from 1-2 hours to cook. Cover with thin slices of tomato so the okra won't dry out.

Spinach-Rice in Pita Bowls

Serves 6
Preparation time 1 hour and 30 minutes
Cooking time 30 minutes

3 lb (1½ kg) fresh spinach
1 cup olive oil
1 small onion, grated
5 green onions, finely chopped
2 medium tomatoes, diced
salt and freshly ground pepper
1/2 cup finely chopped dill
1/3 cup short-grain rice
1 recipe for cornmeal and flour pitas (see basic recipes)

Wash the spinach and cut off most of the tough stalks. Chop the leaves and plunge into boiling water. Parboil 5 minutes and drain. Heat the oil in a large pan, and saute both kinds of onions until wilted. Add the tomatoes, salt, pepper, dill, spinach, and mix well. Spread the mixture on the bottom of the pan with a wooden spoon, making cavities here and there. Put the rice in a strainer and rinse until the water runs clear. Distribute the rice evenly into the cavities. Cover the pan and simmer for 20 minutes without stirring. Take the pan off the heat, remove the cover, place sheets of absorbent towels on top and replace the cover. Allow the dish to stand 10 minutes before serving. Prepare the dough for the pitas as described in the recipe. Put the dough in a plastic bag and allow to rest for 15 minutes. Divide into 12 equal pieces and roll out into 8-inch (20-cm) rounds. Heat a large non-stick frying pan and cook the pitas one at a time, turning once. While still warm, soft, and pliable, place each pita in a small round heat-proof or metal bowl pleating the edges with your hands so it will take the form of the bowl. Bake the pita "bowls" in a hot oven at 400°F (200°C) for 7-8 minutes until crisp and lightly browned. Serve the spinach-rice in the pita bowls garnished with lemon slices.

blossom and carefully fold in the top edges. Arrange them side by side on the bottom of a large pan in one or two layers. Dissolve the tomato paste in 1 cup of water and pour on top of the stuffed blossoms with the remaining oil. Sprinkle the surface with some freshly ground pepper, cover, and simmer 20 minutes until very little sauce remains. They are just as tasty served either hot or at room temperature.

Stuffed Tomatoes and Peppers

Serves 6
Preparation time 1 hour
Cooking time 1 hour 45 minutes

6 large tomatoes
6 large bell peppers
2 tablespoons ketchup
2 tablespoons tomato paste
1¼ cups olive oil
1 cup grated onion
1½ cup short-grain rice
2/3 cup finely chopped parsley
1/4 cup finely chopped fresh mint
4 large potatoes

Stuffed Zucchini Blossoms

Serves 4-5
Preparation time 30 minutes
Cooking time 20 minutes

1/2 cup olive oil
1 cup finely chopped green onions
2 tablespoons grated onion
2 small zucchinis, grated
2 cups finely chopped fresh tomatoes
2 tablespoons lemon juice
1/2 cup finely chopped fresh dill or mint
1/2 cup finely chopped parsley
3/4 cup short-grain rice
25 zucchini flowers
salt and freshly ground pepper
1 tablespoon tomato paste

Saute the onions and the grated zucchini in half the oil until wilted. Add the tomato and lemon juice and cook 5 minutes. Add the herbs, rice, salt, and pepper; mix and remove from the heat. Rinse the blossoms in plenty of water and remove the stamens from the center. Place a tablespoon of filling in each

Slice off the top of each tomato and remove the pulp with a spoon. Cut off the top of each pepper and remove the seeds and veins. Set tops aside. Puree the tomato pulp in a blender at medium speed. Stir the ketchup and the tomato paste into the pureed tomatoes. Heat half the oil in a pan and saute the onions. Add the tomato mixture, salt, and pepper and cook the sauce for 10 minutes. Remove from the heat, cool, and stir in the rice, the parsley, and the mint. Pour in a large strainer and collect the excess juice in a bowl. Fill the tomatoes and the peppers 3/4 full, allowing for the rice to swell. Arrange in a baking dish and close each piece with its top. Peel and cut the potatoes lengthwise into wedges. Place between the stuffed vegetables and pour the juice collected in the bowl on top. Spoon the remaining oil over each piece and sprinkle with a little salt and pepper. Bake in a 350°F (180°C) oven for 1 hour and 45 minutes or until the rice is tender and the juice has cooked down almost to the oil. It may be necessary to add some water during the baking. May be served hot or cold. Alternatively, add 2 tablespoons of pine nuts and 1/4 cup black raisins to the stuffing.

Assorted Stuffed Vegetables

Serves 6
Preparation time 1 hour
Cooking time 2 hours

3 large tomatoes
1 each, green, red, and yellow bell pepper
1 large round eggplant
1 thick zucchini
2 large onions
2 large potatoes
1½ cup olive oil
1¼ cup short-grain rice
1/2 cup finely chopped fresh mint
3 tablespoons tomato paste
1 tablespoon ketchup
salt and pepper
1/4 teaspoon ground allspice
1 cup tomato juice

Rinse all the vegetables and wipe dry. Slice off the tops from the tomatoes and peppers and reserve. Scoop out the pulp from the tomatoes with a spoon, deseed the peppers, and set aside. Cut the eggplant and the zucchini in half lengthwise, and scoop out most of the pulp to form 4 shells. Peel the onions, slice off the tops, and set aside. Scoop out most of the center portion to form two shells. Finely chop the onion centers and set aside. Parboil the eggplant, zucchini, and onion shells in boiling water for 5 minutes and drain. Arrange all the vegetable shells in a large baking dish. Heat half the olive oil in a pan on high heat and lightly saute the finely chopped onion. Finely chop the pulp from the tomatoes, the eggplants, and the zucchini. Add to the sauteed onions and cook, stirring on high heat for 10 minutes. Remove from the heat, stir in the rice, mint, tomato paste, ketchup, salt, pepper, and allspice. Fill the empty shells 3/4 full with the stuffing and replace caps on tomatoes, peppers, and onions. If there is any stuffing left over, use to stuff zucchini blossoms. Peel and cut the potatoes into wedges and place between the stuffed vegetables. Pour the tomato juice on top and sprinkle with a little salt and pepper. Spoon the remaining olive oil over the potatoes and the stuffed vegetables. Bake in a 360°F (180°C) oven for about 2 hours or until lightly browned. If the tops begin to brown too quickly, cover loosely with a piece of aluminum foil. It may be necessary to add some water during the baking to prevent sticking. Serve hot or cold.

Stuffed Tomatoes Arabia

Serves 3-4
Preparation time 15 minutes
Cooking time 40-50 minutes

7-8 medium tomatoes, not too ripe
2 teaspoons salt
1 teaspoon pepper
1/4 cup olive oil
1 onion, finely chopped
4 cloves garlic, mashed
4 tablespoons pine nuts
1/3 cup water
1/2 cup short-grain rice
1/8 teaspoon each ground cumin, cinnamon, and clove
1/4 cup black currants or raisins
1 tablespoon finely chopped parsley
1 teaspoon oregano

Wash the tomatoes and cut off the tops. Scoop out most of the pulp with a spoon, taking care the tomatoes don't lose their shape. Rub the pulp through a sieve or puree in a food processor. Sprinkle the tomato shells with salt and pepper and drain upside down on a rack. Saute the onion and garlic in the olive oil until wilted. Add the pine nuts and saute lightly. Stir in the tomato puree, rice, spices, and water and simmer for about 10 minutes until the rice is half-cooked. Remove from the heat, stir in the currants, parsley and oregano. Fill the tomatoes about 3/4 full allowing room for the rice to expand. Cover with the tops and brush with olive oil. Arrange side by side in a lightly oiled baking dish and bake in a 350°F (180°C) oven for 40-50 minutes. May be served hot or cold.

Stuffed Vine Leaves (Dolmas Yialantzi)

Serves 6-8
Preparation time 2 hours
Cooking time 30 minutes

1 lb (500 g) vine leaves, fresh or canned
2½ cups finely chopped green onions
2½ cups grated dry onions
1 lb (500 g) short-grain rice
1 cup finely chopped parsley
1 cup finely chopped dill or
1/2 cup finely chopped mint
1 oz (35 g) pine nuts (optional)
1/4 cup black raisins or currants (optional)
2 cups olive oil
1/3 cup lemon juice
2½ cup boiling water
salt and freshly ground black pepper

Rinse and blanch the vine leaves, a few at a time, for 2-3 minutes in boiling water. Combine the chopped green and dried onions in a strainer, rub with a little salt until wilted. Rinse with cold water and drain well, squeezing out excess moisture with your hands. Combine onions in a bowl with the remaining ingredients except for the oil and water. Stir in half the oil, salt, and pepper. Put 1 teaspoon of filling at the stem-end of each vine leaf and roll up loosely, folding in the sides. Line the bottom of a large heavy-bottomed pan with broken vine leaves and arrange the stuffed leaves side by side in layers. Take care to allow room for the rice to expand. At this point, the vine leaves can be frozen. Put the pan on the heat, pour in the remaining oil, boiling water, and lemon juice. Place a heavy plate just large enough to fit into the pan, on top of the stuffed leaves. Cover the pan, and simmer on medium heat until the "dolmas" have absorbed all the liquid and the sauce has cooked almost to the oil. Taste and if the rice is not tender enough, add more water and continue simmering. After removing from the heat, put an absorbent towel between the top of the pan and the cover and allow to cool. These meat-less vine leaves, always served at room temperature, are a very special Greek appetizer.

Stuffed Zucchini

Serves 4
Preparation time 1 hour
Cooking time 45 minutes

10 medium zucchini
3/4 cup olive oil
1/2 cup finely chopped green onions
1¹/₂ cups pulped canned or ripe tomatoes
1/3 cup short-grain rice
1/2 cup finely chopped parsley
1/2 cup finely chopped mint or dill
salt and freshly ground pepper
1/2 teaspoon sugar or
1 tablespoons ketchup

Rinse the zucchini and cut off both ends. Parboil 5 minutes and drain. Cool and remove pulp from the centers with an apple-corer, taking care not to cut through to the outside. Finely chop half of the zucchini pulp or coarsely grate. Sprinkle with a little salt and allow to drain well in a colander. Heat the oil in a pan on high heat and saute the onions until wilted. Add the drained zucchini and stir until wilted. Add the tomatoes and cook 5 minutes. Remove from the heat, stir in the rice, parsley, mint, salt, pepper, and sugar. Empty the mixture into a large sieve and collect the excess liquid. Stuff the zucchini cases with the mixture and arrange the stuffed zucchini on the bottom of a large heavy-bottomed pan. Pour the strained zucchini liquid on top. Cover and simmer until the zucchini are tender and the sauce has cooked down almost to its oil. It may be necessary to add additional water. Serve hot sprinkled with freshly ground pepper and, if desired, a little lemon juice.

Bulgur with Leeks and Cabbage

Serves 4-5
Preparation time 30 minutes
Cooking time 1 hour

26 oz (750 g) leeks
26 oz (750 g) cabbage
2/3 cup olive oil
1 large carrot, finely chopped
1 red bell pepper, finely chopped
2 stalks of celery, finely chopped
1 cup finely chopped fresh ripe or canned tomatoes

salt and freshly ground pepper
1/2 cup bulgur
3 tablespoons lemon juice

Trim and rinse the leeks, discarding the tough dark green leaves. Cut into small pieces, blanch, and drain. Do the same with the cabbage. Heat the oil in a pan on medium heat and saute the carrot, pepper, and celery until wilted. Stir in the tomatoes, leeks, cabbage, salt, and pepper and gently mix. Cover and simmer until the leeks and cabbage are half-cooked, about 15 minutes. Using a spoon, make several depressions here and there in the cooking vegetables and fill them with small portions of the bulgur. Continue cooking until the bulgur is tender and the sauce has cooked down. Pour the lemon juice on top and shake the pan to distribute. Serve hot or cold. The bulgur may be substituted with short-grain rice.

Artichokes Constantinople Style

Serves 4
Preparation time 30 minutes
Cooking time 30 minutes

8 fresh or frozen artichokes
1 cup olive oil
1 medium onion, grated
4 green onions, sliced
2 large carrots, diced
3 large potatoes, in pieces
3-4 oz (100 g) frozen peas
1/2 cup finely chopped dill
salt and freshly ground pepper
1/4 cup lemon juice
1 tablespoon flour (optional)

If using fresh artichokes, trim the tough dark green outer leaves so that the bottoms with the tender light green or yellow portion remains. Carefully remove the choke (fuzzy part) with a spoon. Peel the stalks down to the tender core in the center, and cut them in pieces. Rub each trimmed artichoke liberally with lemon juice and put in a bowl of water containing a little flour and lemon juice to prevent discoloration. Heat the oil in a large wide pan on high heat and lightly saute both kinds of onions until wilted. Add the carrots and peas and continue sauteeing. Arrange the artichokes in the pan, add the potatoes and 1 cup of hot water. Sprinkle with dill, salt, and pepper. Cover, lower heat, and simmer 30 minutes until the artichokes and potatoes are tender and sauce has cooked down. It may be necessary to add a little water. Remove from the heat and add the lemon juice. If a thick white sauce is desired, dissolve 1 tablespoon of flour into the lemon juice with 2-3 tablespoons of the hot cooking liquid, pour into the pan and shake to distribute evenly. Cook another 5 minutes. Arrange the artichoke bottoms filled with the chopped vegetables on a platter surrounded by the potatoes and pour sauce on top. Serve hot or at room temperature.

Artichokes with Broad Beans

Serves 6
Preparation time 1 hour
Cooking time 1 hour

3 lb (1½ kg) fresh broad (fava) beans
6 artichokes
1 cup olive oil
8 green onions, finely chopped
1/2 cup finely chopped dill
salt and freshly ground pepper
2 tablespoons lemon juice

Pull off the fibrous strings and cut the bean pods in half. Remove shells from the mature pods and discard. Rinse and drain thoroughly. Blanch in water briefly to prevent discoloration. Prepare the artichokes as described in the previous recipe for Constantinpole Artichokes. Heat the oil on high heat and saute the onions. Add the beans, artichokes, dill, salt, pepper, and 1 cup hot water. Cover and simmer until the sauce cook down and the vegetables are tender. Remove from the heat and pour the lemon juice on top. Shake the pan to distributed evenly. Serve with a salad of fresh greens. Serve hot or at room temperature. The broad beans may be cooked by themselves. Alternatively, add one ripe tomato and 1 lb (500 g) of fresh garden peas to the other ingredients.

Baked Artichokes with Mixed Vegetables

Serves 4-5
Preparation time 1 hour
Cooking time 2 hours

8 fresh trimmed artichokes, in bite-sized pieces or
28 oz (800 g) canned artichoke hearts
1 lb (500 g) frozen mixed vegetables
1 medium onion, finely chopped
1/2 cup finely chopped dill
2/3 cup olive oil
salt and freshly ground pepper
2 large potatoes, in bite-sized cubes
1/4 cup lemon juice

Arrange the prepared chopped artichokes in an oven dish. If using canned artichokes, drain, rinse, squeeze lightly to remove excess moisture and cut in half, if large. Rinse the frozen mixed vegetables, combine with the onions and dill and arrange on top of the artichokes. Pour the olive oil all over the vegetables and sprinkle with salt and freshly ground pepper. Add 1 cup of water and cover the dish with aluminum foil. Bake the vegetable dish in a 400°F (200°C) oven about 1 hour until half-cooked. Meanwhile lightly fry the potatoes in olive oil, drain and add to the vegetables. Carefully mix and pour in the lemon juice. Continue baking until all the vegetables are tender and the sauce has cooked down. If necessary, add some water.

ARTICHOKES CONSTANTINOPLE STYLE

dish substituting the dill with 1/4 cup finely chopped mint and the lemon juice with 1 ripe tomato added along with the other ingredients at the beginning of the cooking.

Baked Green Beans

Serves 4-5
Preparation time 35 minutes
Cooking time 2 hours

3 lb (1½ kg) fresh green beans or
2 lb (1 kg) frozen green beans
1 cup olive oil
1 small onion, grated
4 green onions, finely chopped
2 cloves garlic, sliced
26 oz (750 g) ripe tomatoes or
14 oz (400 g) canned tomatoes
1/2 cup finely chopped parsley
1/2 teaspoon sugar
salt and pepper

Trim the beans and rinse. Cut in half or in several pieces if they are very long. Heat the oil in a pan on high heat and saute the onions and garlic. Add the tomatoes and cook several minutes. Add the parsley, sugar, salt, and pepper. Arrange the beans in a ceramic or glass oven-proof dish and pour the sauce and 1/2 cup water on top. Cover with aluminum foil and bake at 400°F (200°C) 1-2 hours until the beans are tender and the sauce has cooked down. Remove the foil during the last 15 minutes of baking. Depending on the tenderness of the beans, it may be necessary to add some water. Serve hot or lukewarm accompanied by beet salad.

Broad Beans with Peas

Serves 6
Preparation time 40 minutes
Cooking time 1 hour

3 lb (1½ kg) fresh broad beans
1 cup olive oil
8 green onions, finely chopped
1 lb (500 g) shelled fresh peas
1/2 cup finely chopped dill
salt and freshly ground pepper
2 tablespoons lemon juice

Destring the broad beans and cut in half. Remove shells from mature pods and discard. Rinse and drain thoroughly. Heat the oil on high heat and saute the onions. Add the beans, peas, dill, salt, pepper, and 1 cup hot water. Cover and simmer until the beans and peas are tender and the sauce has cooked down to the oil. Remove from the heat and pour in the lemon juice. Shake the pan to distribute evenly. Serve hot or at room temperature. This recipe can be made without peas. Alternatively, prepare the

Lemon- or Tomato-Baked Potatoes

Serves 4-5
Preparation time 1 hour
Cooking time 1 hour 30 minutes

4 lb (2 kg) potatoes
1/3 cup lemon juice or
2 cups tomato juice
salt and pepper
1 teaspoon oregano
2 cloves garlic, slivered
2/3 cup olive oil

Peel, rinse, and cut the potatoes into pieces. For lemon potatoes, toss them with the lemon juice, salt, pepper, oregano, and garlic. Put in a ceramic or glass oven-proof dish. Pour the olive oil on top. Cover with aluminum foil and bake in the oven at 325°F (175°C) for 1 hour. Remove foil and continue baking 30 minutes, basting and stirring occasionally until the potatoes are tender and the sauce has cooked down to the oil. If necessary, add a little water. For tomato-baked potatoes, substitute the lemon juice with 2 cups of tomato juice and the remaining ingredients. Follow the same procedure as for the lemon-baked potatoes. Best served freshly baked and piping hot.

Jacket-Baked Potatoes, Stuffed or Not

Serves 5
Preparation time 15 minutes
Cooking time 1 hour 30 minutes

5 large baking potatoes of equal size
1/2 cup finely chopped green onions
1/4 cup finely chopped fresh parsley, dill, or, mint
1 cup vegetarian cream, whipped
1/4 cup finely chopped red bell pepper
salt and freshly ground pepper

for the stuffed potatoes
1/4 cup olive oil
1/2 cup finely chopped green onions
5 oz (150 g) spinach, chopped, blanched, and well-drained
1/2 cup finely chopped parsley, dill, or mint
1/4 cup vegetarian cream
1/4 cup grated vegetarian cheese (optional)
2 tablespoons prepared mustard
1 tablespoon lemon juice

Scrub the potatoes and pat dry. Wrap each one in aluminum foil and bake at 400°F (200°C) about 1 hour and 30 minutes until soft. Slash the skins of the potatoes with a sharp knife, once lengthwise down the center and crosswise across the middle. Squeeze the bottom of the slashed potato with your fingers to open like a flower. Sprinkle with salt and plenty of pepper. Serve with the herbs, cream, and chopped onion. To make stuffed or twice-baked potatoes: cut the potatoes in half after baking and remove most of the pulp with a spoon. Set the shells aside and mash the pulp with a fork. Saute the onions in the olive oil. Add spinach and stir for 5 minutes on the heat. Combine with the mashed potatoes along with the herbs, cream, cheese, mustard, lemon juice, salt, and pepper. Fill the potato shells and bake at 350°F (180°C) for about 30 minutes. Sprinkle with finely chopped red pepper sauteed in a little olive oil. Serve immediately.

eggplants. Cover the dish with aluminum foil and bake at 400°F (200°C) for 25-30 minutes until the sauce has cooked down to the oil and the vegetables are lightly browned and tender. Serve hot or at room temperature. This is a convenient and attractive dish for a buffet.

Baked Eggplant and Pepper Casserole

Serves 5-6
Preparation time 2 hours
Cooking time 1 hour

4 lb (2 kg) eggplant
1 lb (500 g) long sweet green peppers
1 lb (500 g) long sweet red peppers
1/3 cup olive oil
5-6 cloves garlic, slivered
2 lb (1 kg) pulped ripe tomatoes
2 tablespoons ketchup
salt and freshly ground pepper
1/4 cup finely chopped parsley
pinch of oregano (optional)

Slice the eggplant lengthwise into thick pieces, salt, and drain. Rinse and pat dry with paper towels. Fry lightly in olive oil. Fry or grill the peppers, deseed, and peel. Heat the oil in a pan and saute the garlic. Add the tomatoes, ketchup, salt, pepper, parsley, and oregano. Cook the sauce for 5 minutes. Arrange the fried eggplant and peppers in a ceramic or oven-proof baking dish in several layers, spreading the sauce between. Cover and bake at 350°F (175°C) for about 40 minutes until tender and the sauce has cooked down to the oil. Serve hot or at room temperature.

Eggplant Special

Serves 4-5
Preparation time 1 hour 30 minutes
Cooking time 30 minutes

4 lb (2 kg) medium round eggplant
4-5 large green bell peppers, in 1/2-inch (1-cm) rings
3-4 tomatoes, thinly sliced crosswise
1/4 cup olive oil
1 large onion, thinly sliced
1½ cups tomato juice
2 tablespoons finely chopped fresh mint
salt and freshly ground pepper

Wash the eggplant, wipe dry, and slice crosswise into rounds 1-1½ inch (3-4 cm) thick. Sprinkle with salt and allow to drain 1 hour in a colander. Rinse under running water and gently squeeze out excess water with your hands. Lightly fry in olive oil and arrange side by side in one layer in the bottom of a large baking pan. Place a pepper ring on top of each eggplant round. Heat the olive oil in a large saucepan and lightly saute the onions until wilted. Add the tomato juice, mint, pepper, and a little salt. Cook the sauce until slightly thickened. Remove the onions with a slotted spoon, allowing some of the sauce to drain off and put them on top of the eggplant rounds inside the pepper rings. Put a slice of tomato on each round, sprinkle with a little salt and pepper. Pour the sauce on top and around the

Hot Couscous with Tomato Sauce

Serves 4
Preparation time
Cooking time

1½ cups couscous
1/3 cup live oil
3½ cups boiling water
1 onion, thinly sliced
10 oz (300 g) canned plum tomatoes, halved
2 cloves garlic, slivered
1 cup green and black olives, pitted

1/4 cup parsley, dill, or mint, finely chopped
1 teaspoon oregano
2 tablespoons capers
salt and pepper, to taste

Put the couscous in a bowl, pour in the boiling water, 2 tablespoons olive oil, salt, and pepper. Cover and set aside for 5 minutes. Heat the remaining oil in a frying pan and saute the onions and garlic for about 3 minutes, until wilted. Add the tomatoes and cook on high heat for 2-3 minutes until golden. Add the olives, salt, and pepper and continue cooking for 1-2 minute more. Sprinkle the couscous with the parlsey and oregano, toss to mix, and then toss with the capers. Divide the couscous among four plates and spoon the tomatoes on top. Garnish with sprigs of parsley and lemon slices. Serve hot.

Baked Onions Naousa

Serves 5-6
Preparation time 1 hour
Cooking time 2-3 hours

5 lb (2½ kg) fresh or frozen pearl onions
1 cup olive oil
6 cloves garlic
2 lb (1 kg) ripe tomatoes, finely chopped
1 cup dry red wine
2 tablespoon vinegar
3 bay leaves
20 peppercorns
10 allspice berries
salt and freshly ground pepper

If using fresh onions, plunge them into a pot of boiling water. Turn off the heat and allow to stand 1-2 hours. The outer skins of the onions will easily slip off. Heat the oil in a pan and saute the peeled onions and the garlic, until slightly wilted. Toss the onions with the remaining ingredients and empty into a glass or ceramic oven pan. Cover with foil and bake in a 400°F (200°C) oven for 2-3 hours until tender and sauce has almost cooked down to the oil.

Stuffed Celeriac

Serves 4
Preparation time 30 minutes
Cooking time 45 minutes

24 oz (700 g) celery leaves

14 oz (400 g) celeriac
1/2 cup olive oil
1/2 cup green onions, finely chopped
1 cup tomato juice
2 ripe tomatoes, finely chopped
salt, to taste
freshly ground pepper
juice of 1 lemon
1/2 cup water

Rinse the celery leaves, blanch, and chop. Peel and slice the celeriac into thick rounds and blanch. Drain and when they are cool enough, press the center with your fingers to make a depression. Heat the oil and saute the onions. Add the tomato juice, tomatoes, celery leaves, celeriac, lemon juice, salt, and pepper. Add the water, cover, and simmer for about 45 minutes without stirring, until the vegetables are tender. To serve, arrange the celeriac rounds on a platter. With a slotted spoon, fill the centers with the cooked vegetables. Pour the sauce on top and garnish with lemon slices and sprigs of parsley. Serve hot. VARIATION: Cut small balls from two potatoes and add to the vegetables while they are cooking. This recipe is from the Messinias region of the Peloponnese where it is served as a main dish.

Eggplant Stuffed with Onions and Garlic

Serves 4-6
Preparation time 1 hour 30 minutes
Cooking time 1 hour

6 round eggplants (4 lbs or 2 kg)
2/3 cup olive oil
4 large onions, sliced
8 cloves garlic, slivered
1³/₄ cups canned or fresh tomato pulp
1/2 cup finely chopped parsley
salt and freshly ground pepper

Rinse and cut each eggplant in half lengthwise. Make two or three slashes in the flesh of each with a knife, taking care not to cut into the outer skin. Sprinkle with salt and drain 1-2 hours in a colander. Rinse and squeeze out excess moisture with your hands. Lightly brown in hot olive oil and drain. Arrange in one layer in a large oven-proof baking dish. Heat the oil and saute the onions and the garlic until wilted and transparent. Add the tomatoes, parsley, salt, and pepper and cook for 10 minutes. Make an opening down the middle of each eggplant with a spoon and fill with some of the onion mixture. Pour remaining sauce on top. Sprinkle with freshly ground pepper and bake in 350°F (180°C) oven for about 1 hour until the sauce has almost cooked down to the oil. It may be necessary to add a little water while baking. Serve hot or at room temperature.

Caponata

Serves 6
Preparation time 24 hours

3 lb (1¹/₂ kg) eggplant, cut in
1-inch (2¹/₂-cm) cubes
salt
1 cup finely chopped onion
1/4 cup olive oil
3/4 cup finely chopped celery
1/2 cup finely chopped green bell pepper
1/2 cup finely chopped red bell pepper
1 lb (500 g) ripe tomatoes, finely chopped
2 tablespoons balsamic vinegar
1 teaspoon sugar
1/2 cup sliced green olives
2 tablespoons capers
2 tablespoons finely chopped parsley

Salt the eggplant and drain 1 hour. Rinse with plenty of cold water and gently squeeze out the excess moisture with the palms of your hands. Fry them lightly in olive oil and drain well on paper towels. Saute the onions in the oil on medium heat until wilted. Add the celery and peppers and stir until wilted. Add the tomatoes, cover, and simmer 5 minutes. Stir in the vinegar, sugar, olive, and capers into the tomato sauce and simmer another 10 minutes until sauce is thick. Add the eggplant and the parsley, mix well, and remove from the heat. The flavor develops the longer the dish is allowed to stand. Prepare 24 hours in advance and serve at room temperature.

Vegetable-Stuffed Dolmas Cyprus

Serves 6
Preparation time 1 hour
Cooking time 40 minutes

4 lb (2 kg) chard or
1 lb (500 g) vine leaves
1¹/₂ cup olive oil
2 cups grated onion
1 leek, white part only, finely chopped
2 small zucchini, grated
2 medium carrots, grated
1/2 cup finely chopped cabbage
2 artichoke bottoms, finely chopped
1/4 cup finely chopped parsley
1/4 cup finely chopped mint
2 tablespoons finely chopped celery
2 cups short-grain rice
2 large ripe tomatoes, pureed or

14 oz (400 g) tomato juice
1/4 cup lemon juice
1 teaspoon sugar
salt and freshly ground pepper, to taste

Rinse and blanch the chard, taking care not to over-cook. Drain well. Heat half the oil in a pan and saute the onions, and leeks until wilted. Add the zucchini, carrots, cabbage, and artichoke and stir over medium heat until wilted. Remove from the heat, stir in the herbs, rice, salt, and pepper. Cut the blanched leaves into desired size and lay out on the worktop. Put one tablespoon of the rice mixture on the bottom end of each leaf, turn in the edges, and roll up as for "dolmas." Arrange some remaining and broken leaves on the bottom of a large pan. Arrange the rolls side by side in several layers. Combine the pureed tomatoes with the lemon juice, remaining olive oil, sugar, salt, and pepper and 1 cup of water. Pour the mixture on top of the rolls and place a heavy plate upside down on top to hold them while cooking. Cover the pan, and simmer the dolmas until nearly all the liquid has been absorbed and the rice is tender. Add a small amount of hot water, if necessary. May be served hot or at room temperature.

Chicory Salad

Serves 4-6
Preparation time 10 minutes

2 heads of chicory, leaves separated
4 cups rinsed, chopped curly endive or frisee
2 cups chopped Italian radicchio or red lettuce
1 medium onion, sliced into rings

for the dressing
1 tablespoon water
2 tablespoons vinegar
2 teaspoons prepared mustard
3 tablespoons olive oil
1/8 teaspoon pepper
1/4 teaspoon salt

Combine the ingredients for the dressing in a well-sealed jar and shake vigorously. Sprinkle the chicory leaves with 2 tablespoons of dressing and set aside in a bowl to marinate. Lightly toss the remaining chopped greens with the rest of the dressing. Turn out onto a deep platter and arrange the chicory around the edges. Serve immediately.

Cabbage Salad

Serves 4-5
Preparation time 30 minutes

3 cups finely shredded white cabbage
3 tablespoons each finely chopped red and green bell pepper
1/4 cup finely chopped celery
1 large carrot, grated
1/4 cup olive oil
2 tablespoons vinegar
salt and freshly ground pepper

Combine the prepared vegetables in a bowl. Shake the oil, vinegar, salt and pepper in a jar and pour over the salad shortly before serving.

Noodle and Vegetable Salad

Serves 4
Preparation time 20 minutes

3-4 oz (100 g) cooked noodles
1 large red bell pepper, julienne
1 large carrot, julienne
1 medium zucchini, julienne
7 oz (200 g) broccoli florets, blanched
mustard dressomg (see following recipe)

Combine the noodles and vegetables in a bowl and pour the mustard dressing on top.

Asparagus Salad with Mustard

2 lb (1 kg) fresh asparagus, blanched

for the dressing
1/4 cup olive oil
2 tablespoons white vinegar
2 teaspoons Dijon mustard
1 clove garlic, minced
1/4 teaspoon sugar
salt and pepper

Combine the ingredients for the dressing in a jar and shake vigorously. Pour over the blanched asparagus and allow to marinate at least 2 hours before serving.

Carrot Salad Vinaigrette

Serves 4
Preparation time 24 hours

4 large carrots, very thinly sliced
2 stalks of celery, thinly sliced
1 medium red onion, in rings
1 small green bell pepper, julienne
1/2 cup olive oil
1/4 cup vinegar
1 small garlic clove, minced
salt and freshly groundpepper
tender lettuce leaves

Combine the prepared vegetables except for the lettuce in a

bowl. Sprinkle with the oil, vinegar, garlic, salt, and pepper. Cover the bowl with plastic wrap and refrigerate overnight or 8 hours. Drain the salad and serve on the bed of lettuce.

Spinach and Mushroom Salad

Serves 4
Preparation time 15 minutes

5-6 oz (150 g) chopped young spinach leaves
1½ cups sliced fresh white mushrooms
3 tablespoons balsamic vinegar
3 tablespoons olive oil
1/2 teaspoon red pepper flakes
1 teaspoon toasted sesame seeds
salt and pepper

Combine the spinach and the mushrooms in a bowl. Combine the vinegar, oil, pepper flakes, sesame seeds, salt, and pepper in a well-sealed jar and shake vigorously until blended. Pour over the salad shortly before serving.

Peel and rinse all the vegetables. Deseed and devein the peppers. Slice the vegetables into 1/4-inch (1/2-cm) thick rounds. Remove the centers from the eggplant slices with a round cookie cutter. It is imperative that all the slices be of uniform size to ensure even cooking. Salt the eggplant and zucchini slices and drain 30 minutes. Rinse and gently squeeze out excess moisture. Combine the oil with the garlic, herbs, salt, and pepper in a well-sealed jar and shake vigorously until well-blended. Arrange the prepared vegetables in a large shallow bowl and sprinkle with the herbed oil mixture. Toss until all the vegetables are coated evenly. Line a baking sheet with baking paper and oil lightly. Arrange the vegetables in one layer on top. Bake in a 450°F (230°C) oven for 25 minutes. Arrange the spinach and rocket leaves on a large platter and lay the roasted vegetables on top. Sprinkle with the balsamic vinegar and serve immediately.

Grilled Vegetables

Roasting or grilling eggplant, zucchini, mushrooms, or tomatoes over hot coals or under the broiler gives them a wonderful flavor and aroma. Cut eggplant and zucchini lengthwise in half and make cross-hatch cuts in the flesh with a sharp knife. If desired, slice the larger ones into thick pieces, especially when cooking over live coals. Brush with olive oil and sprinkle with herbs. Marinate in the oil several minutes before placing the cut side under the broiler or over the hot coals. Turn to cook the other side. During the grilling, brush several times with olive oil. If desired, put one clove of finely minced garlic in the oil. Mushrooms should simply be wiped with a damp towel and grilled whole. Cut the tomatoes in half, stand on their sides, and gently press the bottom to squeeze out the seeds and the excess juice. Arrange in an oven dish. Combine some breadcrumbs with finely chopped parsley, mint, or oregano, finely minced garlic, salt, and pepper. Sprinkle the cut sides of the tomatoes with some of the mixture and dribble olive oil on top. Grill under the oven broiler pre-heated to 400°F (200°C) and grill 12 inches (30 cm) from the heat source for 20 minutes until done, taking care not to scorch.

Roasted Vegetable Salad

Serves 4
Preparation time 1 hour
Cooking time 25 minutes

1 large carrot
1 small celeriac root
1 medium onion, sliced
1 medium zucchini, sliced crosswise
1 each red and yellow bell pepper
2 medium beet roots
1 long medium eggplant
1 medium potato
1/3 cup olive oil
1 clove garlic, minced
1 teaspoon thyme, rosemary, and oregano mixture
1½ teaspoon salt
1/2 teaspoon freshly ground pepper
3-4 oz (100 g) fresh young spinach leaves
3-4 oz (100 g) rocket
4 tablespoons balsamic vinegar

Escarole and Wild Asparagus Salad

Serves 6
Preparation time 15 minutes

1 lb (500 g) escarole or curly endive
8 oz (250 g) wild asparagus
2 tablespoons olive oil
1 clove garlic, slivered
2 slices of bread, cubed
1/4 cup coarsely chopped walnuts
2 tablespoons vinegar
1/4 cup olive oil
salt and freshly ground pepper

Rinse and pick over the escarole and the asparagus. Pull off and discard the tough outer leaves of the escarole, retaining the tender leaves at the center. Cut off the thick woody portions of the asparagus, retaining the tender shoots and tips. Cut the escarole and asparagus into pieces and drain. Heat the 2 tablespoons of oil and saute the garlic briefly. Remove garlic with a slotted spoon and discard. Lay the cubes of bread on a baking sheet and sprinkle with the garlic oil. Toast in a 350°F (175°C) oven until lightly browned. Shortly before serving the salad, arrange the escarole and asparagus in layers on a platter with the croutons and walnuts in between. Combine the vinegar, olive oil, salt, and pepper in a well-sealed jar and shake vigorously until blended. Pour on top of the salad and serve immediately.

Roasted Eggplant Salad

Serves 4
Preparation time 30 minutes

4 large round eggplants
salt
5-6 cloves garlic, finely minced
1/4 cup vinegar
1/3 cup olive oil
10 drops Tabasco sauce
2 tablespoons finely chopped parsley
1 small green bell pepper, finely chopped (optional)
1 small ripe tomato, seeded and finely chopped
(optional)

Rinse the eggplants and pat dry. Wrap each one separately in aluminum foil and grill over hot coals or on the stove, gas or electric, turning on all sides until skin is almost completely charred. Unwrap and slit down one side lengthwise forming a boat. Arrange eggplants on a platter and separate the pulp from the skins in pieces without mashing. Sprinkle the pulp with salt, minced garlic and a little parsley. Beat the vinegar with oil and Tabasco sauce until well-blended and pour into each eggplant boat. If desired, sprinkle with chopped pepper and tomato or garnish each boat with half a cherry tomato and a small clove of garlic.

Potato Salad

Serves 4
Preparation time 45 minutes

4 large potatoes
1 small onion, thinly sliced in rings
3 green onions, chopped
2 tablespoons finely chopped parsley
1 carrot, blanched and thinly sliced
Vinaigrette dressing (see basic recipes)

Scrub the potatoes and put them in a pan with water to cover. Cook until tender, drain, and peel. Cut into bite-sized pieces and toss in a bowl with the onions, parsley, and carrot. The parsley can be substituted with mint or dill. Pour the vinaigrette on top and refrigerate several hours before serving.

Marinated Beets with Garlic Sauce

Serves 4
Preparation time 30 minutes
Cooking time 1 hour

2 lb (1 kg) medium fresh beets with tops
1/2 cup olive oil
1/4 cup vinegar
1 clove garlic, finely minced
salt to taste

Cut the beet roots from the stalks and scrub well under running water. Separate the leaves from the stalks and rinse well. Put the beets in a pan with boiling water to cover and cook until almost tender. About 15 minutes before they are done, add the leaves and continue cooking until the beets are fork tender and leaves are cooked but not soggy. Do not over-cook the leaves. Drain and separate the roots from the tops. Peel the beets, slice, and arrange on a platter with the cooked tops. Combine the oil, vinegar, garlic, and salt in a well-sealed jar and shake until well-blended. Pour over the beets and allow to marinate several hours before serving. They taste even better when prepared a day ahead. Serve with garlic sauce (see basic recipes).

Tabbouleh (Parsley Salad)

Serves 4-6
Preparation time 1 hour

1 cup medium bulgur
2 cups tap water
1/2 cup lemon juice
1/3 cup olive oil
1/2 teaspoon salt
1 teaspoon freshly ground black pepper
1 cup finely chopped green onions

3 cups finely chopped parsley
3 medium tomatoes, peeled and seeded
1/2 cup finely chopped mint

Soak the bulgur in the water 30 minutes to absorbed the water and drain the excess. Put the drained bulgur in a bowl with the parsley, mint, tomatoes, and half the lemon juice. Set aside for another 30 minutes. Beat the oil with the remaining lemon juice, salt, and pepper and pour over the salad. Serve on a bed of lettuce or in "cheese baskets." To make the cheese "basket," heat an 8½-inch (22-cm) non-stick fry pan on low and sprinkle 1/4 cup grated vegetarian cheese on the bottom. When it has melted, sprinkle 1/4 cup ground walnuts on top of the cheese. Continue cooking and when it begins to brown around the edges, remove from heat, cool briefly, and remove from the pan with a wooden spatula. Immediately put the cheese "pancake" on the outside of an inverted 4-inch (10-cm) round metal bowl. Allow to cool until the cheese sets, about 20 minutes. Repeat the procedure to make several more cheese baskets. Garnish the salad with lemon slices, parsley leaves, and tomato rosettes.

Baked Mushrooms

Serves 6
Preparation time 15 minutes
Cooking time 1 hour

1/4 cup olive oil
4 cloves garlic, slivered
1 large onion, grated
14 oz (400 g) canned chopped tomatoes
3 tablespoons ketchup
25 drops Tabasco sauce
2 tablespoons tomato paste
2 bay leaves
1/4 cup white wine
salt and freshly ground pepper
2 lb (1 kg) fresh white mushrooms, rinsed and patted dry
1/4 cup margarine, in small pieces
1/4 cup finely chopped parsley

Saute the garlic and onion in the oil until wilted. Add the tomatoes, ketchup, Tabasco, salt, and pepper. Cook the sauce for 15 minutes. Stir in the parsley. Arrange the whole mushrooms in an oven-proof dish and dot with the pieces of margarine. Pour the sauce on top and bake in a 350°F (175°C) oven for 1 hour, until the sauce has cooked down. Serve hot or at room temperature.

Stuffed Mushrooms

Serves 6
Preparation time 15 minutes
Cooking time 15 minutes

18 large fresh white mushrooms
2 tablespoons lemon juice
1/4 cup olive oil
2 cloves garlic, finely minced
1/3 cup finely chopped green onions
2 tablespoons finely chopped fresh mint or
1 tablespoon dried mint
2 tablespoons ketchup
2 tablespoons dried breadcrumbs
1/3 cup grated vegetarian cheese (optional)
salt and freshly ground pepper

Rinse the mushrooms briefly under running water and pat dry. Remove the stems and brush with lemon juice. Chop the stems and set aside. Saute the garlic and onions in the oil until wilted. Add the chopped stems and saute 2-3 minutes. Remove from the heat and add the mint, ketchup, breadcrumbs, cheese, salt, and pepper. Mix well and fill the mushroom caps with the mixture. Arrange in a small baking dish and broil 15 minutes until lightly browned. Serve immediately.

Fried Vegetables in Red Sauce

Serves 4-5
Preparation time 1 hour
Cooking time 1 hour

1/4 cup olive oil
1 small onion, grated or
4 cloves garlic, slivered
3 lb (1½ kg) ripe tomatoes or
28 oz (800 g) canned tomatoes, finely chopped
2 tablespoons ketchup
1/4 cup finely chopped parsley
salt and pepper
2 lb (1 kg) eggplant, sliced
2 lb (1 kg) potatoes, sliced
2 lb (1 kg) sweet green peppers, quartered
2 lb (1 kg) zucchini, sliced

In a large wide pan heat the oil and saute the onions or garlic. Add the tomatoes, ketchup, parsley, salt, and pepper, cover and simmer the sauce until it thickens. Meanwhile, sprinkle the sliced eggplant with salt and put in a colander for 1 hour. Rinse and squeeze out excess moisture with your hands. Fry them in olive oil and drain well on absorbent paper. Fry the potatoes and peppers separately. Sprinkle the zucchini lightly with salt and drain well. Dip first in flour, then in cold water, and fry in olive oil. Toss the fried vegetables in the sauce until well-coated. Serve hot or at room temperature.

Zucchini Mushroom Casserole

Serves 6
Preparation time 1 hour
Cooking time 2 hours

5 sun-dried tomatoes
2 lb (1 kg) zucchini, sliced
1 lb (500 g) portobello or oyster mushrooms, chopped
2/3 cup olive oil
1 medium onion, finely chopped
2 cloves garlic, finely minced
1 cup tomato juice
2 tablespoons ketchup
1/2 cup finely chopped parsley
salt and freshly ground pepper

Soak the sun-dried tomatoes in water several hours to swell. Drain and pat dry with paper towels. Arrange the sliced zucchini, mushrooms and tomatoes in an oven-proof baking dish. Heat the oil and saute the onions and the garlic. Add the tomato juice and ketchup. Cook until the sauce is slightly thick. Stir in the parsley, salt, and pepper and spoon evenly on top of the vegetables. Cover with foil and bake in a 350°F (180°C) oven for about 2 hours. During the last half hour remove the foil and bake until lightly browned.

Spaghetti with Roasted Garlic Sauce

Serves 6
Preparation time 40 minutes
Cooking time 30 minutes

5 whole heads of garlic
3 tablespoons olive oil
1/4 cup Dijon mustard
1 tablespoon lemon juice
1/2 teaspoon black pepper
3 zucchini, julienne
14 oz (400 g) canned sliced mushrooms, drained
1/3 cup olive oil
14 oz (400 g) canned tomatoes, drained and chopped
1lb (500 g) spaghetti

Put the whole heads of garlic in the middle of a large piece of aluminum foil, pour 3 tablespoons of oil on top, enclose the garlic in the foil and bake in a 400°F (200°C) oven for 35 minutes until soft. Remove from the oven and cool slightly. Separate the cloves, squeeze out the soft pulp, and discard the skins. Put the garlic pulp in the food processor, add the mustard, lemon juice, and pepper. Process until well-blended. Saute the zucchini and mushrooms in the remaining oil. Add the pureed garlic and tomatoes and simmer the sauce 20 minutes. Meanwhile, cook the spaghetti in boiling salted water with 2 tablespoons olive oil al dente. Drain, empty into a heated baking dish, pour the hot sauce on top and toss until the spaghetti is well coated. Serve immediately.

Fried Vegetables

Serves 6
Preparation time 30 minutes
Cooking time 30 minutes

1 large eggplant, sliced in thin rounds
12 large white mushrooms, cut in half
2 large zucchini, sliced into thin rounds
1 small cauliflower, cut into florets
1 small broccoli, cut into florets
2 large onions, sliced into rings
tahini sauce (see basic recipes)
batter for frying (see basic recipes)

Prepare the batter about 1 hour before using or it will not stick to the vegetables. Meanwhile, sprinkle the eggplant and zucchini slices with salt, drain separately for 30 minutes, rinse, and pat dry. Dip the vegetables in the batter and fry in hot olive oil. Drain on paper towels and arrange on a platter. Drizzle with the tahini sauce and serve immediately.

Individual Macaroni Timbales

Serves 6
Preparation time 2 hours
Cooking time 35 minutes

1/2 lb (250 g) thick macaroni or ziti
2 cups bechamel sauce (see basic recipes)
1/8 teaspoon ground nutmeg
2 tablespoons margarine
1 cup grated vegetarian cheese
2 large eggplants, in small cubes
1 medium onion, grated
2 cloves garlic, finely minced
1/3 cup olive oil
1 lb (500 g) white mushrooms, finely chopped
14 oz (400 g) canned tomatoes, finely chopped
1 tablespoons tomato paste
2 tablespoons ketchup
1 teaspoon chili powder
1/8 teaspoon cinnamon
1/8 teaspoon ground clove
salt and freshly ground pepper
2 tablespoons dried breadcrumbs

Cook the macaroni al dente in salted boiling water with 2 tablespoons olive oil. Drain well and empty into a bowl. Prepare the bechamel seasoned with the ground nutmeg. Toss the cooked macaroni with the margarine, half the bechamel, and half the cheese. Salt the eggplant and drain 30 minutes. Meanwhile, saute the onions and the garlic in the oil. Add the mushrooms and cook 5 minutes. Add the tomatoes, ketchup, tomato paste, spices, salt, and pepper. Cover and simmer until the sauce thickens. Rinse and drain the eggplant. Fry in hot oil until crisp. Drain on absorbent paper and stir into the mushroom sauce. Allow to cool and stir in the remaining cheese and bechamel sauce. Grease the bottoms and sides of the 6 cups of a jumbo muffin tin with margarine and sprinkle with the dried breadcrumbs. Pat the strands of macaroni evenly onto the sides of the muffin cups in a spiral beginning at the bottom center. Fill each one almost to the top with the mushroom sauce. Cover the surface with the remaining macaroni mixture. Bake the timbales in a 400°F (200°C) oven for 35 minutes. Remove from the oven and cool for 8 minutes before unmolding on a serving platter. Alternatively, the macaroni can be layered in a 8x10-inch (20x25-cm) baking dish with the mushroom sauce as a filling and the bechamel on top, as for Greek pastitsio. Bake in a 400°F (200°C) oven for 50 minutes. Serve hot.

Finocchio Saute

Serves 4
Prepare time 20 minutes
Cooking time 20 minutes

8 small fennel bulbs, cut in half
6 cloves garlic, peeled
1/3 cup olive oil
salt and pepper
1/2 cup water or tomato juice
1/4 cup finely chopped fennel leaves
2 tablespoons lemon juice

Heat the oil in a large heavy-bottomed frying pan. Saute the fennel and garlic for 10-15 minutes, turning often until lightly browned on all sides. Add the water or tomato juice, the salt, and the pepper, cover and simmer 20 minutes until the fennel is tender and the sauce cooked down almost to the oil. One minute before taking off the heat, stir in the finely chopped fennel leaves and lemon juice. Shake the pan lightly to distribute and serve immediately.

Leeks with Celeriac

Serves 4-5
Preparation time 15 minutes
Cooking time 1 hour

3 lb (1¹/₂ kg) trimmed leeks, in
1¹/₂-inch (4-cm) slices
1 lb (500 g) peeled celeriac, quartered or
celery stalks, in 1-inch (2-cm) pieces
3/4 cup olive oil
salt and freshly ground pepper
1/3 cup lemon juice
2 medium potatoes, quartered

Steam the leeks and celeriac separately and drain. Heat the oil and saute the leeks several minutes. Add 1/2 cup water, the salt, and the pepper. Cover and simmer until half-cooked. Add the celeriac and the potatoes, stir lightly to mix. Cover and simmer until the vegetables are tender but not mushy and the sauce has almost cooked down to the oil. It may be necessary to add a little water during the cooking. Add the lemon juice and shake the pan to distribute. Sprinkle with freshly ground pepper and serve hot or at room temperature. Alternatively, prepare the dish substituting the potatoes with 1/2 cup of short-grain rice.

Pasta Shells with Peas

Serves 4
Preparation time 15 minutes

2 cups medium shell pasta
1 cup fresh shelled peas
2 roasted red peppers, in thin strips
vinaigrette dressing (see basic recipes)

for the garnish
1 bunch of rocket, cress, or purslane
fresh zucchini blossoms, rinsed and patted dry

Cook the pasta in boiling salted water with 2 tablespoons olive oil for about 8 minutes and drain. Cook and drain the peas. Allow both to cool. Prepare the vinaigrette according to the recipe. Put the pasta, peas, and peppers in a bowl, pour the dressing on top and toss lightly. Arrange the rocket leaves on a platter with the salad on top. Garnish with the zucchini blossoms.

Lasagne Rolls with Vegetables

Serves 6
Preparation time 1 hour
Cooking time 40 minutes

8 oz (250 g) – 12 sheets lasagne
2½ cups blanched broccoli florets
2½ cups fresh white mushrooms, thinly sliced
2 green onions, finely chopped
2 tablespoons finely chopped parsley
1 teaspoon oregano
1 teaspoon basil or pizza seasoning
2½ cup grated vegetarian cheese
1 cup vegetarian cream
1 tablespoons cornstarch
salt and freshly ground pepper

for the sauce
4 large ripe tomatoes
1/3 olive oil
3 tablespoons tomato paste
1 clove garlic, minced
1 teaspoon oregano
1 teaspoon dried basil or pizza seasoning
1 bay leaf
salt and freshly ground pepper

First, prepare the tomato sauce. Peel and deseed the tomatoes, and puree the pulp in the food processor. Empty into a saucepan with the remaining ingredients for the sauce. Cover and simmer for 10 minutes until thick. Bring water to boil in a large pan with 1-2 tablespoons olive oil. Cook the lasagne in two batches for about 5 minutes until softened. Remove with a slotted spoon and plunge into cold water until cool enough to handle. Drain until dry on cotton towels. Meanwhile, combine the vegetables, the cheese, and the seasonings in a large bowl. Cook the cream with the cornstarch until thick and pour into the vegetable mixture with the salt and plenty of freshly ground pepper. Toss gently until well blended. Spread half the prepared tomato sauce into the bottom of a rectangular baking dish 9x13 inches (22 x 30 cm). Divide and spoon the vegetable mixture evenly onto the 12 cooked lasagne sheets and roll up loosely. Place side by side in the baking dish with the seam side down. Pour the remaining tomato sauce on top. Bake in a 350°F (180°C) oven for 45-50 minutes. Remove from the oven, sprinkle with a little cheese, and serve immediately.

Vegetable Farfalle

Serves 4
Preparation time 40 minutes
Cooking time 15 minutes

1/4 cup olive oil
1 cup small white mushrooms, sliced
1/2 cup finely chopped onion
2 cloves garlic, slivered
1 cup finely chopped sweet red pepper
10 oz (300 g) pasta farfalle
1 tablespoon margarine
1 tablespoons flour or cornstarch
1 cup vegetarian cream or soya milk, scalded
1/8 teaspoon ground nutmeg
salt and freshly ground pepper
1½ cups blanched broccoli florets or asparagus

1 large carrot, in paper thin slices
3 tablespoons finely chopped parsley
2 tablespoons finely chopped fresh basil
1/3 cup shredded vegetarian cheese

Heat the oil and saute the onions, garlic, mushrooms, and red pepper until wilted. Cook the pasta in boiling salted water with 2 tablespoons olive oil and drain well. Melt the margarine in a small pan and stir in the flour and cook 1 minute. Add the cream or the scalded milk, stirring continuously until the sauce is thick. Remove from the heat, stir in the nutmeg, the salt, and plenty of freshly ground pepper. Combine the broccoli florets, the carrots, the sauteed mushroom mixture and the pasta in a large bowl. Add the cream sauce, the herbs, and more salt and pepper, if desired. Alternatively, the cream sauce can be served separately. Sprinkle with the cheese and serve immediately.

Farfalle al Pesto

Serves 5-6
Preparation time 30 minutes
Cooking time 8 minutes

1 cup finely chopped parsley
1 cup finely chopped fresh basil
2-3 cloves garlic, finely minced
2 oz (60 g) pine nuts
1/2 cup olive oil
salt and freshly ground pepper
1 lb (500 g) farfalle pasta
1/2 cup shredded vegetarian cheese

Combine the parsley, basil, garlic, pine nuts, 1/4 cup of the oil, salt, and pepper in a blender or food processor container. Process until well-blended. Using the medium setting, add the remaining oil in a steady stream and continue blending until the mixture is thick and smooth, the consistency of mayonnaise. Cook the pasta in boiling salted water with 2 tablespoons olive oil for about 8 minutes. Drain and while still hot, toss with the pesto sauce. If desired, the pesto can be prepared using 2 cups of basil instead of parsley and basil. Sprinkle the pasta with grated cheese and serve immediately.

Linguine with Bell Peppers

Serves 4
Preparation time 15 minutes
Cooking time 15 minutes

1/4 cup olive oil
1 teaspoon grated fresh ginger or
1 clove garlic, finely minced
1 each red, green, and orange bell peppers, julienne
1 small fennel bulb, sliced
3 green onions, julienne
3 oz (100 g) blanched sliced almonds or cashews
10 oz (300 g) linguine or spaghetti

Heat the oil in a deep frying pan and saute the ginger or the garlic. Add the peppers, fennel, and green onions and stir-fry until wilted. In a small pan brown the almonds lightly in 1 tablespoon olive oil. Cook the pasta in boiling salted water with 2 tablespoons olive oil al dente and drain. Arrange on a deep platter with the sauteed vegetables and nuts on top. Toss lightly to mix and serve immediately.

Tagliatelle with Creamed Squash

Serves 4
Preparation time 15 minutes
Cooking time 30 minutes

2 lb (1 kg) winter squash, peeled, seeded, and cubed
2 medium leeks, thinly sliced
1/4 cup olive oil
1/8 teaspoon ground nutmeg
1 lb (500 g) tagliatelle (eggless)
1½ cup vegetarian cream
1/4 cup water
1/4 cup toasted pine nuts
salt and freshly ground pepper

Heat the oil and saute the leeks until wilted. Add the squash, nutmeg, salt, and pepper and simmer 10 minutes. Stir in the cream and the water and when the sauce comes to a boil again, lower the heat and simmer 10 minutes, until the squash is tender. Meanwhile, cook the tagliatelles in boiling salted water with 2 tablespoons olive oil. Drain and serve in hot bowls with the creamed squash and pine nuts. Sprinkle with plenty of freshly ground black pepper.

Tagliatelle with Mushrooms and Olive Sauce

Serves 4
Preparation time 15 minutes
Cooking time 15 minutes

10 oz (300 g) tagliatelle (eggless)
1 cup olive sauce (see basic recipes)
1/4 cup olive oil
2 cloves garlic, slivered
10 oz (300 g) white mushrooms, sliced

Cook the tagliatelle al dente in boiling salted water with 2 tablespoons of olive oil. Prepare the olive sauce according to the directions in basic recipe. Heat the oil and saute the garlic and the mushrooms until wilted. Drain the pasta and toss with the sauce and sauteed mushrooms. Serve immediately accompanied by fresh green salad.

Oyster Mushrooms with Mustard Sauce

Serves 6
Preparation time 30 minutes
Cooking time 45 minutes

1/3 cup olive oil
2 cloves garlic, minced
2 lb (1 kg) oyster mushrooms
1 oz (35 g) dried porcini mushrooms (optional)
1/2 cup dry white wine
1 teaspoon cornstarch
1/2 cup vegetable stock (see basic recipes)
1/4 cup Dijon mustard
1/4 cup vegetarian cream
2 tablespoons finely chopped parsley
salt and freshly ground pepper
1 small cauliflower, cut into florets
1 large broccoli, cut into florets

Rinse the oyster mushrooms, pat dry, and cut into pieces. Heat the oil in a large pan and saute the garlic. Add the mushrooms and saute briefly. Remove with a slotted spoon to a hot platter and keep warm. If using the dried porcinis, soak in a cup of hot water until soft, about 15 minutes. Rinse well and add to the pan along with the wine. Dissolve the cornstarch in the stock and stir in the mustard and cream. Pour the mixture into the pan, stir to mix, cover, and simmer until thick. Meanwhile, cook the cauliflower and broccoli florets in boiling water until crisp-tender. Serve the oyster mushrooms on hot plates with the vegetables accompanied by mashed potatoes. Pour the hot mustard sauce on top and serve immediately.

Mushroom Pilaf

Serves 4-5
Preparation time 1 hour
Cooking time 30 minutes

1 oz (35 g) dried porcini mushrooms
3 cups boiling water
1/4 olive oil
5 cloves garlic, slivered
5 green onions, finely chopped
2 cups long-grain rice
2 teaspoons salt
7 oz (200 g) fresh white mushrooms, sliced
1 red or yellow bell pepper, finely chopped
1/2 cup finely chopped parsley or dill
freshly ground pepper

Soak the porcini mushrooms in the boiling water for 1 hour to swell. Remove from the water one by one, shake off excess water, and finely chop. Allow the water to settle and remove 2 cups from the top. Heat half the oil in a pan and saute the finely chopped mushrooms, half the garlic, and half the onions. Add the rice and stir in the oil until well-coated. Add the salt, the mushroom liquid, and 2 cups of boiling water. Cover and simmer the rice 20 minutes, until all the liquid is absorbed. Meanwhile, in a small pan heat the remaining oil and saute the other half of the onions and garlic until wilted. Add the white mushrooms and peppers and stir for about 15 minutes until wilted. Add the cooked rice, the parsley or dill, and sprinkle with freshly ground pepper. Stir lightly for 1 minute on the heat to blend. Pack the rice into an oiled form to shape and unmold onto a platter. Serve immediately.

Garlic Spaghetti with Olives

Serves 4
Preparation time 15 minutes

1/3 cup olive oil
3-4 cloves garlic, thinly slivered
10 Calamata olives, pitted and sliced (optional)
1 hot red chili, minced (optional)
14 oz (400 g) spaghetti
salt and freshly ground pepper

Cook the spaghetti 8 minutes in boiling salted water with 2 tablespoons olive oil and drain. Meanwhile, heat the oil in a large pan and saute the garlic until soft. Add the sliced olives and saute for 1-2 minutes. Add the drained spaghetti and toss until well-coated with the oil. Sprinkle with freshly ground pepper and, if desired, minced hot red chili. Serve immediately accompanied by grated vegetarian cheese.

Pasta with Mushrooms and Black Truffle

Serves 4
Preparation time 15 minutes
Cooking time 15 minutes

10 oz (300 g) leaf-shaped pasta or spaghetti
3 tablespoons olive oil
10 oz (300 g) oyster mushrooms
1 oz (30 g) jar of black truffles
1 cup vegetarian cream
2 tablespoons truffle oil
salt and white pepper

Cook the pasta al dente in salted boiling water with 2 tablespoons olive oil and drain. Rinse the mushrooms, drain and pat dry with paper towels. Arrange on a piece of aluminum foil, sprinkle with salt and pepper, brush with the oil, and broil 15 minutes. To prepare the sauce, scald the cream and stir in the truffle oil, some salt, and a little pepper. If you cannot find truffle oil, use the liquid from the jar of truffles. Finely chop half the truffles and stir into the cream sauce. Serve the drained pasta with the broiled mushrooms on heated plates, pour the cream sauce on top, and garnish with the remaining truffles, a lemon slice, and a sprig of dill.

Mashed Potatoes

Serves 4
Preparation time 40 minutes

2 lb (1 kg) large potatoes, peeled and quartered
1/3 cup margarine
1/2 cup soy milk or vegetarian cream
salt and pepper
1/8 teaspoon ground nutmeg

Cook the potatoes in boiling about 1½ cups of salted water until all the water has been absorbed and they are very soft. Mash them with the margarine and as much soy milk or cream as necessary to make a smooth puree. Add the salt, pepper, and nutmeg. Stir over very low heat for another 5 minutes. Serve immediately.

Velvet Vegetable Soup

Serves 4
Preparation time 30 minutes
Cooking time 1 hour

1/4 cup margarine
8 oz (250 g) peeled cubed potatoes
1 carrot, thinly sliced
1 large onion, chopped
1 small stalk of celery root or celeriac, and
a few tender leaves, chopped
1 tablespoon flour
6 cups vegetable stock (see basic recipes)
salt and freshly ground pepper
1 cup vegetarian cream (optional)
3 tablespoons finely chopped parsley
10 thin slices of celery, for garnish

Melt the margarine in a pan and saute the vegetables until wilted. Add the flour and stir several minutes. Add the stock, salt, and pepper. Cover and simmer until the vegetables are very soft. Cool slightly and empty into the container of a food processor. Blend until smooth. Pour back into the pot and if the soup too thick, add a little water. Cook 5 minutes. Add the cream and stir until hot. Serve immediately sprinkled with the chopped parsley and the sliced celery.

Stuffed Cabbage Leaves

Serves 4-5
Preparation time 1 hour
Cooking time 30-40 minutes

5 lb (2½ kg) cabbage
1½ cups olive oil
1 cup grated onion
1 cup finely chopped green onions
1 large carrot, finely grated
2 cups pulped fresh or canned tomatoes
1/2 cup finely chopped dill
1/2 cup finely chopped parsley
1½ cups short-grain rice
salt and freshly ground pepper
1/4 teaspoon cayenne
1 oz (30 g) pine nuts

Rinse the cabbage and cut a piece around the core at the stem-end with a sharp knife and remove. Put the cabbage cut side down into a large pan of boiling water and cook until leaves are half tender. Remove, allow to cool and separate the leaves. If the interior is still tough, return to the pan of boiling water and cook until all the leaves are softened. Remove the tougher stem-ends and cut each leaf into 2 or 3 large pieces. Heat half the oil on high heat and saute the onions and carrots until wilted. Add the tomatoes and the remaining ingredients, except for the rice and pine nuts. Cook the sauce for 10 minutes. Remove from the heat and stir in the rice and pine nuts. Strain the mixture and reserve the excess liquid. Place 1 tablespoon of rice mixture at the center of one end of the cabbage leaf. Fold in the sides over the stuffing and roll up loosely allowing room for the rice to expand. Repeat until all the stuffing and leaves are used up. Use the tough pieces and left-over leaves to line the bottom of a large casserole. Arrange the stuffed cabbage leaves seam-side down and side by side in layers into the casserole. Pour the reserved juice on top, set a heavy plate slightly smaller than the diameter of the pan, on top of the rolls. Cover and simmer until the sauce has almost cooked down to the oil and the rice is tender. It may be necessary to add a little water during cooking. Serve hot or at room temperature accompanied by olives.

Fusilli with Eggplant Sauce

Serves 4
Preparation time 1 hour
Cooking time 30 minutes

3 lb (1½ kg) eggplant
1/4 cup olive oil
2 cloves garlic, slivered
2 lb (1 kg) ripe tomatoes, peeled,
seeded, and chopped
2 tablespoons ketchup
20 drops Tabasco sauce
1/4 cup finely chopped basil or mint
10 oz (300 g) fusilli pasta
grated vegetarian cheese (optional)

Chop the eggplant into 1/2-in (1-cm) cubes. Sprinkle with a little salt and drain in a colander for 1 hour. Rinse in and squeeze out excess water with your hands. Fry lightly in olive oil and drain on paper towels. Heat the oil and saute the garlic. Add the tomatoes, ketchup, and Tabasco sauce. Simmer until the sauce is slightly thick. Shortly before the sauce is done, add the herbs and the eggplant and continue simmering a while longer. Cook the pasta 8-10 minutes in boiling salted water with 2 tablespoons olive oil and drain. Serve on hot plates topped with the eggplant sauce and sprinkled, if desired, with grated cheese.

Spaghetti Neapolitan with Vegetables

Serves 4
Preparation time 30 minutes
Cooking time 30 minutes

1/3 cup olive oil
1 onion, finely chopped
1 leek, trimmed and sliced
2 stalks of celery, trimmed and sliced
7 oz (200 g) small white mushrooms
2 carrots, sliced
14 oz (400 g) canned chopped tomatoes, drained
2 tablespoons ketchup
2 tablespoons finely chopped basil
1/4 teaspoon cayenne
10 oz (300 g) pesto-flavored or plain spaghetti
salt and freshly ground black pepper

First, prepare the sauce. Saute the onions in the oil until wilted. Add the leeks, celery, mushrooms, and carrots. Stir over medium heat for 10 minutes until wilted. Add the tomatoes, ketchup, basil, salt, and cayenne. Stir over high heat, and when the sauce comes to a boil, lower the heat, cover, and simmer 30 minutes. Meanwhile, cook the pasta al dente in salted boiling water with 2 tablespoons olive oil. Drain the pasta, transfer to a deep platter and pour the hot sauce on top. Serve immediately.

Spaghetti Bolognese with Mushrooms

Serves 4
Preparation time 15 minutes
Cooking time 30 minutes

28 oz (800 g) canned mushrooms
1/4 cup olive oil
1 medium onion, grated
2 cloves garlic, finely minced
28 oz (800 g) canned tomatoes, finely chopped
1 tablespoons tomato paste
2 tablespoons ketchup
1 bay leaf
1/4 teaspoon ground allspice
3 tablespoons finely chopped parsley
salt and freshly ground pepper

14 oz (400 g) spaghetti
2 tablespoons margarine
grated vegetarian cheese (optional)

Drain the mushrooms and pat dry with absorbent paper towels. Mince finely in the food processor. Heat the oil and saute the onions, and garlic until wilted. Add the minced mushrooms and saute lightly. Add the tomatoes, the tomato paste, ketchup, bay leaf, allspice, parsley, salt, and pepper. Cover and simmer the mushroom sauce until thick, about 20 minutes. Cook the pasta al dente in boiling salted water with 2 tablespoons olive oil and drain. Melt the margarine in the same pan, return the cooked pasta to the pan and toss until well-coated. Serve on hot plates accompanied by the mushroom sauce and grated cheese, if desired.

Pasta with Pink Sauce

Serves 4
Preparation time 10 minutes
Cooking time 15 minutes

3 tablespoons olive oil
5 green onions, white part only, finely chopped
3 sun-dried tomatoes
14 oz (400 g) tomato juice
1/2 cup vegetarian cream
14 oz (400 g) fussili or farfalle pasta
salt and freshly ground pepper
3 tablespoons finely chopped fresh basil

Soak the sun-dried tomatoes several hours in hot water to cover. Strain and cut into strips. Heat the oil in a pan and lightly saute the onions. Add the tomatoes, and stir over medium heat for several minutes. Stir in the tomato juice, and simmer until the sauce thickens. Shortly before taking off the heat, stir in the cream which will turn the sauce a beautiful pink color. Taste and correct the seasonings. Cook the pasta al dente and drain. Transfer to a platter and pour the sauce on top and toss. Sprinkle with finely chopped fresh basil and serve immediately on heated plates.

SPAGHETTI NEAPOLITAN WITH VEGETABLES

Snail and Onion Stew

Serves 4
Preparation time 30 minutes
Cooking time 2 hours

2 lb (1 kg) fresh live snails
1 cup flour (to feed the snails)
1 cup olive oil
2 lb (1 kg) onions, peeled and sliced
2 cloves garlic, sliced
1½ cups tomato juice
2 tablespoons tomato paste
2-3 bay leaves
3-4 whole allspice berries
salt and pepper
1/4 cup dry red wine

If you collect fresh live snails from the field, put them in a container (box or basket) for 8-10 days, sprinkle with a handful of flour every 2-3 days to clear their digestive tracts. If you buy snails which are hibernating, put them in cold water, remove the membrane (operculum), and discard those which do not move when their foot is touched. Place the snails in a colander and rinse several times with plenty of fresh water. Sprinkle with a little salt, toss, and allow to stand 5 minutes. Rinse several times in plenty of water to rid them of slime. Put them in a pan with enough water to cover and a little salt and place on low heat so they will come out of their shells. Increase the heat and cook them until tender, about 1 hour, occasionally skimming the foam which rises to the surface. Remove the snails with a slotted spoon and set aside. Allow the cooking liquid to settle and reserve 1 cup of clear liquid from the top and discard the remainder. Heat the oil on high heat and lightly saute the onions and garlic until wilted. Add the snails, tomato juice, paste, bay leaf, allspice, pepper, and the reserved cooking liquid. Cover and simmer until the snails are tender and the sauce has cooked down almost to the oil. Serve at room temperature. This dish tastes even better the day after it is prepared.

Snails with Vegetables

Serves 4-5
Preparation time 30 minutes
Cooking time 1 hour 35 minutes

1 lb (500 g) eggplant, cubed
1 lb (500 g) zucchini, cubed
1 lb (500 g) potatoes, peeled and cubed
2 lb (1 kg) snails
1 cup olive oil
1 large onion, chopped
4 cloves garlic, sliced
2 lb (1 kg) ripe tomatoes, chopped
2 bay leaves
6 whole allspice berries
10 peppercorns
salt and freshly ground pepper

Salt the eggplant and drain in a colander for 1 hour. Rinse and squeeze out excess moisture with your hands. Fry the eggplant, zucchini, and potatoes lightly in olive oil. Prepare the snails as described in the recipe above and cook in boiling water for 1 hour. Remove snails with a slotted spoon and allow the cooking liquid to settle. Reserve 1 cup of the clear liquid from the top and discard the remainder. Heat the oil in a large pan on high heat and saute the onions and garlic until wilted. Add the tomatoes and cook for 5 minutes. Add the remaining ingredients along with the snails and the reserved liquid. Cover and simmer until the vegetables are tender, about 35 minutes.

It may be necessary to add a little water. The sauce should cook down almost to the oil. Sprinkle with freshly ground black pepper and serve warm.

Onion Soup

Serves 8
Preparation time 1 hour 30 minutes

4 large onions, thinly sliced
1/3 cup margarine
2 tablespoons flour
8 cups hot vegetable stock
8 thin slices of bread, toasted

1/4 cup olive oil
7 oz (200 g) grated vegetarian cheese (optional)
salt and freshly ground pepper

Melt the margarine in a pan and add the onions. Sprinkle with a little salt, cover, and allow them to simmer in their own juices. Cook for about 40 minutes, stirring occasionally until tender but not browned. Remove the cover, add the flour, and increase the heat. Stir the onions continuously until golden brown, about 30 minutes. If they start to color too quickly, lower the temperature slightly. Add the stock and simmer 10 minutes. Add salt and freshly ground pepper and ladle into 8 oven-proof bowls. Put a piece of toast dribbled with a little olive oil in each bowl and sprinkle with cheese. Place the bowls under a hot broiler until the cheese melts and is lightly browned. Serve immediately.

Archestratus in his much feted poem:
But leave aside a lot of the fancy
nonsense and buy yourself a lobster
which has long and heavy hands
but small feet and advances
only slowly over the land.
They are most numerous and the best
of all for quality in the Lipari islands.
The Hellespont also gathers many
together. Archestratus the Daedalus
of tasty dishes advises: If you ever go to
Iasus, the city of the Carians, you will
get a good-sized prawn, but it is rarely
for sale, while in Macedonia
and Ambracia there are a good many.

S H E L L F I S H

Archestratus, *The Life of Luxury*,
Fragments 24 & 25 in Athenaus 105e.
(Wilkins & Hill translation, Prospect Books, 1994)

The oceans and salt-water seas of the world offer a great variety of shellfish which are harvested wild or "cultivated" in carefully controlled areas where the food supply is supplemented with nutrients to produce succulent animals high in protein, Omega-3 fatty acids, vitamins, and trace elements. The shellfish family can be divided into roughly three separate categories: *crustaeans* include prawns, shrimp, lobsters, crayfish and crabs. *Molluscs* include clams, scallops, mussels, and oysters. These two types are probably the best known and most popular of the world's shellfish. The third, *cephalopods*, which include octopus, squid and cuttlefish, are less well-known in the Western world outside the Mediterranean, but nevertheless, can also be used in a wide-variety of tasty dishes. In coastal areas most fresh shellfish is sold either in the shells or shucked, meaning the shells have been removed. Since shellfish is highly perishable, much of it is fresh-frozen or vacuum-packed aboard sea-going processing plants immediately after being caught, making it more widely available and safer to eat. Avoid eating raw shellfish unless you are absolutely sure it comes from unpolluted waters. Take particular care in preparing seafood

S H E L L F I S H

dishes – shellfish become tough when improperly cooked.

NOTE: Surimi is often sold as crab sticks or seafood legs. They are not real crab but white fish fillets highly processed into seafood "analogs" complete with red-dyed edges. Read package label to be sure. To make sure you are getting the "real thing" shop from a reliable fishmonger or market.

PRAWNS AND SHRIMP: In this cookbook "prawn" refers to jumbo and large shellfish while medium and smaller size are called "shrimp." Both fresh and frozen raw shrimp and prawns appear bluish-gray turning deep pink when cooked. For maximum flavor, shrimp may be either steamed, simmered, fried or grilled whole in the shells. Some recipes call for peeling and removal of heads and/or tails before cooking. To do this break off heads and gently pull off legs with shell attached. Head, tails, and shells may be simmered and the liquid used to add flavor to the dish. "De-veining" refers to the removal of the black line which is the intestine running along the back of the animal, usually containing sand. To devein, gently pierce the flesh along this line with a pointed wooden skewer or knife and lift or scrape out.

CRAYFISH: Crayfish resemble mini-lobsters. Their shells are tougher than those of prawns and are pink when raw, turning redder as they cook. Most of the meat is in the tail. If very large, they should be parboiled and split down the middle with a pair of scissors or knife before grilling. Devein before eating or using in a recipe. Prawns, shrimp and crayfish are an excellent source of niacin, vitamin B_{12}, iron, calcium, and selenium.

LOBSTER: True lobsters come from the cold Northern waters of the Atlantic. They have large edible claws (one usually larger than the other) as opposed to spiny or rock lobsters from warmer waters which lack large claws. The most of their edible meat is in the tail. The European lobster is generally

food in the fishmonger's holding tank or they may have moulted recently and not yet grown enough to fill their new shells with firm flesh. White spots on the shell are a sign of age. To prepare for cooking, tie the claws and bend the tail toward the head and tie. Plunge lobster into a pot of boiling water head-first, allow to come to a boil again, cover, and cook for 20 minutes for a 2 lb (1 kg) lobster until it turns red. Increase cooking time, about 10 minutes for every 1 lb (450 g). If desired, add seafood seasoning or aromatics such as celery, carrot, onions, paprika, cayenne, and bay leaf to the cooking liquid. Remove lobster, place on a board belly down with a heavy weight on top to straighten it. When cool, cut lobster through shell lengthwise down the middle with a sharp knife or a pair of scissors. Remove coral if there is any and retain liver for salad or sauce or serve as a garnish. Discard vein and stomach sack. Carefully remove meat from claws and legs with a special fork without breaking, retaining whole claws for garnish. Serve prepared lobster in the shell-halves.

CRAB: There are many varieties of crab including blue crab, king crab, Dungeness, and stone crab (claws only). As crab is very perishable, it is seldom sold fresh except very near the source. Crab must be sold either alive and kicking or cooked. Picked or lump crabmeat is sold fresh, frozen, pasteurized and packed into containers, or cooked and canned. Live crabs are usually steamed, boiled, or grilled. To clean, crack the underside open, split and remove meat with a special spoon. Pick over to remove any hard bits. Crack legs and claws and remove meat.

regarded as the finest flavored. Lobsters are blue-black when raw but turn deep pink when cooked. Female lobsters are preferred as they are larger and tastier and often contain a pink roe called "coral" which is excellent in sauces or lobster salad. The soft grey-green liver, or tomalley is also edible. Choose fresh lobsters which are relatively heavy for their size. Underweight specimens may have been kept for days without

CLAMS: Soft-shell clams are those with soft, easily broken shells which include steamers, gapers, razor, geoduck. Never eaten raw, they should be soaked in salt-water for 2 hours, then steamed or fried. Large geoducks are cut up for chowder or soup. Hard-shell species include cockles and littlenecks, and larger cherrystones, hardshell or quahogs. Clams must be alive (or cooked, canned, or frozen) when you buy them.

Fresh clams should smell pleasantly of the sea. Store in refrigerator covered with a damp towel for at least 2-3 hours. Those that are alive will open slightly. Discard those that do not open. To clean, rinse in several changes of water, and if gritty, scrub with a stiff brush. To shuck or open, insert a paring or clam knife in the opening opposite the hinge. Those

that are alive will immediately snap shut (discard those that don't!). Run the knife along the edge to the hinge and twist blade to upright position to open. Clams also open easily when steamed or briefly micro-waved. Carefully remove meat discarding the "sack" with its sandy contents. Rinse flesh briefly of extraneous matter and cook according to recipe.

SCALLOPS: Most are sold already shucked but uncooked. Fresh scallop meat should be firm, shiny pale beige or cream-colored, and moist. Beware of very white scallops, an indication they may have been soaked to increase their weight. Freezing somewhat spoils their texture. Since they are so fragile, try to find those which have been individually quick-frozen. If buying unshucked scallops, open as for clams, remove flesh, trim off tough parts, remove innards, retain red or white roe (eggs), an excellent addition to sauces or spread on crackers. Scallop shells make a perfect serving dish for the cooked meat. Cook by briefly sauteeing or steaming no longer than 8-10 minutes depending on size. Over-cooking toughens them.

MUSSELS: Like clams, mussels must be alive. Check for movement by tapping shells, avoid those that are broken. Mussels in their shells should be scrubbed under running water with a brush. Remove "beard" by simply pulling it off. Shuck or open by steaming in a pan with a small amount of water, and aromatic herbs, if desired. Remove from heat as soon as they open (discard those that don't). In many places, cultivated mussels are sold already shucked. Put in a colander in cold water for 30 minutes, rubbing gently with fingers to

release sand and dark matter. Drain and repeat 1-2 times until water runs clear. Mussels toughen if over-cooked; 5 minutes should be enough to keep them soft and juicy.

OYSTERS: Most oysters, even native wild ones, are "plumped up" in sheltered areas or beds. They should be stored, cleaned and shucked in a manner similar to that for clams and mussels. To be appreciated fully, European and Portuguese oysters should be eaten raw, with their juices, from the half shell. Oriental oysters does not have the exquisite flavor of their smaller European relatives and are usually baked or sliced and fried. Oysters are popular along the US Atlantic coast where they are sold fresh in vacuum-pack containers. Often eaten raw, avoid overcooking. Stew, grill, or fry only until their edges curl, no more than 4-5 minutes.

OCTOPUS: Meaty octopus – all flesh, no bones, and little waste – is widely available cleaned, frozen, and ready to cook. If caught or purchased fresh, it needs to be tenderized, either by beating with a mallet, or throwing against a hard surface (40 times, it's said in Greece!) or simply by placing it in the freezer for a few days. To clean, turn the "hood" inside out and pull off innards, including ink sac. Pinch out the beak-like mouth in the center of the 8 tentacles. It can be skinned before or after cooking, but the skin (and suckers) are edible. To precook, place in a pan with water to cover and 1/2 cup vinegar. Simmer until it starts to soften. Shrinkage is considerable so try to buy larger ones, 2-3 lbs (1-1.5 kg). For grilling, however, choose baby octopus, one for each serving.

SQUID & CUTTLEFISH: Squid are popular the world over, easy and quick to prepare in a variety of ways. Squid are long and slender, ranging from finger-size for frying to large ones for stuffing. Cuttlefish are related, but rounder and fleshier. Both can be found fresh in coastal areas, but frozen squid and cuttlefish are now widely available. To clean, pull out the head, to which the innards are connected. Remove the plastic-like "back-bone" or quill from the body, remove other extraneous matter from inside, pull off skin from outside, and discard. Cut off the tentacles just below the eyes which should be discarded with the beak-like mouth. Rinse thoroughly under running water and drain well before cooking. At this point, they can be cut into rings for frying or left whole. Cuttlefish ink is often used in sauces or to color homemade pasta. It is preferable to simmer large squid and cuttlefish in a small amount of water in a covered pan until all the juices evaporate to tenderize before further cooking. This step reduces shrinkage and toughening. Small squid or cuttlefish can be "sweated" without water to tenderize.

Tagliatelle Mediterraneo

Serves 4
Preparation time 45 minutes
Cooking time 30 minutes

1/3 cup olive oil
1 medium onion, finely chopped
1 clove garlic, minced
1 small carrot, finely chopped
1 small green pepper, finely chopped
4 large ripe tomatoes, finely chopped
15 drops Tabasco sauce or
1/4 teaspoon cayenne
1 teaspoon Italian Herbs
salt and freshly ground black pepper
1 small fresh lobster (2 lb/1 kg) or frozen lobster
tail (1/2 lb/500 g)
2 lb (1 kg) mixed shellfish (shucked clams, mussels,
oysters, scallops)
or crabmeat
14 oz (400 g) fine tagliatelle

1 cup grated vegetarian cheese (optional)
2 tablespoons finely chopped fresh basil

Heat the oil in a heavy-bottomed pan and saute the onion, garlic, carrot, and pepper on high heat until wilted. Add the tomatoes, seasonings, salt, and pepper. Cover and cook until the sauce thickens. To bring the freshness of the sea to your dish, cook the sauce with some of the shellfish in their shells. Hardshell clams with their lovely colors make an attractive garnish for your seafood platter. Add the remaining shucked shellfish and continue cooking 5-10 minutes stirring occasionally. Cook the tagliatelle in salted boiling water with 2 tablespoons olive oil. Drain and arrange on a large deep platter. Pour the sauce with shellfish on top, sprinkle with grated cheese and chopped basil. Serve immediately in hot plates.

Shellfish Pilaf

Serves 6
Preparation time 45 minutes
Cooking time 40 minutes

1 lb (500 g) shucked mussels or oysters
1 lb (500 g) peeled, deveined shrimp, chopped
8 oz (250 g) squid, cleaned and chopped
3/4 cup olive oil
1 large onion, sliced
2 cloves garlic, sliced
2 small green bell peppers, finely chopped
2 lb (1 kg) ripe tomatoes, finely chopped
3 tablespoons ketchup
1/4 cup finely chopped parsley
salt and freshly ground pepper

1/4 teaspoon cayenne
2 cups long-grain rice
2½ oz (70 g) pine nuts, toasted, for garnish
5-6 large whole shrimp for garnish

Parboil the mussels in 1/4 cup water. Drain and reserve the liquid. Parboil the chopped and whole shrimp in 1/4 cup water; drain and reserve the liquid. Combine and measure the reserved liquids. Add water as needed to make 4 cups. Sweat the squid in a small pan over medium heat until all their liquid has evaporated and they are half-cooked. Heat the oil in a heavy-bottomed pan and saute the onion, garlic, and peppers until wilted. Stir in the tomatoes and cook several minutes over high heat. Add the ketchup, all but 2 tablespoons of the parsley, cayenne, salt, pepper, and squid. Lower the heat, cover, and simmer until the squid are tender and the sauce is thick. Stir in the 4 cups of reserved shellfish cooking liquids and bring to a boil. Add the rice, cover, and simmer for about 15 minutes. Stir in the parboiled shellfish (reserving the whole shrimp) and cook another 5 minutes. Pack the rice into a lightly oiled star-shaped mold. Turn out onto a large round platter and garnish the pilaf with the pine nuts, remaining chopped parsley, and the reserved whole cooked shrimp.

Grilled Seafood with Sauce of Choice

Serves 6
Preparation time 2 hours
Cooking time 20 minutes

1 lb (500 g) mussels in their shells
1 small octopus
4 medium squid or cuttlefish, cleaned
1 lb (500 g) large shrimp, shelled, deveined, without heads and tails
assorted sauces (see basic recipes)

Prepare mussels according to directions at beginning of this section. Several hours in advance brush the octopus, squid, and shrimp with olive oil. Cover the seafood and refrigerate. Plan on grilling the seafood shortly before serving. Arrange the shrimp, squid, and octopus on three separate double-sided grilling baskets and clamp securely shut. Broil the seafood quickly over hot coals taking care not to overcook, 2-3 minutes on each side for the shrimp, and 8-10 minutes each side for the squid and the octopus. Put the mussels in a baking dish sprinkle with a little white wine, cover and place the dish on the grill for about 6-8 minutes until they open. Serve the seafood hot accompanied by a sauce of your choice such as garlic, thousand island, pesto, hot pepper, or lemon tartar sauce (see basic recipes). Alternatively, grill the seafood on an electric or gas broiler, brushing with olive oil when you turn over to cook the other side. **Lemon tartar sauce:** Mix in a bowl 1 tablespoon mashed caper, 2 tablespoons finely chopped pickles, 1 tablespoon finely chopped green onion, 1/2 teaspoon minced mint, 1 cup eggless mayonaise, 1 tablespoon lemon juice, salt and freshly ground pepper.

the cooked shellfish pieces and remove from heat. Heat the remaining margarine and saute the flour. Pour in the reserved liquid, and cook, stirring continuously, until the sauce thickens. Stir in the vegetable cream, salt and pepper and continue cooking for one more minute. Finally, stir in the cream sauce and chopped parsley. Spoon the shellfish filling evenly into the 4 pastry shells. Shortly before serving, put the stuffed pastries in a hot oven until thoroughly heated. Serve immediately accompanied by sauteed vegetables (see basic recipes).

Shellfish in Choux Pastry Puffs

Serves 4
Preparation time 1 hour 10 minutes

1 cup water
1/2 cup white wine
1 small onion, with cross-wise slash in center
7 oz (200 g) frozen scallops
1 lb (500 g) fresh clams
1 lb (500 g) crab claws
6 tablespoons margarine
3 tablespoons flour
1/2 cup vegetarian cream
salt and pepper
1 medium eggplant, in small cubes
3 green onions, finely chopped
2 tablespoons finely chopped parsley
4 large choux pastry shells, fish-shaped or round

Put the water, wine, and onion in a pan; bring to a boil and cook for 5 minutes. Add the scallops and cook for 15 minutes. Remove the scallops with a slotted spoon and set aside. Add the clams and crab claws; when they come to a boil, immediately remove and drain. Strain and reserve 1½ cup of the liquid. Carefully remove the meat from the clam shells, discard the hard sandy portion and reserve the meat. Crack the crab claws, carefully remove the meat, and set aside. Salt the eggplant cubes and set aside for 30 minutes. Rinse and squeeze out excess water. In another pan, heat half the margarine and saute the onions and eggplant until wilted. Add

artichoke bottoms. Cook the artichokes in salted water with lemon juice until tender. Drain and brush with olive oil. Prepare the filling. Heat the oil and saute the onion, celery, garlic, and peppers until wilted. Stir in the crabmeat, parsley, salt and pepper and cook for 1-2 minutes. Remove from the heat and stuff the artichoke cups with the mixture. Prepare the bechamel sauce and spoon on top of the stuffed artichokes. Bake stuffed artichokes in a 350°F (175°C) oven for 30-35 minutes, until tops are lightly browned. Serve while still warm.

Fried Seafood

Serves 4
Preparation time 30 minutes
Cooking time 10 minutes

1 lb (500 g) squid
1 lb (500 g) shrimp
1/2 cup dried bread crumbs
1 cup flour
1/4 cup olive oil
1 teaspoon garlic powder
2 teaspoons salt
2 teaspoons seafood seasoning
1 carrot, julienne
1/2 each red and green bell pepper, julienne
5 radishes, sliced
1 zucchini, julienne
1 green onion, julienne
3-4 oz (100 g) blanched almonds or cashews

Peel and devein the shrimp leaving the tails intact. Prepare the squid according to the directions at the beginning of this section. Cut the bodies into rings. In a plastic bag, combine the flour, garlic powder, salt, and seafood seasoning. Dredge the prepared seafood in flour by shaking them in the bag. Transfer to a colander and shake gently to remove the excess flour. Dip each piece separately in water, roll in the bread crumbs, and refrigerate until the coating is firm. Heat the oil in a deep frying pan and stir-fry the vegetables and the nuts. Drain and arrange on a platter. Deep fry the prepared seafood for 2-3 minutes until lightly browned. Remove with a slotted spoon, drain well on absorbent paper. Serve hot with the fried vegetables accompanied by asparagus or carrot salad vinaigrette.

Crab-Stuffed Artichokes

12 buffet servings
Preparation time 1 hour
Cooking time 30-35 minutes

12 fresh artichokes

for the filling
8 oz (250 g) canned crabmeat
1/4 cup olive oil
1/2 cup finely chopped green onions
1/2 cup finely chopped celery
1 clove garlic, minced
1/4 cup finely chopped green pepper
1/4 cup finely chopped parsley
salt and freshly ground pepper
1½ cup bechamel sauce (see basic recipes)

Drain the crabmeat, pick over and remove bits of shell and other foreign matter. Trim artichoke stems and leaves, remove choke, leaving only the bottom "cups." Or use prepared frozen

Creamed Shrimp and Broccoli with Pasta

Serves 4
Preparation time 35 minutes
Cooking time 20 minutes

10 oz (300 g) eggless tagliatelle
1/3 cup margarine
1/2 cup finely chopped onion
2-3 cloves garlic, minced
2 lb (1 kg) large shrimp
1½ cup vegetarian cream
1 cup shredded vegetarian cheese
salt and freshly ground pepper
10 oz (300 g) broccoli florets, parboiled and drained

Peel and devein the shrimp leaving heads and tails intact. Rinse and drain well. Cook the pasta in salted water with 2 tablespoons olive oil and drain. In a large deep pan, melt 3 tablespoons margarine and lightly saute the onions and garlic. Add the shrimp and stir over high heat until they turn pink. Remove with a slotted spoon to a bowl and keep warm. Add the remaining margarine and cream and stir until margarine has melted; then stir in the cheese, salt, and pepper. Toss the tagliatelle with the broccoli and the cream sauce. Empty onto a hot platter and arrange the shrimp on top. Serve immediately sprinkled with lots of freshly ground pepper.

in the rice or the couscous, sun-dried tomatoes, reserved liquid, saffron, parsley, cayenne, salt and pepper. Cover and simmer until the rice is tender and all the water has been absorbed. Stir in the cooked seafood and the peas. Serve hot or cold garnished with lightly sauteed green pepper rings.

Seafood Flambe with Couscous

Serves 4
Preparation time 20 minutes

4 large or 8 medium shrimp
8 oz (250 g) shucked mussels, rinsed and drained
1 cup couscous
1/3 cup olive oil
3 cloves garlic, thinly sliced
7 oz (200 g) frozen scallops
2 tablespoons brandy
1 large or 2 small ripe tomatoes, chopped
1/2 cup cooked peas
3 tablespoons finely chopped dill
1/4 teaspoon cayenne
salt and freshly ground pepper

Peel and devein the shrimp, leaving heads and tails intact. Rinse well and allow to drain in a colander. Meanwhile bring a small amount of water to a boil in a saucepan and cook the mussels rapidly for 3-4 minutes. Do not overcook. Remove with a slotted spoon. Strain the liquid, measure, and add water as needed to make 1½ cups. Add a little salt and bring to a boil. Stir in the couscous, remove from the heat, cover and allow to stand 5 minutes. Meanwhile, in a heavy-bottomed frying pan heat the oil and saute the garlic. Remove garlic and discard. Fry the shrimp in the garlic-oil until they turn pink. Add the scallops and stir over high heat until all their liquid has evaporated. Pour in the brandy and carefully light with a match. When the flame dies down, stir in the tomatoes and cook for 3 minutes. Add the peas, dill, cayenne, salt, pepper, and mussels. Continuously stirring, cook another 3 minutes and remove from the heat. Serve the shellfish accompanied by the couscous.

Seafood Paella

Serves 6
Preparation time 20 minutes
Cooking 30 minutes

15 mussels, with or without shells
12 medium shrimp
6 oz (200 g) frozen scallops
4 large crab claws
1/3 cup dry white wine
2 cloves garlic, minced
1 medium onion, finely chopped
1/3 cup olive oil
1½ cups rice or couscous
4 sun-dried tomatoes julienne
1 teaspoon saffron stigmas, powdered
1/4 cup finely chopped parsley
1/4 teaspoon cayenne
salt and freshly ground pepper
1/2 cup cooked peas (optional)

Scrub the mussels with a brush, de-beard and shuck, removing any remaining bits of shell. Peel and devein the shrimp leaving the heads and tails intact. In a saucepan combine the wine with 1/2 cup water and bring to a boil. Add the scallops and cook for 10 minutes. Add the shrimp and continue cooking another 7 minutes. Add the mussels and crab claws and cook until the mussels open. Remove the seafood with a slotted spoon to a platter. Strain the liquid, and measure, adding water as needed to make 3 cups. Set aside. In a large heavy-bottomed casserole, heat the olive oil and saute the garlic and onion. Stir

SEAFOOD FLAMBE WITH COUSCOUS

Grilled Shrimp with Oinomelo

Serves 4
Preparation time 6 hours
Cooking time 8 minutes

24 large shrimp
24 large fresh white mushrooms

for the Honey-wine marinade (oinomelo)
1/3 cup Greek honey
1/3 cup olive oil
1/4 cup red wine vinegar
1 teaspoon thyme or rosemary
salt and freshly ground pepper
1 clove garlic, minced

Shell and devein the shrimp, removing the heads but leaving tails intact. Rinse and drain well in a colander. Put the ingredients for the marinade in a jar and shake vigorously until thoroughly blended. In a large bowl, toss the shrimp and mushrooms with the marinade until well-coated. Cover and refrigerate 6 hours, occasionally stirring. Shortly before you are ready to cook them, drain the shrimp and mushrooms well before broiling. Alternatively, you can skewer the shrimp and mushrooms before grilling. Broil 4 minutes on each side. It is preferable to serve hot but they are just as delicious at room temperature.

Shrimp Creole

Serves 4
Preparation time 20 minutes
Cooking time 30 minutes

20 large shrimp
1 cup water
2 tablespoons olive oil
1 teaspoon seafood seasoning

for the sauce
1/4 cup olive oil
1 medium onion, finely chopped
3 cloves garlic, minced
1 small hot green pepper, finely chopped
14 oz (400 g) canned tomatoes, finely chopped
1/4 cup ketchup
2 tablespoons lemon juice
salt and freshly ground pepper
1/4 cup finely chopped parsley

Rinse and devein shrimp leaving the shells, heads, and tails intact. In a pan bring the water, olive oil, and seafood seasoning to a boil. Add the shrimp and cook for 5 minutes until they turn pink. Remove to a plate with a slotted spoon and reserve the liquid. Cool slightly and peel, leaving heads and tails intact. In a large deep fry pan heat the oil and saute the onions, garlic, and chopped hot pepper. Stir in the tomatoes, ketchup, lemon juice, reserved shrimp liquid, salt, and pepper. Simmer for 20 minutes until the sauce thickens. Stir in the cooked shrimp and parsley. Simmer for 5 more minutes. Serve the shrimp Creole with rice pilaf garnished with sprigs of parsley.

Shrimp-Eggplant Rolls

Serves 5
Preparation time 1 hour
Cooking time 10 minutes

5 long thin eggplants
20 large shrimp
2/3 cup olive oil
2 cloves garlic, thinly sliced
1 cup pureed canned or fresh tomatoes
1 tablespoons tomato paste
1 tablespoon ketchup
1 teaspoon thyme
1 bay leaf, broken into small pieces
salt and freshly ground pepper
1/4 cup finely chopped parsley

Wash the eggplants and slice each one lengthwise into 4 pieces. Salt and drain in a colander for 1 hour. Rinse off salt and gently squeeze out excess water between the palms of your hands. Peel and devein the shrimp, leaving heads and tails intact. Heat the oil in a fry pan, lightly brown the eggplants on each side, and drain on absorbent paper. Roll the shrimp in some flour and fry in the oil until they turn pink. Remove from the pan and drain on absorbent paper. Heat two tablespoons of the oil in a sauce pan and saute the garlic. Add the tomatoes, tomato paste, ketchup, thyme, bay leaf, salt and pepper. Stir and simmer the sauce uncovered until slightly thickened. Meanwhile, roll a piece of eggplant around each shrimp and secure with a toothpick. Arrange in an oven-proof dish and pour the sauce on top. Bake in a 400°F (200°C) oven for about 10-15 minutes. This dish is an excellent buffet item or appetizer.

Shrimp in Cream Sauce with Dill

Serves 4
Preparation time 10 minutes
Cooking time 10 minutes

1/4 cup olive oil
2 lb (1 kg) shrimp, peeled and deveined
1 tablespoon flour
1/4 cup ouzo
1/4 cup finely chopped dill weed
1 cup vegetable cream
salt and freshly ground pepper

Heat the oil in a pan and saute the shrimp over high heat. Sprinkle with the flour and stir for 1 minute. Pour in the ouzo. Add the dill, salt, and pepper, and cream; stir and allow to come to a boil. Remove from the heat. Serve immediately accompanied by cooked tagliatelle sauteed in a small amount of margarine.

on both sides until lightly browned. Serve on burger buns garnished with lettuce leaves, sliced tomato, pickle relish, and store-bought cocktail sauce or prepare your own sauce. Stir in the cream, lemon juice, dill, garlic powder, ketchup, salt and white pepper, to taste. Chill the sauce 30 minutes in the refrigerator before serving.

Braised Shrimp Saganaki

Serves 4-6
Preparation time 20 minutes

2 lb (1 kg) medium shrimp
1/3 cup olive oil
1/4 cup water
1 teaspoon seafood seasoning
1 long green hot pepper, cut into thirds
1/4 cup finely chopped parsley
salt and freshly ground pepper
1/4 cup lemon juice

Peel and devein the shrimp, leaving the heads and tails intact. Put the oil, water, seafood seasoning, parsley, hot pepper, salt, and pepper in a large pan, cover and simmer until the liquid cooks down almost to the oil. Add the shrimp and cook 8 minutes shaking the pan vigorously 2 or 3 times so the shrimp cook evenly. Avoid overcooking or the shrimp will toughen. Remove from the heat and pour the lemon juice over the shrimp. Serve immediately.

Shrimp Patties

Serves 4
Preparation time 10 minutes
Cooking time 10 minutes

2 lb (1 kg) small fresh or frozen cooked shrimp
1/2 cup finely chopped green onions
1 clove garlic, minced
7 oz (200 g) fresh breadcrumbs
1 tablespoon Italian Herbs or dried basil
2 tablespoons finely chopped dill
1 tablespoon balsamic vinegar
2 tablespoons olive oil
salt and freshly ground pepper

for the sauce
1 cup vegetable cream
2 tablespoons lemon juice
2 tablespoons finely chopped dill
1/4 teaspoon garlic powder
1 tablespoon ketchup (optional)
salt and white pepper

Mince cooked shrimp in the food processor. Add remaining ingredients and process for 1 minute until well-blended. Shape shrimp mixture into 4 patties. Dust with flour and fry in hot oil

Crayfish with Pesto

Serving 4
Preparation time 30 minutes
Cooking time 15 minutes

16 large crayfish (3 lb/ 1½ kg)
salt and pepper
1/4 cup olive oil
1 tablespoon seafood seasoning
1 recipe pesto sauce (see basic recipes)

Rinse the crayfish and slit the undersides lengthwise with a pair of scissors to facilitate peeling after cooking. Bring the water, seafood seasoning, oil, salt, and pepper to a boil in a large pan. Drop in the crayfish and cook for 10 minutes. Drain well. Prepare the pesto sauce and serve the crayfish on large plates accompanied by the pesto, slices of lemon and fresh basil or mint leaves.

Shrimp in Tomato Sauce

Serves 4
Preparation time 15 minutes
Cooking time 15 minutes

1/4 cup olive oil
1/2 cup finely chopped onion
1 cup finely chopped canned tomatoes
1/3 cup dry white wine
1 teaspoons oregano
salt and pepper
16 medium shrimp, peeled and deveined
3 tablespoons finely chopped
parsley or mint
1/2 cup shredded vegetarian cheese

Saute the onions in the oil until transparent. Add the tomatoes, wine, oregano, salt, and pepper. Simmer the sauce uncovered until thick. Add the shrimp and continue cooking until the sauce thickens again. Stir in the chopped parsley. Empty into a small oven-proof baking dish and sprinkle the shredded cheese on top. Put under the broiler for about 5 minutes, until cheese is melted. Serve immediately.

Octopus Croquettes Kalymnos

Serving 4
Preparation time 1 hour
Cooking time 15 minutes

1 octopus, 2-3 lb (1½ kg) cooked
as for pickled octopus, page 100
1 large onion grated
2 cloves garlic, grated or mashed
1/4 cup finely chopped green onion
5 oz (150 g) stale crustless bread,
soaked and squeezed
1 medium tomato, peeled, seeded, and pulped
2 teaspoons oregano
3 tablespoons finely chopped fresh mint
salt and freshly ground pepper
olive for frying, flour for coating

Grind the octopus in a food processor or mince with two knives. Combine with the remaining ingredients and knead lightly until mixture spongy and smooth. Cover and refrigerate 1 hour. Form small round balls, coat with flour, and deep-fry in ample hot oil. Serve hot accompanied by garlic sauce or taramosalata (see basic recipes.)

Grilled Crayfish

Serves 2
Preparation time 15 minutes
Cooking time 6 minutes

8 large crayfish (24 oz/800 g)
salt and pepper
1/2 cup margarine
1 clove garlic, minced
finely chopped dill
10 drops Tabasco sauce

Rinse, drain, and sprinkle the crayfish with salt. Cut in half lengthwise with a sharp knife or pair of scissors and devein. Cream the margarine with the garlic, dill, pepper, Tabasco, and a little salt. Spread the cut surfaces of the crayfish halves with the herbed margarine using a small spatula. Arrange on the broiler rack 4 inches (10 cm) from the heat source and grill 5-6 minutes. Serve at once garnished with lettuce leaves and lemon wedges. Good with sauteed vegetables such as zucchini and carrot rounds.

Crayfish Stew

Serves 4-5
Preparation time 15 minutes
Cooking time 1 hour 15 minutes

3 lb (1½ kg) crayfish
1 cup olive oil
3 lb (2 kg) onions, sliced
3 lb (1½ kg) ripe tomatoes pureed or
28 oz (800 g) canned tomatoes
1 stick cinnamon
2 bay leaves
5-6 whole allspice berries
salt and freshly ground pepper

Rinse and drain the crayfish. Slit the undersides lengthwise with a pair of scissors without removing the shell, to facilitate peeling after cooking. Heat the oil in a large pan and saute the onions until wilted. Add the tomatoes, bay leaves, cinnamon, allspice, salt, and pepper and simmer until the onions are tender and the sauce has cooked down almost to the oil. Add the crayfish and toss until well-coated with the sauce. Cover and cook for another 10 minutes until the onions and crayfish are tender and the sauce is thick. Serve the crayfish stew with rice pilaf or tagliatelle.

Fried Crayfish

Serves 4
Preparation time 15 minutes
Cooking time 5 minutes

4 lb (2 kg) crayfish
1 cup flour
2 teaspoons salt
1 teaspoon pepper
oil for frying
cocktail sauce (see basic recipes)

Slit the shell on the undersides of the crayfish with a pair of scissors and carefully peel. Devein the crayfish meat and place in a colander. Rinse with a little water and drain well. Combine the flour with the salt and pepper in a plastic bag and coat the crayfish with the flour. Put the floured crayfish in a colander and shake to remove excess flour. Heat the oil in a deep fryer and fry the crayfish for 2-3 minutes. Serve at once with the cocktail sauce.

Squid and Eggplant Lasagne

Serves 8
Preparation time 1 hour
Cooking time 1 hour 40 minutes

26 oz (750 g) squid or cuttle fish
3 lb (1½ kg) eggplant
3/4 cup olive oil
1 cup chopped onion
2 cloves garlic, finely minced
28 oz (800 g) canned pulped tomatoes
1 tablespoon tomato paste
2 tablespoons ketchup
1 bay leaf
1/8 teaspoon ground allspice
salt and freshly ground pepper
1/2 cup finely chopped parsley or basil
1 lb (500 g) lasagna noodles
1 cup vegetarian cream
2 cups shredded vegetarian cheese
1/3 cup margarine, melted

Rinse the squid and slice into thin strips. Chop the strips into small pieces. Drain well in a colander. Sweat the squid by stirring the pieces in a pan over medium heat until all their liquid has evaporated. Peel the eggplants and slice crosswise.

Cut the slices into thin strips. Chop the strips into small pieces. Place in a bowl of salted water and set aside for 1 hour. Drain, rinse in ample water and squeeze out the excess with your hands. Heat half the oil in a pan and saute the eggplant lightly, stirring occasionally. Heat the remaining oil and saute the onions and the garlic. Add the squid and stir over high heat for 2-3 minutes. Add the tomatoes, tomato paste, ketchup, bay leaf, allspice, a little salt, and pepper. Lower the heat, cover, and simmer until the sauce cooks down and the squid are tender. Stir in the fried eggplant and parsley. Remove from the heat and adjust the seasonings. Parboil the lasagna noodles in ample water with a little salt and 2 tablespoons oil, to soften them. Remove with a slotted spoon and drop in a bowl of cold water. Drain well and place them on a cotton towel to dry. Oil an oblong oven-proof glass dish 11x15 inches (28x38 cm) and cover the bottom with noodles. Spread some sauce, vegetarian cream, and shredded cheese on the noodles. Repeat 3 times ending with the sauce, cheese, and cream on top. Bake the lasagne in a 400˚F (200˚C) oven for 35-40 minutes, until top is well-browned. Allow to stand 10 minutes before serving.

their liquid has evaporated. In another pan, heat the oil and saute the garlic, pepper, and onions until wilted. Add the squid and the remaining ingredients for the sauce. When it comes to a boil, lower the heat, cover and simmer for 35-40 minutes. Meanwhile, cook the spaghetti al dente in salted water with 2 tablespoons oil. Drain the pasta. Empty onto a hot platter and pour the squid sauce on top. Toss lightly and serve immediately.

Stuffed Squid

Serves 4
Preparation time 30 minutes
Cooking time 1 hour

3 lb (1½ kg) squid (10-12 pieces)
3/4 cup olive oil
1/2 cup grated onion
1/4 cup long-grain rice
1/2 cup finely chopped dill
2 tablespoons dark raisins/currants
2 tablespoons pine nuts
salt and freshly ground pepper
1/2 cup white wine
1 cup water
1 tablespoon lemon juice

Spaghetti with Squid Sauce

Serves 4
Preparation time 30 minutes
Cooking 40 minutes

26 oz (750 g) squid
1 lb (500 g) spaghetti

for the sauce
1/4 cup olive oil
1 clove garlic, minced
1 hot red pepper, finely chopped
1/2 cup finely chopped green onions
14 oz (400 g) finely chopped canned tomatoes
2 tablespoons ketchup
1/4 cup dry red wine
1 teaspoon chili powder
1 teaspoon salt
1/4 teaspoon ground allspice

Clean and rinse the squid. If they are large, cut into bite-sized pieces. Sweat the squid by simmering in a saucepan until all

Detach the heads from the bodies of the squid. Prepare for cooking as described in the beginning of this section. Pierce the squid bodies in several places with a wooden skewer. Heat half the oil and saute the onions and the chopped tentacles. Remove from the heat and stir in the rice, dill, raisins, pine nuts, salt, and pepper. Stuff each squid only half-full with the rice mixture, allowing space for the rice to expand and also keeping in mind that squid shrinks with cooking. Close the open end with wooden toothpicks. The squid can be "pre-shrunk" before stuffing by "sweating" them in a pan over high heat for 5 minutes until most of their liquid is evaporated. In that case, they can be stuffed two-thirds full. Lay the stuffed squid in a wide shallow pan, pour the remaining oil on top and lightly saute, turning on all sides. Pour in the wine, water, and lemon juice, cover, lower heat, and simmer until squid are tender and sauce is cooked down. The sauce can be thickened with 1 teaspoon of cornstarch dissolved in a little cold water. Remove from the heat and sprinkle freshly ground pepper on top. Serve with lemon slices.

mushrooms and chop in the food processor until finely minced. Lightly saute the mushrooms in 2 tablespoons of oil. In a saucepan heat the oil and saute the onions and garlic. Add the squid and mushrooms. Stir in the tomatoes, tomato paste, ketchup, bay leaf, allspice, a little salt and freshly ground pepper. Cover and simmer until the sauce is thick and squid are tender. Remove from the heat, taste, and adjust the seasonings before adding the parsley. Combine the cream with the cornstarch in a small pan and cook until slightly thickened. Stir in the nutmeg, the salt and pepper. Cook the pasta al dente in salted water with 2 tablespoons olive oil. Drain and toss with the cream sauce and the cheese. Oil a large rectangular lasagne dish and line the bottom with 4 sheets of phyllo pastry, brushing each one with melted margarine. Arrange half the pasta mixture on top of the phyllo and spread the sauce on top of it. Cover the sauce with the remaining pasta and lay the remaining phyllo on top, brushing each sheet with melted margarine. Cut through the phyllo layer with a sharp knife into 8 pieces and sprinkle the surface with a little water. Bake the pastitsio in a 400°F (200°C) oven for 40-50 minutes. Allow to cool 10 minutes serving.

Squid Pastitsio

Serves 8
Preparation time 2 hours
Cooking time 40 minutes

26 oz (750 g) squid or cuttlefish
28 oz (800 g) canned sliced mushrooms
1/2 cup olive oil
1/2 cup grated onion
2 cloves garlic, finely minced
28 oz (800 g) pulped tomatoes
1 tablespoon tomato paste
2 tablespoons ketchup
1 bay leaf
1/8 teaspoon ground cinnamon
salt and freshly ground pepper
1/2 cup finely chopped parsley
1½ cup vegetarian cream
2 tablespoons cornstarch dissolved in
3 tablespoons water
1/8 teaspoon ground nutmeg
1 lb (500 g) Greek pastitsio macaroni or ziti
2 cups shredded vegetarian cheese
1/3 cup margarine, melted
8 sheets phyllo pastry

Clean, rinse, and finely chop the squid with a sharp knife or a pair of scissors. Drain well. Sweat the squid by stirring over medium heat until all their liquid has evaporated. Drain the

Pasta with Garlic Squid

Serves 6
Preparation time 20 minutes
Cooking time 1 hour

1 lb (500 g) farfalle pasta
2lb (1 kg) squid, preparing for cooking
1/3 cup olive oil
6 cloves garlic, slivered
1/3 cup dry white wine
2 teaspoons rubbed thyme
1 small radicchio
1/2 cup finely chopped green onions
salt and freshly ground pepper

Cook the pasta al dente in salted water with 2 tablespoons of olive oil. Cut the squid into 3/4-inch (2-cm) rings. Leave the tentacles whole. Heat the oil in a pan and saute the garlic. Add the squid and stir 1 minute over high heat. Pour in the wine, add the thyme, and cover. Simmer until the squid are tender and and the sauce is thick. Reserve 6 whole radicchio leaves for the garnish and finely shred the remainder. Add the green onions, shredded radicchio, salt, and pepper to the squid and stir over heat until the radicchio and the onions are cooked. Strain the pasta and toss with the squid sauce. Spoon the mixture into the whole radicchio leaves and serve with plenty of freshly ground pepper sprinkled on top.

Spaghetti with Mussels and Squid

Serves 4
Preparation time 30 minutes
Cooking time 1 hour

1 lb (500 g) squid, cleaned and cut into bite-sized
pieces
2 lb (1 kg) mussels in shells
1/4 cup dry white wine
1 tablespoon lemon juice
14 oz (400 g) linguine or
basil or pepper-flavored bavette
1/4 cup olive oil
1 red bell pepper, julienne
2 cloves garlic, minced
1 teaspoon red pepper flakes
zest of 1 lemon
2 tablespoons finely chopped parsley

Scrub and de-beard the mussels. Pour the wine and lemon juice into a large pan and bring to a boil. Add the mussels, cover, and simmer for 5 minutes, until they open. Remove with a slotted spoon to a bowl and reserve the liquid. Sweat the squid by stirring over medium heat until their liquid is evaporated. Saute the garlic and the peppers in the oil until wilted. Add the pepper flakes, zest, squid, and reserved mussel liquid. Cover and simmer until the squid are tender. Cook the pasta in ample salted water with 2 tablespoons olive oil. Shuck the mussels and reserve several shells to garnish the platter. Stir the mussels into the sauce with the squid. Drain the pasta and transfer to a heated platter. Pour the mussels and squid in their sauce on top of the pasta. Serve immediately sprinkled with the parsley and 2-3 tablespoons extra virgin olive oil.

Squid with Peppers and Eggplant

Serves 6
Preparation time 30 minutes
Cooking time 1 hour

2 lb (1 kg) cleaned squid, cut into bite-sized pieces
3/4 cup olive oil
1/4 cup white wine
10 peppercorns
salt and freshly ground pepper
2 medium eggplants, cubed
3 cloves garlic, thinly sliced
5 large onions, sliced
5-6 long pointed green peppers, cut into rings
1 hot red or green pepper, chopped

Sweat the squid in a saucepan over low heat until all their liquid has evaporated. Add half the oil and lightly saute. Pour in the wine, add the peppercorns and a little salt. Cover and simmer until tender, adding water if needed. Meanwhile salt the eggplant and allow to stand for 30 minutes. Rinse, drain well, and squeeze out excess water. Heat the remaining oil and saute the garlic and onions until wilted. Add the peppers and eggplant and stir over the heat until wilted. Add the squid, cover, and simmer until the sauce cooks down almost to the oil. Serve hot with rice pilaf.

Octopus with Split Green Peas

Serves 5-6
Preparation time 20 minutes
Cooking 1 hour 20 minutes

1 large onion, finely chopped
1 green bell pepper, finely chopped
1/4 cup olive oil
10 oz (300 g) dried split green peas
1 tablespoon paprika
1/2 teaspoon cayenne
salt and freshly ground pepper
2 lb (1 kg) octopus, cooked and chopped
3 tablespoons finely chopped fresh oregano or marjoram

Heat the oil in a large pan and saute the onions and peppers until wilted. Add the peas, paprika, cayenne, salt, and pepper. Add enough water to cover the peas, cover, and simmer for 1 hour and 15 minutes, until peas are tender but retain their shape. Skim during cooking to remove scum. Stir in the octopus and the parsley and simmer another 5 minutes. Serve the peas in deep plates with finely chopped onion, paprika, olive oil and lemon juice on top.

Octopus and Onion Stew (Stifado)

Serves 6
Preparation time 30 minutes
Cooking time 1 hour 30 minutes

1 large octopus (6 lb/3 kg)
1/2 cup vinegar
5 lb (2½ kg) small boiling or pearl onions
10 cloves garlic
1 cup olive oil
1/4 cup balsamic vinegar
1 tablespoon peppercorns
10 allspice berries
2 bay leaves
14 oz (400 g) canned pulped tomatoes
1/4 cup ketchup
salt and freshly ground pepper

Rinse, trim and carefully skin the octopus. Place in a large pan, add water to cover, and the vinegar and half-cook, about 45 minutes. Drain and cut into bite-size pieces. Parboil the onions by soaking them in boiling water for several hours before slipping off the skins. Heat the oil and saute the skinned onions with the garlic. Add the wine, balsamic vinegar, spices, tomatoes, ketchup, salt, and pepper and stir. Cover and simmer until onions are half-cooked, about 50 minutes. Add the octopus and continue cooking until both onions and octopus are tender and sauce has cooked down almost to the oil. If the octopus and onions are done but the sauce has not cooked down, strain and pour into another pan, cook until thick, and return to the pan with the onions and octopus. This dish is just as good served either hot or at room temperature.

OCTOPUS AND ONION STEW

about 35 minutes. Rinse the eggplant, drain, and squeeze out the excess moisture. Lightly fry in olive oil and drain on absorbent paper. Add to the sauce along with the chopped parsley. Simmer for another 10 minutes. May be served hot or at room temperature.

Pickled Octopus

Serves 6
Preparation time 15 minutes
Cooking time 2 hours 30 minutes

1 octopus (4-5 lb/2-3 kg)
1 cup wine vinegar
2 stalks of celery
2 small carrots
1 medium onion
10 black peppercorns and salt
several sprigs of parsley

for the marinade
1/2 cup olive oil
1/3 cup wine or balsamic vinegar
10 peppercorns
salt

If you buy a fresh octopus be sure it is well-tenderized. Freezing automatically tenderizes octopus so keep it in your freezer for several days before cooking or buy a commercially frozen one. No further treatment is required. Thaw, rinse well and peel off the glutinous skin. Put in a large pan with water to cover, add the vinegar, cover, and put on high heat. When it comes to a boil, lower heat, and simmer for 1 hour and 30 minutes. Remove from the pan, drain, and allow to cool enough to handle. Pull off remaining membranes and rinse with a little tap water. Put in a pan with some fresh water, celery, carrots, onion, peppercorns, and salt. Cover and simmer for 30 minutes, remove, and drain well. Shake the ingredients for the marinade in a well-sealed jar and pour over the octopus while it's still hot. Allow to marinate for 24 hours, turning often so all sides are "pickled." Arrange the whole octopus on a platter and garnish with pimento and parsley sprigs. If desired, cut into pieces and pour marinade on top. Olive oil can be left out of the marinade and the octopus served with the vinegar only. Pickled octopus is an excellent "mezes" (appetizer) with ouzo.

Octopus with Eggplant

Serves 4-5
Preparation time 1 hour
Cooking time 1 hour 30 minutes

4 lb (2 kg) octopus
4 lb (2 kg) eggplant, cut into bite-sized pieces
1/4 cup vinegar
1 bay leaf
20 black peppercorns
1/2 cup olive oil
1/2 cup grated onion
1 clove garlic, slivered
3 large ripe tomatoes, finely chopped
2 tablespoons ketchup
1/4 cup finely chopped parsley
salt and freshly ground pepper

Prepare octopus according to directions at the beginning of this section. Put it in a large pan with enough water to cover, the vinegar, bay leaf, and peppercorns and cook about 45 minutes. Meanwhile, sprinkle the eggplant with salt and set aside for 1 hour. Heat the oil in another pan and saute the onions and garlic until wilted. Add the tomatoes, ketchup, salt, and pepper and cook the sauce for 5 minutes. Drain the octopus, cut into bite-sized pieces, and put into the sauce. Cover and simmer until octopus is tender and sauce is thick,

Octopus and Macaroni in Red Sauce

Serves 4
Preparation time 30 minutes
Cooking time 1 hour

1 lb (500 g) elbow macaroni
3 lb (1½ kg) frozen octopus
1/4 cup wine vinegar
1/4 cup olive oil
2 cloves garlic, minced
14 oz (400 g) canned tomatoes, chopped
2 tablespoons tomato paste
2 tablespoons ketchup
1/2 cup dry white wine
1 tablespoon chili sauce or
1/4 teaspoon cayenne
4-5 whole allspice berries
1-2 bay leaves
salt and freshly ground pepper

Cook the octopus in salted water with the vinegar and bay leaves until tender. Drain and cut into pieces. Reserve 1 cup of the octopus liquid. Heat the oil in a saucepan and saute the garlic and onions. Add the remaining ingredients, reserved liquid, salt, and pepper. Cover and simmer the sauce for 10 minutes. Add the octopus and continue simmering for another 10-15 minutes. Meanwhile, cook the macaroni al dente in salted water with 2 tablespoons of olive oil. Drain and place on a heated platter. Pour the octopus sauce on top and serve immediately.

1 large onion, finely chopped
2 ripe tomatoes, finely chopped
salt and freshly ground pepper

Octopus and Beans

Serves 4
Preparation time 12 hours
Cooking time 2 hours

1 teaspoon oregano
1 teaspoon dried rosemary
1 teaspoon dried basil
1/2 cup olive oil
10 oz (300 g) medium white beans
1 liter vegetable stock (see basic recipes)
3 lb (1½ kg) octopus
1/4 cup vinegar
1 bay leaf
20 black peppercorns

In a well-sealed jar, combine the oil with the dried herbs and allow to stand 12 hours. Soak the beans in water to cover for 12 hours. Drain and cook in the vegetable stock for 1 hour, until half-cooked. Meanwhile, skin and rinse the octopus. Put it in a large pot with the vinegar, bay leaf, and peppercorns and simmer for 1 hour, until half-cooked. Heat the herbed oil in another pan and saute the onions until wilted. Add the beans with their cooking liquid, tomatoes, the half-cooked octopus, salt, and pepper. Simmer until the beans and octopus are tender and the sauce has cooked down to the oil.

Cuttlefish with Spinach

Serves 4
Preparation time 1 hour
Cooking time 40 minutes

2 lb (1 kg) fresh or frozen cuttlefish
3/4 cup olive oil
1 large onion, sliced
1/2 cup dry white wine
1 tablespoon tomato paste
salt and freshly ground pepper
2 lb (1 kg) fresh spinach or 1 lb (500 g) frozen
1/2 cup finely chopped dill

Prepare the cuttlefish according to general directions at the beginning of this section and cut into bite-sized pieces. Sweat them in a pan over medium heat until all their liquid has evaporated. Heat the oil in another pan and saute the onions. Add the cuttlefish and saute for 5 more minutes. Add the wine, tomato paste, salt, pepper and stir. Cover and simmer for 10 minutes. If using fresh spinach, trim and rinse well. Chop, blanch, and drain. If using frozen spinach, it is not necessary to blanch. Thaw in a colander and drain well. Add the spinach and dill to the cuttlefish and simmer until the spinach is tender and the sauce has cooked down, about 15 minutes. Serve hot or at room temperature.

Shellfish in Phyllo Parcels

Yield: 18 pieces
Preparation time 40 minutes
Oven time 15 minutes

1 lb (500 g) shrimp
8 oz (250 g) crabmeat, shredded
2 tablespoons olive oil
4-5 spring onions with long green leaves
1 clove garlic, finely minced
2 teaspoons flour
1/4 cup vegetarian cream
2 tablespoons chopped dill
salt and freshly ground pepper
9 sheets of phyllo
1/3 cup olive oil, for brushing

for the sauce
2 tablespoons lemon juice
1/4 cup olive oil
2 cloves garlic, minced
2 tablespoons finely chopped green onion
2 tablespoons finely chopped dill
2 tablespoons finely chopped parsley
salt and freshly ground pepper

Peel and devein the shrimp. Rinse, drain well, and cut into small pieces. Set aside. Clean the onions and remove wilted leaves. Cut off the white part and finely chop. Blanch the green leaves in boiling water until soft and pliable. Drain and set aside. Heat the oil in a saucepan over medium heat and saute the chopped onions and garlic until wilted. Add the shrimp and stir over the heat until they turn pink, about 5 minutes. Sprinkle with the flour and continue stirring for 1 more minute. Stir in the cream and remove from the heat. Add the crabmeat, dill, salt, and freshly ground pepper. Cut the phyllo sheets in half lengthwise. Brush the top half of each piece with oil and fold the bottom half over it. Brush again with oil, place a tablespoon of seafood filling on the center bottom of each piece of phyllo, and roll up. Slightly twist the ends and tie each with one or two blanched onion leaves. Arrange side by side on an oiled baking sheet. Brush rolls with oil and sprinkle with a little water. Bake in a 350°F (180°C) for 10-15 minutes, until lightly browned. Meanwhile, prepare the sauce by combining all the ingredients in a blender container and processing until uniform and thick. Serve the seafood parcels hot accompanied by the herb-sauce.

Macaroni Timbale

Serves 6
Preparation time 40 minutes
Cooking time 1 hour 30 minutes

10 oz (300 g) thick long (Greek) macaroni or ziti
4 tablespoons soft margarine
1/4 cup + 2 tablespoons finely chopped dill
1 cup stale breadcrumbs
salt and pepper
12 oz (350 g) frozen cooked shrimp, ground
8 oz (250 g) frozen spinach
2 tablespoons flour
1 cup vegetarian cream
pinch of nutmeg
1½ cups grated vegetarian cheese (optional)

Cook the macaroni for 10 minutes in salted water with 1 tablespoon olive oil. Drain and carefully lay the strands on absorbent paper so they are not touching each another. Grease the interior of a 9-cup round metal bowl with 2 tablespoons of softened margarine. Sprinkle evenly with 2 tablespoons of chopped dill. Starting at the bottom center, wind strands of macaroni in a spiral, completely covering the entire inside surface of the bowl up to the rim. Cover and chill in refrigerator until set. Cut the remaining macaroni into 1-inch (2-cm) lengths and set aside. In the food processor blend the breadcrumbs, cream, onions, salt, and pepper. Add the ground shrimp and the 1/4 cup dill and process at medium speed 3 minutes. Spread this mixture evenly on the macaroni in the bowl. Cover and refrigerate again. Blanch the spinach, drain, and squeeze out the excess liquid. Melt the remaining margarine in a saucepan, stir in the flour and cook for 1 minute over medium heat. Stir in the cream and cook until the sauce thickens. Remove from the heat and stir in the nutmeg, salt, and pepper. Add the drained spinach, chopped macaroni, and cheese (if used) and mix well. Carefully spoon the mixture into the prepared bowl dressed with the macaroni and shrimp. Cover the edge of the bowl with aluminum foil

leaving a small opening in the center. Place the bowl in a pan with 1/2 inch (1 cm) of hot water. Bake in a 350°F (180°C) oven for 1 hour and 30 minutes or until cooked through. Remove the bowl from the oven and allow to stand for 15 minutes before unmolding on a round platter. Garnish with the remaining 1 tablespoon of chopped dill and a tomato rosette.

Seafood-Stuffed Sweet Potatoes

Serves 3
Preparation time 30 minutes
Cooking time 20 minutes

3 large sweet potatoes
1/2 cup olive oil
3 cloves garlic, minced
1 leek, white part only, finely chopped
3 green onions, finely chopped
12 oz (350 g) frozen scallops
4 medium shrimp, chopped
1 tablespoon flour
1/2 cup white wine
1/2 cup vegetarian cream
salt and freshly ground pepper
1 cup shredded vegetarian cheese (optional)
2 tablespoons finely chopped parsley
2 tablespoons dried breadcrumbs
A small jar of brik (red caviar) (optional)

Cook the potatoes in salted water until just tender, taking care not to overcook. Or microwave until tender. Cut the potatoes in half lengthwise and scoop out the centers. Brush all surfaces of the potatoes with olive oil and arrange on a baking sheet. Heat the oil in a pan and saute the leek, garlic, and onions until wilted. Add the scallops and shrimp, and cook for 1 minute. Sprinkle with the flour and continue stirring over the heat for 2 more minutes. Pour in the wine and cream and simmer, stirring gently until the mixture thickens. Remove from the heat, add the salt, pepper, and half the shredded cheese (if used) and mix. Stuff the prepared potato shells with the seafood mixture. Combine the remaining cheese with the chopped parsley and breadcrumbs and sprinkle on top of the stuffed potatoes. Bake in a 350°C (180°F) oven for 15-20 minutes, until the tops are well-browned. Garnish each potato with a teaspoon of brik (red caviar), if desired, and serve immediately.

Shellfish Cocktail Salad

Serves 4
Preparation time 30 minutes

1 cup long-grain rice
1 teaspoon prepared mustard
1/4 cup eggless mayonnaise (see basic recipes)
2 tablespoons lemon juice
salt and pepper
5 oz (125 g) frozen cooked shrimp
5 oz (125 g) shelled mussels, steamed
4 green onions, chopped
1 small cucumber, chopped
6 cherry tomatoes, quartered
1/4 cup chopped celery
1 small hot pepper, in rings

Cook the rice for 20 minutes in 2 cups of salted water until tender. Set aside to cool. Meanwhile, make the dressing: combine the mustard, mayonnaise, lemon juice, salt, and pepper in a small bowl and mix until blended. In another bowl, combine the cooked rice with the shellfish and the vegetables and pour the dressing on top. Serve the salad in cocktail glasses garnished with lemon slices.

Crab and Macaroni Salad

Serves 4
Preparation time 30 minutes

6 oz (150 g) elbow macaroni, cooked
7 oz (200 g) crabmeat, in bite-sized pieces
1 orange bell pepper julienne
1 green pepper, julienne
2 green onions, sliced
1 clove garlic, thinly sliced
2 cups finely chopped lettuce
vinaigrette dressing or cocktail sauce (see basic recipes)

Toss the salad ingredients together in a bowl. Pour the dressing on top and serve in cocktail glasses. Garnish with slices of lemon and, if desired, put a little brik or caviar in the center.

Mussel Salad with Saffron

Serves 4
Preparation time 30 minutes

1 small onion, sliced
1 small leek, thinly sliced into rounds
1 lb (500 g) shucked mussels
1/4 cup olive oil
2 green onions, sliced
1/4 cup vegetarian cream
1/4 teaspoon powdered saffron
1 head of iceberg lettuce
2 tablespoons lemon juice
2 tablespoons finely chopped celery
2 tablespoons finely chopped green onion
2 tablespoons finely chopped fresh tarragon or parsley
salt and freshly ground pepper

Put the onion, leek, and a cup of water in a pan and simmer for 5 minutes. Add the mussels and when the water comes to a boil again, remove them from the pan, and reserve 1 cup of the liquid. Heat the oil and saute the green onions. Stir in the cream, saffron, and reserved liquid. Simmer for 1 minute. Add the mussels, mix gently, and remove immediately from the heat. Cut the lettuce into four sections, put one on each plate, and sprinkle with lemon juice. Divide the mussel mixture evenly on the plates and sprinkle with chopped celery, onions, tarragon, salt, and pepper. Garnish with lemon slices and hot red peppers.

Seafood Salad in Crabshells

Serves 4
Preparation time 30 minutes

4 medium crabs, cooked
1½ cups alfalfa sprouts
4 green onions, finely chopped
8 oz (250 g) oysters or scallops, parboiled
8 oz (250 g) frozen cooked shrimp
1/4 cup finely chopped pickles
2 tablespoons finely chopped parsley
3/4 cup mayonnaise or cocktail sauce
salt and freshly ground pepper

Slit open the underside of the crab and scoop out the interior. Break the claws and the legs and remove the flesh. Chop into bite-sized pieces and combine with the remaining ingredients. If using scallops, cook for 20 minutes in 1/4 cup dry white wine with 1 bay leaf. Divide the salad among 4 crab shells. Serve on radicchio or red cabbage leaves.

Braised Mussels Saganaki

Serves 4
Preparation time 30 minutes

1 lb (500 g) fresh mussels, shucked
1/3 cup olive oil
1/4 cup water
3 tablespoons finely chopped parsley
1 hot green pepper, in rings
salt and freshly ground pepper
1/3 cup lemon juice

Rinse and drain the mussels on absorbent paper. Put the oil, water, parsley, hot pepper, salt, and pepper in a large pan and bring to a boil. Cover and simmer 5 minutes until all the water evaporates. Increase the heat, add the mussels to the pan and cook for only 5 minutes, shaking the pan once or twice. Do not overcook or the mussels will toughen. Remove from the heat and pour in the lemon juice. Serve immediately. Alternatively, for a spicier dish, substitute one chopped red hot pepper for the green hot pepper. Dissolve 1 tablespoon tomato paste in the cooking liquid and substitute 1 tablespoon fresh or dried oregano for the parsley. Do not use lemon juice for this version.

Curried Mussel Pilaf

Serves 4
Preparation time 20 minutes
Cooking time 20 minutes

3 lb (1½ kg) mussels in shells
1/3 cup olive oil
1/3 cup grated onion
1/3 cup finely chopped green onions
1 small hot pepper, finely chopped
1 cup long-grain rice
1/2 teaspoon salt
1 teaspoon curry powder
freshly ground pepper

Scrub the mussels under running water and de-beard. Place in a pan with a small amount of water over high heat until they open. Drain the mussels and set aside. Measure the cooking liquid and add enough hot water to make 2 cups. Heat the oil in another pan and saute the onions and hot pepper. Add the rice and stir 1-2 minutes over high heat. Bring the cooking liquid to a boil and add to the rice. Add the salt and curry powder. Cover and simmer until rice is tender, about 20 minutes. Shuck the cooked mussels and add to the rice with plenty of freshly ground pepper. Toss to evenly distribute mussels and cool the mixture slightly. Fill several of the more attractive shells with the mussel pilaf. Spoon the remaining rice mixture onto a shallow platter and garnish with the stuffed shells. Serve hot or at room temperature.

Mussel Pilaf with Dill

Serves 4
Preparation time 50 minutes
Cooking time 25 minutes

3 lb (1¹/₂ kg) fresh mussels in shells
1/2 cup olive oil
1/2 cup grated onion
1/2 cup finely chopped green onions
1¹/₂ cups long-grain rice
1/2 cup finely chopped dill
2 tablespoons finely chopped fresh mint
salt and freshly ground pepper

Prepare the mussels according to the general directions at the beginning of this section. Put 1/4 cup water in a large pan with the mussels and cook on high heat until they open. Drain the mussels and reserve the cooking liquid. Measure and add enough hot water to make 3 cups. Heat the oil in a large pan and saute the onions until wilted. Add the rice and stir over the heat for 1-2 minutes. Bring the 3 cups of cooking liquid to a boil and pour into the rice. Add 1 teaspoon of salt, cover, and simmer until all the liquid has been absorbed, about 20 minutes. Stir in the dill, mint, the cooked mussels, and plenty of freshly ground pepper. Mix well. Cover the pan lightly with a cotton dishtowel and put the lid on top. Turn off the heat but leave the pan on the stove to fluff up the rice. Turn out onto a hot shallow platter and sprinkle with a little fresh lemon juice and freshly ground pepper, along with some cayenne. Garnish with some shells filled with rice. Serve hot or at room temperature.

Risotto with Shellfish

Serves 4-5
Preparation time 30 minutes
Cooking time 30 minutes

1/3 cup olive oil
2 cloves garlic, sliced
8 oz (250 g) frozen crab legs
8 oz (250 g) frozen shrimp
8 oz (250 g) frozen scallops
8 oz (250 g) sliced fresh mushrooms
2/3 cup grated onion
1²/₃ cup short-grain rice
2 qt (2 lt/8 cups) vegetable stock (see basic recipes)
salt and freshly ground pepper
3 tablespoons margarine
1/4 teaspoon cayenne
3 tablespoons finely chopped parsley

Heat half the oil in a saucepan and saute the garlic until lightly browned. Remove the garlic with a slotted spoon and discard. Add the shellfish and mushrooms and stir over high heat until all their liquid has evaporated. In another pan heat the remaining oil and saute the onion. Add the rice and saute for 2-3 minutes. Stirring constantly over high heat, add the stock in 1-cup portions over the next 15 minutes, allowing it to be absorbed by the rice before adding the next. Add the shellfish, margarine, cayenne, salt, and pepper. Gently stir until the seafood is evenly distributed and heated through. Serve the risotto hot, sprinkled with the parsley and freshly ground pepper.

Mussel Soup

Serves 4
Preparation time 20 minutes
Cooking time 30 minutes

3 lb (1¹/₂ kg) mussels in shells
1 tablespoon tomato paste
4 ripe tomatoes, pulped
3 tablespoons pepper sauce (see basic recipes) or
2 tablespoons ketchup
3 cloves garlic, minced
1/3 cup olive oil
1/4 cup finely chopped parsley
1/4 cup finely chopped basil
4 slices of wholewheat bread
salt and freshly ground pepper

Prepare the mussels according to the general directions at the beginning of this section. Put the prepared mussels in a large pan with 1 cup of water and simmer on high heat until they open. Remove with a slotted spoon and reserve 1 cup of the cooking liquid. Dissolve the tomato paste in 2 tablespoons of water and combine with the pulped tomatoes and pepper sauce. Heat the oil and saute the garlic in a large pot. Add the tomatoes, the cooking liquid from the mussels, herbs, and 1 teaspoon salt. Simmer for 30 minutes, add the cooked mussels, stir, and remove from the heat. Brush the bread with some garlic-flavored olive oil and toast them under the broiler. Serve the mussels and some of the liquor in soup bowls with plenty of freshly ground pepper and the slices of toasted bread.

Italian Style Lobster with Pasta

Serves 2
Preparation time 1 hour
Cooking time 30 minutes

1 lobster (about 3 lbs or 1¹/₂ kg)
1/4 cup margarine
7 oz (200 g) spaghetti or linguine
1/4 cup olive oil
1 clove garlic, finely minced
14 oz (400 g) finely chopped tomato, without juice
1 tablespoon vinegar
1/4 teaspoon sugar
1 teaspoon tomato paste
1/3 cup finely chopped basil or parsley

for the lobster salad
1/2 cup eggless mayonnaise (see basic recipes)
1/2 cup finely chopped parsley
salt and white pepper

Cook the lobster according to general directions at the beginning of this section. Reserve 1 cup of the liquid. Cut the lobster in half lengthwise, cover each half with plastic wrap, and refrigerate until ready to serve. To re-heat, spread the cut side with the margarine and grill under the broiler for 5 minutes. Use the coral (red eggs) and the claw meat to make the salad. Combine with the mayonnaise, parsley, salt and pepper. Refrigerate the salad until ready to serve. If you wish, use the claw meat and the remaining cooking liquid to make lobster bisque to serve as the first course. To prepare the sauce, saute the garlic in the oil. Add the reserved liquid along with the remaining ingredients and simmer until the sauce is thick. Cook the pasta al dente in salted water with 2 tablespoons of olive oil. Drain and put in a hot shallow platter. Pour the sauce on top. Fill the empty head cavities with the salad and place the lobster halves on the platter with the hot pasta. Serve immediately.

Lobster Bisque

Serves 4
Preparation time 1 hour

1 lobster (about 2 lb or 1 kg)
salt and white pepper
2 tablespoons olive oil
1 very small onion, finely chopped
2 cups vegetable stock (see basic recipes)
3 potatoes, peeled and cubed
2 large artichokes, trimmed
2 teaspoons ground saffron
1/4 cup vegetarian cream
8 thin slices French bread spread with margarine and toasted
2 tablespoons finely chopped parsley

Cook the lobster according to general directions at the beginning of this section. Reserve 1 cup of the cooking liquid and set aside to cool. Meanwhile, heat the oil and saute the onions in a large pot. Add the reserved lobster liquid, vegetable stock, potatoes, and artichokes and simmer for 20 minutes until tender. Remove from heat and cool. Puree the vegetables in a food processor until smooth. Return to the pan and bring again to a boil. Stir in saffron, cream, salt, and pepper. Remove the lobster meat from the shell and cut into pieces. Divide among four deep plates and pour the hot bisque on top. Garnish with chopped parsley and serve with toasted French bread. You can prepare the bisque from 4 large lobster claws.

Crab Chowder

Serves 6
Preparation time 20 minutes
Cooking time 10 minutes

1 cup sliced fresh mushrooms
1/4 cup finely chopped celery
1/4 cup finely chopped green onions
2 tablespoons margarine
2 tablespoons flour
1/2 teaspoon salt
3 cups vegetable stock (see basic recipes)
2 medium boiled potatoes, in small cubes
8 oz (250 g) canned crabmeat
1 cup vegetarian cream
2 teaspoons finely chopped dill

Melt the margarine in a small pan and saute the onions, mushrooms, and celery until wilted. Add the flour and salt and cook, stirring for 1 minute. Add the vegetable stock, potatoes, and crab. Cover and simmer until the chowder thickens slightly. Stir in the cream and dill, and when the chowder comes to a boil, remove from the heat, and serve immediately, sprinkled with finely chopped parsley.

Clam Chowder

Serves 4-5
Preparation time 30 minutes
Cooking time 40 minutes

1/4 cup margarine
1/3 cup finely chopped green onions
2 tablespoons finely chopped green bell pepper
2 tablespoons finely chopped celery
1/4 cup finely chopped carrot
1 clove garlic, minced
14 oz (400 g) potatoes in small cubes
3 cups water
1 teaspoon salt
1/2 teaspoon pepper
20 drops Tabasco sauce
2 cups shucked clams or oysters
1 cup vegetarian cream
finely chopped parsley for garnish

Melt the margarine in a large pan over high heat and saute the onions, pepper, celery, carrot, and garlic until wilted. Add the potatoes and remaining ingredients except for the clams and cream. Cover and simmer until the potatoes are tender. Add the clams and cream and when the chowder comes again to a boil, remove from the heat and serve immediately sprinkled with finely chopped parsley.

When Allah created the Mediterranean,
he addressed it saying:

"I have created you and I will send you
my servants who, when they want me to
grant them a favor, will say, 'God is
great' or 'There is no God but Allah.'
How will you treat them?
And the Mediterranean replied,
"I will drown them!"
Then I curse you and impoverish
your appearance and make you
less fishy than the oceans!"

Al-Muquaddasi

F I S H

The diet of the Mediterranean peoples – particularly the inhabitants of the islands and coasts of the Aegean archipelagos – has always included food from the sea. But only when the land failed to yield enough food did man turn to the sea and face its untold dangers to feed his family and eke out a living. Literature throughout history is full of tales of humans pitted against the elements and creatures of the sea, the life of a fisher-folk nearly always equated with poverty and misery. Seafood, on the other hand, from antiquity to the present, has represented a valuable commodity, one which the fisherman at one end of the economic scale risked his life to provide while those at the other paid high prices to obtain, with the "middle man" taking most of the profit. Nowadays, luxury fish in the Eastern Mediterranean are scarcer than ever due to the failure of the countries of the region to institute and enforce efficient conservation policies. Instead, dynamite blasting, driftnet trawling, off-season capture, and pollution have severely depleted wild stocks in many places. That's the bad news. But the good news is that in the past decade aqua-culture (fish-farming) has been able to meet the increasing demand for fresh fish. The UN Food and Agricultural Organization (FAO) estimates that while global wild-capture fishing is on the decline, world aqua-culture production has increased at least 150% in the past 10 years with estimated growth rates on the rise.

THE GREEK AQUA-CULTURE SUCCESS STORY Taking advantage of its favorable geographic and climatic conditions together with European financial support, Greece pioneered

F   I   S   H

the early development of aqua-culture in the Aegean concentrating on two Mediterranean species of fish, the gilthead bream and seabass. From 300 tons in 1988, Greece is now the leading European and Mediterranean producer of these fish with production surpassing 40,000 tons in 1999.

These statistics represent some 50% of the total world-wide farmed-fish production of which 70% is exported. Fish from the 245 Greek Aegean aqua-culture units are shipped fresh daily packed in ice and air-freighted within 24 hours of catch to customers in the European Union as well as those as far away as the North America. These impressive numbers reported by the Federation of Greek Maricultures (FGM) should make Allah himself reconsider his curse! So successful has this venture proved that other Mediterranean countries – Italy, Turkey, Spain, Cyprus, Malta, and Israel – are following suit.

TIPS WHEN PURCHASING FRESH FISH Since the best fish is a fresh fish, it is important to keep in mind these important points: the flesh of your considered purchase should be translucent, firm, and resilient to the touch. Flabbiness, opaqueness and mushiness are signs that frozen fish may have been thawed and is being passed off as fresh. The eyes of fresh fish should bulge and retain their bright, clear, and glistening "gaze." Sniff the fish at the head, it should smell like a sea breeze, or iodine and seaweed, neither sour nor "fishy." Exceptions to this rule are shark, skater, and ray fish whose flesh contains urea, a chemical which breaks down to produce ammonia after death. This should not concern you because the strong ammonia odor disappears within a day or two. Therefore, do not cook these kinds of fish immediately. Any lingering ammonia will be driven off during the cooking process. The gills of the fish should be bright red, not pink or gray. The scales should be shiny and firmly attached and the surface

that of meat, especially if the fish is of the "wild" variety.

PREPARING AND COOKING FRESH FISH To prepare fresh fish for cooking, scale first by rubbing a knife or special de-scaler against the grain. Some fish, such as mackerel, don't have scales. Then slit underside open from just below the head to the tail. Remove innards and gills, rinse well to remove every trace of blood. Cover with plastic wrap, and refrigerate, preferably in cracked ice or ice packs, until ready to cook which should be within a few hours or the next day. In the Mediterranean most fish are cooked with the heads and tails intact. Large fish are often sliced, but the head adds much flavor to the cooking liquid or soup. Fresh fish can be cooked by frying, grilling, stewing, braising or poaching. Since all fish are naturally tender, relatively brief cooking is required. Check for doneness by piercing the fish with the tines of a fork at its thickest part just behind the gills. When the flesh no longer clings to the bone (some say it "flakes off") the fish is considered done. The time required to cook a fish depends on its size and the degree of heat to which it is subjected.

SALT PRESERVED FISH Although fresh fish is available all year round, Mediterranean regional cuisines feature a wide variety of dishes made with salt cod which, unlike other fish preserved by smoking or pickling, can be cooked in the same ways that are suitable for fresh fish. Salt cod is characteristically off-white or grayish in color. A dull yellow color indicates that the fish has been left in salt for too long. Soaking the fish for at least

should not be slimy. Fish with no scales such as mackerel should be iridescent, not dull. Fish steaks should be shaped like a horsehoe, the edges not brown or yellowish. Ask for slices of equal thickness to assure uniform cooking. Remember that fresh fish is expensive, the price per kilo/pound often exceeding

24 hours in 3-4 changes of cold water will remove most of the salt and restore its original plumpness, tenderness and white color. Pieces of soaked cod dipped in batter, fried in hot oil, and accompanied by garlic sauce is one of the great favorites of the Greeks and is often served at festive gatherings.

F I S H

Cod with Shrimp and Mushrooms

Serves 4
Preparation time 30 minutes
Cooking time 30 minutes

4 cod fillets, fresh or frozen
2 tablespoons lemon juice
salt and freshly ground pepper
1 medium onion, finely chopped
1/4 cup olive oil
1/2 cup dry white wine
2 tablespoons finely chopped parsley or dill
2 oz (60 g) dried porcini mushrooms
8 large frozen shrimp or
10 oz (300 g) small frozen shrimp
1 tablespoon cornstarch
1 tablespoon prepared mustard

Brush the cod with the lemon juice, sprinkle with salt and pepper and set aside 10 minutes. Soak the mushrooms in 1/2 cup of water for about 30 minutes. Heat the oil and saute the onions until wilted. Add the fish fillets and saute lightly. Pour in the wine, sprinkle with the parsley, cover and simmer 8-10 minutes. Remove from the heat and arrange the fillets in a heat-proof dish. In the sauce remaining in the pan, simmer the mushrooms and the shrimp for 10 minutes. Dissolve the cornstarch and the mustard in a small amount of cold water, stir into the sauce, and cook until thick. Remove from the heat and pour on top of the cod fillets. Sprinkle with freshly ground pepper and serve immediately. If using prawns, secure one on each fillet half with toothpicks.

Prawn and Cod Stew

Serves 6
Preparation time 20 minutes
Cooking time 35 minutes

12 (1 lb 8 oz/800 g) fresh or frozen prawns
1 lb (500 g) pre-soaked frozen salt cod fillets
2/3 cup olive oil
1 large onion, sliced
1/2 cup chopped celery
1 green bell pepper, in strips
1 red bell pepper, in strips
3 cloves garlic, minced
4 medium ripe tomatoes, finely chopped
1/4 cup basil or parsley, finely chopped
2 teaspoons paprika
1/2 teaspoon cayenne
2 teaspoons cornstarch dissolved in
1 tablespoon water
2 cups long-grain or basmati rice, cooked
with saffron

Defrost the cod and cut into bite-size pieces. Defrost the prawns, remove heads, peel and devein, leaving the tails in tact. Heat the oil in a large casserole and saute the onions, celery, peppers, and garlic until wilted. Add the tomatoes, basil, paprika, cayenne, and a pinch of salt. Cover and simmer 30 minutes. Add the prepared prawns and cod, sprinkle with freshly ground pepper and cook on high heat for 5 minutes until the shrimp turn pink. Stir in the dissolved cornstarch. Continue cooking, stirring occasionally, until the sauce is slightly thickened, and remove from the heat. Pack the cooked saffron-rice into an oiled ring mold and turn out onto a platter. Remove the shrimp and cod from the sauce with a slotted spoon and place in the center and around the outer edge of the rice. Spoon some sauce on top of the rice and serve immediately. VARIATION: The recipe may be prepared using only cod.

Cod with Peppers

Serves 4
Preparation time 12 hours
Cooking time 40-50 minutes

1 lb (500 g) dried salt cod
1/4 cup olive oil
6 cloves garlic, finely chopped
2 leeks, white part only, finely chopped
6 red bell peppers, in strips
6 ripe tomatoes, peeled, seeded,
and finely chopped
salt and freshly ground pepper
1/2 cup dry white wine

Soak the cod 12 hours, drain and cook 20 minutes in water to cover. Drain, remove the bones and divide into small pieces. Heat the oil and saute the garlic and the leeks. Add the peppers and saute lightly. Stir in the tomatoes, and simmer several minutes before adding the wine, a pinch of salt and the pepper. Cook the sauce uncovered about 15 minutes. Combine the pieces of prepared cod with the sauce and empty into an oven-proof dish. Bake at 350°F (180°C) 20-30 minutes. Serve hot.

Cod Stew with Vegetables

Serves 6
Preparation time 12 hours
Cooking time 1 hour 30 minutes

3 lb (1½ kg) dried salt cod
1 cup olive oil
2 cloves garlic, slivered
1 large onion, finely chopped
1 celery root, cut in pieces
1 carrot, sliced
2 lb (1 kg) ripe tomatoes, peeled, seeded, and
finely chopped
1/4 cup finely chopped parsley
2 lb (1 kg) potatoes, in large pieces
1 lb (500 g) zucchini, sliced
salt and freshly ground pepper

Cut the cod in large pieces and soak in cold water 12 hours, changing the water 3-4 times. Heat the oil and saute the garlic, onion, celery, and carrots until wilted. Add the tomatoes, parsley, salt, and pepper and cook for 5 minutes. Lightly brown the zucchini and potatoes in olive oil, drain, and arrange in an oven-proof dish along with cod. Pour the sauce on top and

sprinkle with freshly ground pepper. Bake at 350°F (180°C) for 1 hour and 30 minutes or until the fish and potatoes are tender. If the sauce cooks down, add a small amount of water.

Cod with Chick-Peas

Serves 4
Preparation time 12 hours
Cooking time 1 hour 40 minutes

10 oz (300 g) chick-peas
10 oz (300 g) spinach, blanched and drained
1 lb (500 g) dried salt cod
2/3 cup olive oil
1 medium onion
1/4 cup finely chopped dill
salt and freshly ground pepper
1/4 cup lemon juice

Soak the chick-peas 12 hours in water to cover with 1 tablespoon of salt. Skin the cod and cut into pieces. Rinse well and soak in water to cover 12 hours, changing the water several times. Drain and cook in fresh water to cover until tender, about 20 minutes. Drain, remove the bones, and tear into small pieces. Drain the chick-peas, rinse, and put in a pot with water to cover. Score the onion in the middle and add to the chick-peas. Add the oil, cover, and simmer until tender, about 1 hour and 15 minutes. Remove the onion and discard. Add the prepared cod, spinach, and dill and shake the pot to distribute the ingredients. Sprinkle the surface with plenty of freshly ground pepper, cover, and simmer another 20 minutes, until the sauce cooks down. Remove from the heat, pour in the lemon juice, and shake the pot in a circular motion to distribute. Serve immediately.

Cod with Leek-Celery Rissoto

Serves 4
Preparation time 24 hours
Cooking time 1 hour 20 minutes

2 lb (1 kg) dried salt cod
2 lb (1 kg) leeks, cut into 1½-inch (4-cm) pieces

3 stalks of celery, finely chopped
3/4 cup olive oil
14 oz (400 g) canned tomatoes, finely chopped
1/3 cup short-grain rice
1/3 cup hot water
2-3 tablespoons lemon juice
1/4 cup parsley, finely chopped
salt and freshly ground pepper

Cut the cod into serving pieces and soak in cold water 12 hours, changing the water 2 or 3 times. Drain and put in a pan with cold water to cover on high heat. When the water comes to a full boil, remove from the heat. Drain the cod and remove skin and bones. Blanch the leeks in boiling water for 5 minutes and drain. Heat the oil and saute the leeks and celery until wilted. Add the tomatoes, salt, and pepper. Cover and simmer until the vegetables are almost tender. Add the prepared pieces of cod, rice, and hot water. Cover and simmer another 20 minutes until the water is absorbed and the rice and fish are tender. Sprinkle with the lemon juice, chopped parsley, and plenty of freshly ground black pepper. Toss lightly and serve immediately.

Pasta with Smoked Trout

Serves 4
Preparation time 5 minutes
Cooking time 10 minutes

14 oz (400 g) farfalle or shell pasta
4 fillets smoked trout (14 oz/400 g)
3 tablespoons olive oil
1/2 cup finely chopped green onions
1/4 cup finely chopped dill or fennel weed
2 tablespoons margarine
2 tablespoons flour
1¹/₂ cups vegetable broth (see basic recipes)
salt and freshly ground pepper

Pick over the trout to remove skin or bones, and shred. Heat the oil and saute the onions and dill until wilted. In another pan, melt the margarine and saute the flour 1 minute. Add the vegetable broth and simmer until slightly thick. Add the shredded trout and sauteed onions. Correct the seasonings. Cook the pasta in boiling salted water with 2 tablespoons of olive oil for 8 minutes and drain. Put the cooked pasta on a deep heated platter and pour the trout sauce on top. Sprinkle with freshly ground pepper and serve immediately.

Cod Cooked with Greens

Serves 4
Preparation time 12 hours
Cooking time 1 hour

2 lb (1 kg) dried salt cod, pre-soaked
1 lb (500 g) spinach
1 lb (500 g) assorted greens (chard, amaranth, or fennel)
1 cup chopped green onions
1/4 cup finely chopped dill
2/3 cup olive oil
6 cloves garlic, slivered
14 oz (400 g) canned tomatoes, finely chopped
salt and freshly ground pepper

Cook the cod briefly in water to cover, drain, and remove skin and bones. Cut into serving pieces. Trim the greens, rinse, chop, blanch, and drain well. Heat half the oil and saute the onions until wilted. Mix with the prepared greens and dill and spread on the bottom of an oven-proof dish. Lay the pieces of cod on top. Heat the remaining oil in a small pan and saute the garlic. Add the tomatoes, a pinch of salt, and pepper, to taste. Cook the sauce until it starts to thicken and spoon on top of the cod and greens. Bake at 350°F (180°C) for 1 hour until the sauce has cooked down. Serve hot.

Fried Salt Cod

Serves 5-6
Preparation time 12 hours
Cooking time 15-20 minutes

2 lb (1 kg) dried salt cod
oil for frying
1 batch of batter for frying (see basic recipes)

for the garnish
sprigs of parsley
lemon wedges
garlic sauce (see basic recipes)

Remove the skin from the cod and cut into serving pieces. Soak in cold water to cover 12 hours, changing the water 4-5 times. Drain the cod and remove the bones. Meanwhile, prepare the batter according to the recipe and set aside for 1 hour. Dip the pieces of cod in the batter one by one, allow excess to run off, and fry in hot oil. Garnish with sprigs of parsley and lemon wedges. Serve immediately accompanied by the garlic sauce.

Lefkada Style Cod

Serves 4
Preparation time 12 hours
Cooking time 1 hour 30 minutes

2 lb (1 kg) fresh or dried salt cod
1 small onion, grated (optional)
10 cloves garlic, thinly sliced
5-6 medium potatoes, quartered (3 lb/1¹/₂ kg)
1 cup olive oil
1/3 cup lemon juice
salt and freshly ground pepper

Divide the cod into serving pieces and skin. Soak in water to cover 12 hours, changing the water 3-4 times. Drain and arrange in a large casserole with the potatoes, garlic, onions, 1/3 of the oil, and water to cover. Add the pepper, and, if necessary, a pinch of salt. Cover and simmer until the cod and potatoes are tender and the sauce has cooked down. Beat the remaining oil with the lemon juice until thick and creamy and pour into the casserole. When it comes again to a boil, remove from the heat. Sprinkle with freshly ground pepper and finely chopped parsley. Serve immediately.

Fish-Stuffed Cabbage Rolls

Serves 4
Preparation time 50 minutes
Cooking time 35 minutes

2 lb (1 kg) frozen sole fillets or cod
1 large loose-leafed cabbage
1 large onion, thinly sliced
10 small dill pickles, julienne
1/4 cup prepared mustard
1/2 cup finely chopped dill
1/2 cup olive oil
1/4 cup lemon juice
1 tablespoons flour

Blanch the cabbage and separate the leaves. Defrost the fish and cut into 1x2 inch (3x5 cm) pieces. Lay one cabbage leaf out on the work surface and spread with mustard. At one end place a piece of fish, 3-4 slices of onion, 3-4 pickle strips, and sprinkle with some dill and freshly ground pepper. Turn in the sides, and roll up. Repeat with the remaining ingredients. Lay the rolls, seam-side down, on the bottom of a wide casserole. Pour the olive oil on top and add 1 cup of hot water. Put the casserole on medium heat, cover, and simmer 30-35 minutes until the liquid has cooked down. Dissolve the flour in the lemon juice and stir in a little of the cooking liquid. Pour on top of the rolls and shake the pan in a circular motion to distribute. Simmer another 5 minutes until the sauce thickens and remove from the heat. Serve with salad couscous.

Grilled Salmon with Mustard Sauce

Serves 4
Preparation time 15 minutes
Cooking time 10 minutes

4 fresh salmon fillets (10 oz/300 g each)
1/4 cup olive oil

for the mustard sauce
1/4 cup Dijon mustard
2 tablespoons orange juice
2 tablespoons lemon juice
2 teaspoons honey
1 tablespoons crushed green peppercorns
salt and freshly ground pepper

Prepare the sauce: Combine the mustard with the orange and lemon juices, honey, and green peppercorns. Brush both sides of the salmon fillets with the oil and grill on charcoal or broil 4-5 minutes on each side, turning once. Serve the salmon with sauteed asparagus and artichoke hearts accompanied by the mustard sauce.

Salad Couscous

1 cup quick-cooking couscous
3 tablespoons olive oil
salt and freshly ground pepper
1 small zucchini
1 clove garlic
1/3 cup tomato juice
1 small peeled tomato
1 sprig of rosemary
1 sprig of thyme

Mix the tomato juice with the oil. Stir in the couscous and soak for about 30 minutes. Chop the zucchini and the garlic and saute in 2 tablespoons olive oil until wilted. Stir into the couscous. Chop the tomato, combine with the rosemary and thyme, and stir into the couscous.

Salmon with Artichokes and Fennel

Serves 4
Preparation time 30 minutes
Cooking time 20 minutes

4 salmon fillets, 8 oz/250 g each
1 small onion, grated
1/4 cup olive oil
10 oz (300 g) Florence fennel, chopped
26 oz (800 g) canned artichokes
2 tablespoons margarine, in pieces
1/4 cup lemon juice
salt and freshly ground pepper

Rinse and remove scales from salmon fillets. Arrange them in an oven-proof dish and dot each with several pieces of margarine. Rinse and drain the artichokes, pressing out excess water with your fingers. Heat the oil in a saucepan and saute them. Add the fennel, salt, and pepper, cover and simmer on low heat for 10-15 minutes. Pour the artichokes and fennel on top of the salmon fillets. Bake at 400°F (200°C) for 15-20 minutes. Remove from the oven and sprinkle with the lemon juice and serve immediately.

Salmon with Mustard and Mushrooms

Serves 4
Preparation time 40 minutes

4 fresh salmon fillets (10 oz/300 g each)
1/4 cup olive oil
salt and freshly ground pepper
3 tablespoons olive oil
8 oz (250 g) oyster mushrooms, in strips

for the sauce
1/4 cup prepared mustard
1 tablespoons dry white wine
1 tablespoon vinegar
1/2 cup olive oil
1/4 cup corn oil
1 tablespoons margarine
2 tablespoons finely chopped onion
2-3 tablespoons brandy (optional)
1/2 teaspoon sugar
2 teaspoons finely chopped dill
salt and freshly ground pepper

Prepare the sauce: Blend the mustard, wine, and vinegar in the food processor. Combine the olive oil with the corn oil. With the motor on medium speed, add the oil in a thin steady stream, and process until the mixture thickens like mayonnaise. Melt the margarine in a small pan, add the onions and saute 2-3 minutes on medium heat until wilted. Add the brandy and carefully light with a match. When the flames die down, sprinkle with the sugar and continue stirring over the heat until the onions caramelize. Remove from the heat, cool, and stir into the mustard sauce along with the dill, salt, and freshly ground pepper. The sauce should be thick. Sprinkle the salmon with salt and pepper and brush all sides with oil. Cook in a non-stick fry pan until lightly brown, about 4-5 minutes on each side. Meanwhile, saute the mushrooms in the oil and arrange on a platter with the salmon. Pour the sauce on top and serve immediately accompanied by sauteed vegetables.

Prepare the sauce: Melt the margarine in a small pan on medium heat. Stir in the flour and cook 1 minute. Add the fish stock and stir vigorously. Simmer slowly until thick. Remove from the heat, add the salt and pepper, lemon juice, and 4 mashed asparagus. Puree in the blender or food processor until smooth. Put 1 inch (2 cm) of water in a wide shallow pan fitted with a steaming rack. Bring the water to the boil and arrange the salmon fillets on the rack. Cover and steam the fish 7-10 minutes. Blanch the carrots and the remaining asparagus and serve with the steamed fish and the sauce. Garnish with lemon quarters. Serve hot.

Steamed Salmon with Spaghetti Primavera

Serves 4
Preparation time 2 hours
Cooking time 10 minutes

4 salmon steaks (7 oz/200 g each)
salt and freshly ground pepper
1 bouquet garni

for the spaghetti primavera
2 tablespoons olive oil
1 green bell pepper julienne
1 red bell pepper julienne
2 canned palm hearts, sliced
1 clove garlic, minced
2 tablespoons balsamic vinegar
1 teaspoon Italian herbs
10 oz (300 g) pesto-flavored spaghetti
basil sauce (see basic recipes)

Prepare the spaghetti primavera. Heat the oil in a pan and saute the peppers, palm hearts, and garlic until wilted. Stir in the vinegar and herbs. Remove from the heat and set aside. Prepare the basil sauce according to the recipe. Place a steamer rack in a wide shallow pan. Pour in 1 inch (2 cm) of water. Add the bouquet garni and bring to a boil. Arrange the salmon steaks on the rack, cover, and steam the fish for 7-10 minutes over the simmering water. Meanwhile, cook the spaghetti in salted water with 2 tablespoons of oil. Drain, toss with the prepared vegetables, and divide the spaghetti primavera among 4 heated plates. Place one salmon steak on each plate garnished with 2-3 tablespoons of basil sauce, freshly ground pepper, and a tomato rosette.

Steamed Salmon with Asparagus Sauce

Serves 4
Preparation time 30 minutes
Cooking time 10 minutes

4 fresh salmon fillets
2 large carrots, sliced
14 oz (400 g) canned asparagus
salt and freshly ground pepper

for the sauce
2 tablespoons margarine
2 tablespoons flour
1½ cup fish stock (see basic recipes)
1 tablespoons lemon juice
salt and freshly ground pepper

STEAMED SALMON WITH SPAGHETTI PRIMAVERA

Hot Potato Salad with Salmon

Serves 3-4
Preparation time 15 minutes
Cooking time 30 minutes

1/2 cup mayonnaise, without eggs
2 teaspoons prepared mustard
2 tablespoons lemon juice
3 cups diced cooked potatoes
2 tablespoons grated onion
1/3 cup finely chopped celery
8 oz (250 g) smoked salmon, finely chopped
1/2 cup grated stale breadcrumbs
3 tablespoons corn oil

Combine the first 6 ingredients in a bowl. Spread 1/3 of the potato mixture on the bottom of an oiled oven-proof dish. Sprinkle the top with half the salmon. Spread another third of the potato mixture on top and sprinkle with the remaining salmon. Cover with the remaining potato mixture. Toss the breadcrumbs with the corn oil and sprinkle on top of the casserole. Bake at 350°F (180°C) for about 30 minutes. Serve hot.

Marinated Mackerel

Serves 4
Preparation time 15 minutes

2 lb (1 kg) mackerel
salt, pepper, flour,
oil for frying
2 tablespoons flour
2 cloves garlic, minced
3 tablespoons vinegar
2 lb (1 kg) ripe tomatoes, pulped and strained
1/2 teaspoon sugar
1 bay leaf
1/4 teaspoon rosemary
salt and freshly ground pepper

Gut and rinse the fish. Put in a strainer and drain well. Sprinkle with salt and pepper, dust with flour and fry on all sides in hot oil. Put 2 tablespoons of the frying oil in a clean pan. Add 2 tablespoons flour and cook until lightly browned. Stir in the garlic, vinegar, tomato pulp, sugar, bay leaf, rosemary, salt and pepper. Simmer the sauce about 15 minutes until thick. Pour on the fried fish and sprinkle with finely chopped parsley or mint. Serve hot or cold.

Fish Patties

Serves 4-5
Preparation time 1 hour
Cooking time 10 minutes

2 lbs (1 kg) fresh small fish
1/2 cup grated onion
4 gloves garlic, minced
1/3 cup breadcrumbs
1 large ripe tomato, peeled, seeded,
and finely chopped
1/2 cup finely chopped mint, parsley or dill
1-2 teaspoons oregano or thyme
salt and freshly ground pepper
flour as needed
oil for frying

De-bone the fish and shred. Combine with onion, garlic, breadcrumbs, tomato, herbs, salt, and pepper. Knead adding flour as needed (2-3 tablespoons) to form a rather stiff mixture. Heat the oil on medium heat and fry tablespoonfuls of the mixture until lightly browned on both sides. Serve hot with garlic sauce or another sauce of your choice.

Salad with Sole Fillets

Serves 4
Preparation time 20 minutes

8 sole fillets (2 lb/1 kg)
1 bunch rocket
1 lb (500 g) curly green lettuce or mixed greens
16 cherry tomatoes
1/3 cup olive oil
1 tablespoon lemon juice
2 tablespoons vinegar
1 tablespoon finely chopped parsley
salt and freshly ground pepper
2 tablespoons capers
1/4 cup thinly slivered almonds
12 fresh mint leaves
several lemon twists

Split the sole fillets in half lengthwise and sprinkle with salt and pepper. Roll up with the whiter portion towards the inside and secure with toothpicks. Steam for 10 minutes. Meanwhile, rinse and pick over the rocket and the lettuce and tear into bite-sized pieces. Divide onto 4 salad plates and arrange 4 sole fillet rolls and 4 tomatoes on each plate. Sprinkle with the capers and almonds. Combine the oil, lemon juice, vinegar, parsley, salt, and pepper in a well-sealed jar and shake vigorously. Pour some on each salad and garnish with the mint leaves and lemon twists. Serve immediately.

Swordfish with Vegetables

Serves 4
Preparation time 20 minutes
Cooking time 12-15 minutes

1/3 cup olive oil
1/3 cup chopped celery
1/3 cup chopped onion
1 clove garlic, minced
1/3 cup chopped red bell pepper
2 tablespoons lemon juice
2/3 cup chopped tomatoes
1/2 teaspoon oregano
1/2 teaspoon herbes de Provence
1/4 teaspoon thyme
1/4 teaspoon sugar
10 drops Tabasco sauce
salt and freshly ground pepper
4 swordfish fillets

Heat 3 tablespoons olive oil in a heavy-bottomed pan and saute the celery, onions, garlic, and peppers until wilted. Add the tomatoes, herbs, sugar, Tabasco, salt, and pepper and half the lemon juice, stirring the vegetables until tender and glossy. Remove the vegetables from the heat and keep warm. Brush the swordfish fillets with the remaining oil and lemon juice, sprinkle with a little salt and pepper and broil 5-6 inches (12-15 cm) from the heat source, 4-6 minutes on each side. Alternatively, fry the fish on both sides in a non-stick pan. Serve hot topped with 3-4 tablespoons of the vegetables and accompanied by sauteed carrots and zucchini.

Trout Fillets with Mushrooms

Serves 4
Preparation time 15 minutes
Cooking time 30 minutes

4 trout fillets (10 oz/300 g each)

for the sauce
4 green onions, finely chopped
2 tablespoons olive oil
3/4 cup dry white wine
2 oz (60 g) sliced mushrooms
1/2 cup vegetarian cream

for the stuffing
4 green onions, finely chopped
3 tablespoons olive oil
7 oz (200 g) oyster mushrooms
2/3 cup breadcrumbs

Sprinkle the trout fillets with salt and pepper. Heat the oil in a saucepan and saute the onions until wilted. Add the wine and mushrooms. Cover and simmer until the sauce cooks down to half its volume, about 10 minutes. Stir in the cream and simmer 1 minute. Strain the mixture through a sieve, pressing the onions and mushrooms with the back of a wooden spoon to release all their juices. To prepare the stuffing, heat the oil and saute the onions for 5 minutes until wilted. Add the mushrooms and cook another 5 minutes. Add the breadcrumbs, salt, and pepper. When ready to serve, melt 3 tablespoons of margarine and saute the fish fillets 2-3 minutes on each side. Put a trout fillet on a heated plate, and top with 1/4 of the stuffing. Repeat with the remaining three fillets and stuffing. Pour the sauce on top and serve immediately. Garnish with lemon twists and sprigs of parsley.

Swordfish on Skewers

Serves 4
Preparation time 1 hour
Cooking time 25-20 minutes

2 lb (1 kg) swordfish
1 large onion
1 large green bell pepper
2 large tomatoes or 6-8 cherry tomatoes, halved
1-2 hot peppers (optional)
salt and freshly ground pepper
1/4 cup lemon juice
1/3 cup olive oil
8 wooden or metal skewers

Rinse and drain the fish and pat dry with paper towels. Cut into large bite-sized pieces. Cut the onion, pepper, and tomatoes (outer part) into 1-inch (2½-cm) squares. Thread the fish on the skewers alternately with onion, pepper, and tomato squares between each piece. If desired, put one or two small pieces of hot pepper on each skewer. Thread leftover vegetables on extra skewers. Sprinkle with salt and pepper and brush amply on all sides with olive oil. Broil on charcoal or oven grill 8 minutes on each side. Take care not to overcook or the fish will dry out. Arrange broiled fish on a platter. Combine the lemon juice and 1/3 cup olive oil in a jar, shake vigorously, and pour over the swordfish. Serve immediately with extra grilled vegetables.

Stuffed Sole Fillets

Serves 4
Preparation time 1 hour
Cooking time 20 minutes

8 fresh or frozen sole fillets (2 lb/1 kg)
1/4 cup lemon juice
salt and white pepper
8 oz (250 g) frozen spinach
6 green onions, chopped
1/4 cup finely chopped dill
1/4 cup finely chopped parsley
8 thin tomato slices
1/3 cup olive oil
1/2 cup fish stock
1/2 cup dry white wine
1/4 teaspoon cayenne

Heat half the oil in a pan and saute the onions. Add the spinach and stir for 5 minutes on high heat. Add the dill, parsley, salt, and pepper, cover and simmer until the liquid has cooked down almost to the oil. Sprinkle the fillets with the salt, pepper, and lemon juice. Put 1-2 tablespoons of the spinach mixture on each fillet and roll up. Arrange the fish rolls side by side in an oven-proof dish and put a tomato slice on top of each. Pour the fish stock, wine, and remaining oil on top. Sprinkle with salt, pepper, and cayenne. Bake in a 400˚F (200˚C) oven for 15-20 minutes. Serve immediately.

Baked Seabass with Olives

Serves 4
Preparation time 40 minutes
Cooking time 45 minutes

2 small onions, sliced in thin rings
4 seabass (about 13 oz/400 g each)
4 cloves garlic, sliced
3 tablespoons finely chopped parsley
2 teaspoons thyme
2 medium tomatoes, peeled, seeded, and chopped
2 tablespoons tomato paste
1 large green, red, or yellow bell pepper, cut in strips
salt and pepper
10 black Calamata olives
10 green olives
1/2 cup dry white wine
1/2 cup olive oil

Lightly rub the onion rings with salt until wilted; rinse, and squeeze out excess water with your hands. Scale and gut fish, leaving heads and tails in tact. Rinse well. Sprinkle all surfaces inside and out with salt and pepper and brush with olive oil. Oil a large oven-proof baking dish just large enough to hold the fish. Combine the onions, garlic, parsley, thyme, tomatoes, tomato paste, and peppers, with a pinch each of salt and pepper. Spread half the mixture on the bottom of the pan and lay the whole fish on top. Sprinkle the other half of the vegetable mixture on top of the fish surrounded by the olives. Pour the wine and oil on top and bake at 425°F (220°C) for about 45 minutes. Baste 3-4 times during the baking with the pan juices. Serve hot accompanied by salad and cooked greens.

Baked Stuffed Seabass

Serves 4
Preparation time 45 minutes
Cooking time 30 minutes

4 seabass (13 oz/400 g) each, scaled and gutted
2 green onions, finely chopped
2 tablespoons finely chopped parsley
1/3 cup olive oil
1 lb (500 g) spinach, cleaned and finely chopped
1/4 cup grated onion
salt and freshly ground pepper
1/4 cup dry white wine

Heat half the oil in a pan and saute the green onions. Add the spinach, sprinkle with salt and pepper and stir over medium heat until wilted. Remove from the heat, stir in the parsley. Heat the remaining oil in another pan and saute the grated onion until wilted. Slit the fish open along the length of the belly, from the gills to the tail. Insert a sharp knife into the opening between the flesh and bone just below the gill cover. Release the top fillet from the skeleton by sliding the knife all the way down to the tail taking care not to cut through to the skin. Cut the backbone with a scissors just below the gill cover (head) and at the tail end, leaving the two halves joined and the heads and tails intact. Carefully detach the spine with the attached bones from the bottom fillet with a tweezers. Remove any other visible bones left inside. Rinse the fish thoroughly under cold running water to remove all traces of blood. Drain well and pat all surfaces dry with paper towels. Sprinkle the fish inside and out with salt and pepper and brush with olive oil. Spread the sauteed onions on the bottom of an oven-proof dish large enough to hold the fish. Arrange the fish on the onions with the open sides facing upward. Stuff the fish with the spinach mixture and sprinkle with the wine. Cover with baking paper or foil and bake in a 400°F (200°C) oven for about 30 minutes. Remove from the oven and serve immediately.

Braised Sardines with Oil and Oregano

Serves 4
Preparation time 30 minutes
Cooking time 20 minutes

2 lb (1 kg) fresh sardines, anchovies or smelt
2/3 cup olive oil
5-6 cloves garlic, sliced
2-3 tablespoons vinegar
salt, freshly ground pepper, and oregano

Clean and gut the fish. If convenient, remove the backbone and heads, leaving tails intact. Heat the oil in a heavy-bottomed pan on high heat and lightly saute the garlic. Add the sardines and sprinkle with the vinegar, salt, pepper, and oregano. Cook on high heat until the liquid evaporates nearly down to its oil. Serve hot or cold. Alternatively, arrange the fish in an oiled baking dish, pour the sauteed garlic and oil on top. Sprinkle with the vinegar, salt, pepper, and oregano and bake in a 400°F (200°C) oven until the liquid cooks down to the oil.

Savory Marinated Fish Corfu

Serves 6
Preparation time 3-4 days

3 lb (1½ kg) red mullet, mackerel, or bogue (small bream)
1 cup tomato juice
3 cups olive oil
1½ cups vinegar
15 cloves garlic, whole
1 tablespoon rosemary
salt
2 tablespoons flour

Clean and rinse the fish thoroughly to remove all traces of blood. Sprinkle with salt and drain well in a colander. Coat with flour and fry in hot oil. Allow to cool. Combine the tomatoes, oil, vinegar, garlic, rosemary, and salt in a saucepan and simmer the marinade until the garlic softens, about 10-15 minutes. Put some of the hot marinade in a ceramic dish and lay the fish on top side by side in one layer. Spoon some more hot marinade on top and continue layering the fish in rows with some of the hot marinade in between until all the fish is used up. Cover the top layer of fish completely with the remaining marinade. Refrigerate for at least 3-4 days before ready to serve. May be kept in the refrigerator up to 15 days.

Baked Fresh Anchovies

Serves 4
Preparation time 20 minutes
Cooking time 30 minutes

1 lb (500 g) fresh anchovies
1/2 cup finely chopped parsley
3 cloves garlic, slivered
5-6 Calamata olives, chopped
salt, pepper, oregano
2-3 tomatoes, sliced in thick rounds
1 green bell pepper, cut in strips

Clean and remove heads, innards, and backbones from the anchovies. Rinse and drain well. Combine the parsley, garlic, and olives in a bowl. Arrange the tomato slices in a baking dish and place 1 tablespoon of the parsley mixture, 1-2 anchovies, and two pepper strips on each slice. Sprinkle with a little olive oil, salt, pepper, and oregano. Bake in a very hot oven, 475°F (250°C) for 30 minutes. Serve hot or at room temperature.

Peppers Stuffed with Tuna Salad

Makes 10 pepper cups
Preparation time 2 hours 30 minutes

5 large bell peppers, red, yellow, and green
2/3 cup cooked basmati rice
2/3 cup cooked peas
2/3 cup cooked corn
1 lb (500 g) canned tuna, flaked
1/4 cup chopped sweet red pepper
1/4 cup pickle relish
1 tablespoon capers
2 tablespoons coarsely chopped pistachios or pine nuts

for the sauce/dressing
1/4 cup olive oil
2 tablespoons vinegar or lemon juice
2 teaspoons mustard

salt and freshly ground pepper
lettuce leaves and canned roasted red peppers, for garnish

Cut the peppers in half width-wise, devein, deseed, and rinse. Arrange the lettuce on a platter and place the pepper cups on top. Cut the roasted peppers into 10 narrow strips and roll up to form rosettes. Combine the remaining ingredients for the salad in a large bowl and toss to mix. Put the ingredients for the dressing in a well-sealed jar and shake vigorously to blend. Pour over the salad and toss until well-mixed. Cover with plastic wrap and refrigerate for at least 2 hours. Fill the peppers with the salad and garnish the top of each with a pimento roll. As attractive as they are delicious. A perfect dish for a buffet or luncheon.

Baked Tuna ala Genovese

Serves 4
Preparation time 20 minutes
Cooking time 25 minutes

4 tuna steaks
1 oz (35 g) dried porcini mushrooms or
3 oz (100 g) oyster mushrooms
3 anchovy fillets
2 tablespoons finely chopped parsley
2 cloves garlic
3 tablespoons olive oil
1 tablespoon flour
1 cup dry white wine
1 tablespoon Italian herbs
2 tablespoons lemon juice
2 tablespoons margarine
salt and freshly ground pepper

Rinse the fish steaks and soak in cold water for 30 minutes to remove all traces of blood. Drain and pat dry with paper towels. Meanwhile, soak the dried mushrooms in 1 cup of lukewarm water until soft. Drain the mushrooms and puree in the food processor or blender along with the anchovies, parsley, and garlic. Heat the oil in a large pan, add the flour, and stir over medium heat for 1 minute. Stir in the pureed mushrooms and wine. Bring to a boil and add the fish steaks, herbs, salt, and pepper. Cover and simmer for 5 minutes. Transfer the fish to an oven-proof dish, pour the sauce on top and bake at 400°F (200°C) for 20 minutes. Remove the steaks with a slotted spoon and arrange on a warm platter. Add the margarine and lemon juice to the pan and stir to mix well. Pour over the fish and serve immediately.

Pasta Salad with Tuna

Serves 4
Preparation time 15 minutes
Cooking time 8 minutes

2 pieces canned roasted red peppers
7 oz (200 g) canned tuna, in brine
14 oz (400 g) canned artichoke-hearts
2 tablespoons finely chopped mint
3 tablespoons olive oil
1 tablespoon capers
1 clove garlic, minced
10 oz (300 g) shell pasta
2 tablespoons balsamic vinegar
salt and pepper

Drain the peppers and cut into narrow strips. Drain the tuna and flake with a fork. Drain the artichokes, rinse, and press out the excess water. Cut each one in half and put them in a bowl with the tuna and peppers. Add the mint, olive oil, capers, and garlic. Cover with plastic wrap and refrigerate several hours or until the next day. Cook the pasta in boiling salted water with 2 tablespoons olive oil. Drain well and toss in a bowl with the tuna salad. Sprinkle the vinegar, salt, and pepper on top and serve immediately.

Heat the oil and saute the onions until wilted. Dissolve the cornstarch in the soya milk and add to the onions, stirring until slightly thickened. Remove from the heat and cool slightly. Stir in the cheese, broccoli, carrots, tuna, cilantro, salt, freshly ground pepper, and gently mix. Open a sheet of phyllo out on the work surface and brush with olive oil. Place the remaining phyllo sheets on top, brushing with oil between each. Spoon the tuna mixture along the long edge leaving a 2-inch (5-cm) space at each side. Bring the two sides over the mixture and roll up. Transfer the roll to a baking sheet and brush with oil. Score the surface with a sharp knife to allow steam to escape during baking. Bake in a 400°F (200°C) oven for 40 minutes, until lightly browned. Serve hot.

Smoked Trout with Potato Salad

Serves 6
Preparation time 20 minutes

6 smoked trout fillets, about 1 lb (500 g)
lemon slices
sprigs of dill
tomato slices

for the salad
3 large potatoes, cooked and diced
2 stalks celery, chopped
2 cups pomegranate seeds
1/4 cup olive oil
2 tablespoons vinegar
1 tablespoon lemon juice
1 teaspoon prepared mustard
salt and freshly ground pepper

Combine the olive oil, vinegar, lemon juice, mustard, salt, and pepper in a well-sealed jar and shake. Toss with the remaining salad ingredients, except the pomegranate seeds, in a bowl. Spoon onto the center of a round platter and sprinkle the pomegranate seeds on top. Arrange the trout fillets around the salad and garnish with sprigs of dill and lemon and tomato slices. An attractive appetizer course.

Tuna-Vegetable Phyllo Roll

Serves 4
Preparation time 1 hour
Baking time 40 minutes

1 medium onion, finely chopped
3 tablespoons olive oil
1/2 cup soya milk
1 teaspoon cornstarch
1 cup grated vegetarian cheese
1/8 teaspoon nutmeg
1½ cup parboiled broccoli florets
1½ cup parboiled carrots, in small cubes
7 oz (200 g) canned tuna in brine, flaked
1/4 cup finely chopped fresh cilantro or parsley
8 sheets of phyllo
1/3 cup olive oil, for brushing
salt and pepper

Red Snapper Stifado

Serves 4
Preparation time 30 minutes
Cooking time 1 hour 30 minutes

3 lb (1½ kg) red snapper or other large fish
2 lb (1 kg) small boiling onions, frozen
1 cup olive oil
6 cloves garlic, whole
2 large ripe tomatoes, peeled, seeded, and pureed
2 bay leaves
6 whole allspice berries
salt and freshly ground pepper
1/2 cup dry white wine

Scale, gut, and rinse the fish thoroughly to remove every trace of blood from the belly and head. Cut into thick pieces, cover with plastic membrane and refrigerate until ready to cook. Thaw the onions in a colander, rinse with cold water, and drain well. Heat the oil on high heat and saute the onions and garlic. Pour in the wine, tomatoes, salt, pepper, bay leaves, and allspice. Cover and simmer the onions for about 1 hour, until tender. Add the fish and continue cooking until the sauce has cooked down and the fish is opaque and flaky.

Red Snapper with Peppers

Serves 4
Preparation time 40 minutes
Cooking time 1 hour 30 minutes

3 lb (1½ kg) red snapper, cod, grouper, or
other large fish
1/2 cup olive oil
2 medium onions, sliced
2 cloves garlic, slivered
2 green, 2 red, 2 yellow bell peppers, in wide strips
2 large ripe tomatoes, peeled, seeds, and finely chopped
1/4 cup finely chopped parsley
1/4 cup dry white wine
2 tablespoons lemon juice
salt and freshly ground pepper

Scale, gut, and rinse the fish thoroughly to remove all traces of blood. Cut into large pieces. Heat half the oil on high heat and saute the onions and garlic until wilted. Add the peppers and continue cooking until wilted. Add the tomatoes, cover, lower heat and simmer for 10 minutes. Stir in the parsley and spread the mixture on the bottom of an oven-proof dish. Arrange the pieces of fish here and there, pushing them slightly into the mixture. Pour the remaining oil and wine on top, sprinkle with salt and pepper and bake in a 400°F (200°C) oven for about 1 hour. Remove from

the oven, pour the lemon juice on top and serve immediately.

Braised Carp Kastoria

Serves 4
Preparation time 1 hour

2 lb (1 kg) carp with its roe
1 cup olive oil
1 tablespoon flour
2 tablespoons chopped parsley
salt and hot red pepper flakes or cayenne
1 cup grated stale bread, without crusts
3-4 cloves garlic, minced
2 tablespoons vinegar
1 cup ground walnuts

Prepare the carp for cooking. Boil the fish whole in 4 cups (1 liter) salted water and drain. Set cooking liquid aside to cool. Cut the fish in half lengthwise, remove backbone, and arrange on a platter. Heat half the oil on medium heat and stir in the flour for 1 minute. Pour in 1 cup of reserved fish liquid, add the parsley, salt, pepper, roe, red pepper, and simmer 10 minutes. Combine the bread crumbs with the garlic, remaining oil, vinegar, walnuts, and 1 cup of the fish liquid. Mix well and add the mixture to the sauce in the pan and stir until well-blended and heated through. Serve the fish accompanied by the sauce. Garnish with parsley sprigs and serve with more cayenne.

Baked Red Snapper with Eggplant

Serves 4
Preparation time 1 hour
Cooking time 40 minutes

2 long eggplants, sliced into rounds
1/2 cup olive oil
2 large onions, sliced
1 clove garlic, minced
1/4 cup finely chopped parsley
2 large tomatoes, thinly sliced

4 pieces red snapper (10 oz, 300 g each)
salt and freshly ground pepper
1 teaspoon thyme

Slice the eggplant, sprinkle with salt, and allow to drain for 1 hour in a colander. Rinse well, and press out the excess water with the palms of your hands. Fry lightly in olive oil. Saute the onions and the garlic in the oil until wilted. Stir in the parsley. Arrange the pieces of fish in an oven-proof dish with a few eggplant slices on each. Spoon the sauteed onions on top and cover them with the tomato slices. Sprinkle with salt, pepper, and thyme. Bake the fish in a 400°F (200°C) oven for about 40 minutes, until tender and the sauce has cooked down almost to the oil.

Athenian Style Poached Fish

Serves 4
Preparation time 30 minutes
Cooking time 40 minutes

2 lb (1 kg) grouper, cod, or red snapper
1 large onion, whole
2 stalks celery
1 zucchini
1 large potato
1 large carrot
1/2 cup peas
1 green bell pepper
salt and freshly ground pepper
2 tablespoons lemon juice

for the garnish
2 cups eggless mayonnaise
olives, pickles, capers, parsley sprigs

Clean the fish, leaving head and tail intact. Rinse well and drain. Put the vegetables, oil, and 6 cups (1½ lt) water in a large pan and cook covered for 30 minutes. Remove the vegetables with a slotted spoon and discard the onion and pepper. Add the fish and lemon juice to the hot stock and cook uncovered for 8-10 minutes, until tender. Take the fish out of the pan, cool, and remove the skin and bones. Cut the fish and vegetables into small pieces. Combine the fish and vegetables with half the mayonnaise. Add salt, pepper, and lemon juice to taste. Arrange the fish mixture on an oblong platter in the shape of a fish. Spread the remaining mayonnaise on top or pipe it on with a pastry bag. Garnish with the olives, pickles, capers, and parsley. Cover with plastic wrap and refrigerate until ready to serve.

Baked Red Snapper Spetses

Serves 5-6
Preparation time 1 hour 30 minutes
Cooking time 1 hour

3 lb (1½ kg) red snapper or white fish
salt and pepper
1/4 cup lemon juice
1 cup olive oil
2 tablespoons flour
1 onion, sliced
4 cloves garlic, minced
14 oz (400 g) tomato juice
1/2 cup dry white wine
1/2 cup finely chopped parsley

Clean the fish, leaving head and tail intact. Rinse the belly cavity thoroughly to remove all traces of blood. Make 3 or 4 parallel slashes on both sides of the fish with a sharp knife to ensure it cooks throughout. Put the fish in a baking dish and rub all surfaces with lemon juice, salt, and pepper. Pour half the oil on top, sprinkle with a little flour, and set aside for 1 hour. Heat the remaining oil in a saucepan on high heat, and lightly saute the onion and garlic. Add the tomato pulp, wine, and parsley, cover, and simmer until thick. Pour the sauce over the fish and bake in a 350°F (175°C) oven for about 1 hour, occasionally basting with the pan juices. Serve accompanied by cooked greens, broccoli, or asparagus.

Sole Almondine

Serves 4
Preparation time 10 minutes
Frying time 10 minutes

4 sole fillets
salt and freshly ground pepper
flour for coating
1/4 cup clarified margarine
1 very small onion onion, sliced
1/3 cup slivered almonds

1 tablespoon lemon juice
2 tablespoons finely chopped parsley
lemon slices

Sprinkle the sole with salt, pepper, and coat with flour. Heat the margarine in a small frying pan and saute the onions. Strain the melted margarine into a large non-stick frying pan and discard the onions. Stir the almonds in the margarine over medium heat until lightly browned. Remove the almonds with a slotted spoon and fry the sole in the same fat for 2-3 minutes on each side. Remove the fillets to a hot platter, sprinkle with the almonds, parsley, and lemon juice and serve immediately garnished with sliced lemon. Excellent accompanied by sauteed asparagus or broccoli.

Baked Anchovies

Serves 4-5
Preparation time 1 hour
Cooking time 1 hour

3 lb (1¹/₂ kg) anchovies, sardines, or
other small fish
1¹/₃ cups olive oil
4 large onions, sliced
6 cloves garlic, slivered
1 cup finely chopped parsley
salt and pepper
2 tablespoons tomato paste
1/4 cup dry white wine
2 ripe tomatoes, thinly sliced
3 thinly sliced lemon rounds, without rind

Clean and gut the fish, removing the heads but leaving tails in tact. If time permits, carefully remove the backbones. Rinse the fish thoroughly and drain well in a colander. Heat the oil in a saucepan and saute the onions and the garlic until wilted. Remove from the heat, stir in the parsley, salt, pepper, and the tomato paste diluted in the wine. Arrange the fish side by side in a ceramic or oven-proof baking dish in two rows with some sauce and lemon and tomato slices in between. Pour any remaining sauce on top. Bake the fish in a 400°F (200°C) oven for 1 hour, until the sauce has cooked almost down to the oil. May be served either hot or cold.

Fillet of Sole Valenciana

Serves 4-5
Preparation time 25 minutes
Cooking time 1 hour 20 minutes

1/4 cup olive oil
2 cloves garlic, slivered
2 medium onions, finely chopped
1 green bell pepper, chopped
2 large tomatoes, peeled, seeded, and chopped
4 tablespoons ketchup
1 teaspoon ground coriander seed
1 teaspoon oregano
salt and freshly ground pepper
30 green stuffed olives, sliced
4 tablespoons finely chopped parsley
10 sole or cod fillets (2 lb/1 kg)
1 cup flour
2 teaspoons salt
2 teaspoons clarified margarine

Heat the oil in a large frying pan and saute the garlic, onions, and peppers until wilted. Add the tomatoes, ketchup, coriander, oregano, salt, and pepper. Simmer the sauce for 30 minutes and remove from the heat. Stir in the olives and parsley. Combine the flour and salt in a deep dish. Drain the sole fillets and pat dry on paper toweling. Coat both sides of the fillets with flour and shake off excess. Melt the margarine in a large frying pan and fry the fillets for 5 minutes on each side. Arrange on a deep platter and pour the sauce on top. Serve immediately accompanied by a green salad.

Pickled Anchovies in Garlic

Preparation time 2-3 days

2 lb (1 kg) anchovies
4 tablespoons garlic, thinly slivered
salt, vinegar, olive oil,
oregano or thyme

Rinse the anchovies and gut. Remove heads and backbones taking care they don't lose their shape. Rinse again and drain well. Arrange side by side in a colander, sprinkle each layer with regular salt. Set aside in a cool place for 2-3 hours. Rinse well in water and arrange the fish side by side on the bottom of a deep flat glass dish. Sprinkle with garlic slivers, oregano or thyme. Make another layer with more garlic and oregano. Continue until all the fish are used up. Carefully pour in enough vinegar to cover the fish. Cover with plastic wrap and refrigerate for 10-12 hours. Drain off the vinegar. Remove and discard the garlic. Pour enough olive oil over the fish to cover them. They are ready to serve. May be kept in the refrigerator up to 15 days. Perfect meze for ouzo.

Salt-Preserved Sardines

Preparation time 2-3 days

2 lb (1 kg) fresh sardines
1 lb (500 g) coarse salt
1 lb (500 g) regular salt
vinegar, olive oil

Rinse the sardines, remove heads and gut. Soak in cold water 30 minutes to remove all traces of blood. Rinse again and drain completely. Layer the sardines in a large colander side by side, heads to tails. Cover each layer of fish with both coarse and regular salt so they are completely buried. Allow to drain at least 2-3 days in a cool place until all their juices have run out. Remove from the salt and rinse well. Arrange in a deep glass dish and soak in ample vinegar for 30 minutes. Remove from the vinegar and arrange on a platter. Pour olive oil on top and serve. Desalt only the number of fish you wish to serve and consume each time. Do not keep the fish in the salt more than a week as it dries out. For this reason, preserve only small amounts of fish - not more than 2 lb (1 kg) at a time. Perfect meze for ouzo.

Mackerel Stew Syros

Serves 3
Preparation time 40 minutes
Baking time 45 minutes

1 cup caper buds in brine
3/4 cups finely chopped onion
2/3 cup olive oil
1/2 cup water
1-2 cloves garlic, slivered
1½ cup fresh or canned pulped tomatoes
1/8 teaspoon cayenne
1/2 teaspoon sugar
salt (if needed) and pepper
2½ lb (1¼ kg) mackerel, gutted and rinsed.

Rinse the capers under running water and drain. Soak them in water to cover for 1 hour, changing the water twice. Drain well. Heat the oil on medium heat, add the onions and garlic and lightly saute until wilted. Add the tomatoes, cayenne, sugar, water, and freshly ground pepper. Bring the mixture to a boil, add the drained capers and simmer 10 minutes. Meanwhile, lightly fry the fish in olive oil and drain. Arrange them in an oven-proof dish and pour the caper sauce on top. If desired, drain the caper mixture and stuff the mackerel. Pour the cooking liquid on top. Bake in a 350°F (180°C) oven for 45 minutes or until the sauce has cooked down almost to the oil.

SALT-PRESERVED SARDINES

Oven-Braised Tuna

Serves 4-5
Preparation time 45 minutes
Cooking time 1 hour

3 lb (1½ kg) tuna steaks or
other large fish steaks
salt and vinegar
3 lb (1½ kg) onions, sliced
10 cloves garlic, slivered
1/2 cup finely chopped parsley
1 lb (1/2 kg) ripe tomatoes, peeled, seeded,
and finely chopped
2 large ripe tomatoes sliced
1 cup olive oil
salt and freshly ground pepper

Slice the tuna into thick steaks and soak in cold water for 1 hour to remove all traces of blood. Rinse under cold running water and drain well. Sprinkle with salt and a little vinegar. Arrange the fish steaks side by side in a baking pan. Heat half the oil in a large heavy-bottomed pan and saute the onions and garlic until wilted. Add the tomatoes, salt, and freshly ground pepper and simmer until the sauce is slightly thick. Add the parsley and spread the sauce on top of the fish steaks. Cover with the tomato slices. Sprinkle with a little more salt, pepper, and the remaining oil. Bake at 400°F (200°C) for 1 hour, until pan juices have cooked down almost to the oil. Serve hot or at room temperature.

Grilled Gilt-Head Bream

Serves 4
Preparation time 15 minutes
Cooking time 20 minutes

4 breams (300 g each, total 3 lb/1200 g)
salt and freshly ground pepper
olive oil
olive oil-lemon dressing (See basic recipes)
finely chopped parsley

Scale the fish, remove the innards and gills, but leave heads and tails intact. Rinse thoroughly under cold running water to remove all traces of blood. Also remove the black membrane from the belly opening. Drain well and sprinkle with salt and pepper. If the fish are thick, make 3-4 slashes on both sides with a sharp knife to ensure even cooking. Rub all surfaces of the fish, inside and out with olive oil. Arrange on a hinged wire grill basket which has been oiled and heated. Close securely and barbecue over charcoal or broil under a grill. When one side is done, turn the grill-basket over. Brush the fish once or twice with a little oil during the cooking. Remove to a heated platter or plates and pour the oil and lemon dressing on top. Garnish with finely chopped parsley and serve with cooked greens.

Seafood Cioppino

Serves 4
Preparation time 40 minutes
Cooking time 45 minutes

1/4 cup olive oil
1 large onion, finely chopped
1 green pepper, julienne
1 large carrot, julienne
1 large clove garlic, minced
14 oz (400 g) canned tomatoes, finely chopped
1½ cups dry white wine
1 tablespoons chopped basil, marjoram, or thyme
1/2 teaspoon cayenne
1 bay leaf
salt and freshly ground pepper
2 cups vegetable stock
2 cups chopped chard
1 lb (500 g) white fish fillets,
cod or sole, diced

12 mussels or oysters on the shell,
scrubbed and rinsed
8 oz (250 g) medium shrimp, peeled
1/3 cup finely chopped parsley

Heat the oil in a large casserole and saute the onions, peppers, carrots, and garlic until wilted. Add the tomatoes, wine, herbs, salt, and pepper. Cover and simmer 20 minutes. Add the stock, chard, fish, and mussels. Cover and continue simmering 5 minutes. Add the shrimp and parsley, and cook another 5 minutes until the shrimp turn pink. Serve the steamed seafood in their liquor in deep plates or bowls sprinkled with freshly ground black pepper.

Fish Soup with Vegetables

Serves 4
Preparation time 1 hour
Cooking time 1 hour

4 large carrots
1 stalk of celery and leaves
1 leek
1 small onion
1 large green bell pepper
3 small zucchini
4 large potatoes
2/3 cup olive oil
20 peppercorns
3 lb (1½ kg) fresh cod, grouper, bream or
any fish suitable for soup
1/3 cup lemon juice
salt and freshly ground pepper

Prepare the various vegetables for cooking. Bring 4 cups (1 liter) of water to a boil with the peppercorns, salt, and all the vegetables except for the potatoes. Cover and simmer for 30 minutes. Meanwhile, clean and thoroughly rinse the fish. If it is large, cut into two pieces so it will fit into the pan. Remove the vegetables with a slotted spoon to a platter and put the fish into the boiling broth. Cook for 10-15 minutes until the fish is tender but not falling apart. Remove the fish with a slotted spoon to the platter. Strain the fish broth into another pan to remove any bones. Cut the potatoes into pieces and cook in the broth until tender, for about 20 minutes. Remove half the potatoes to a bowl and mash with a fork or put through a food mill. Add some of the broth to the mashed potatoes and return to the soup. Cut the cooked carrots, celery, and zucchini into small pieces and add to the soup. Drain the onion, leek, and pepper. Discard and add the drained liquid to the soup. Bring the soup to a boil again, remove from the heat, stir in the lemon juice and some freshly ground pepper. Serve the soup hot accompanied by the cooked fish.

Bouillabaisse

Serves 6-8
Preparation time 50 minutes
Cooking time 40 minutes

2 lb (1 kg) assorted fresh fish
1 lobster
6 crayfish
12 mussels or 6 scallops
1/2 cup olive oil
2 medium onions, sliced
3 cloves garlic
1 leek, white part only, in pieces
4 tomatoes, peeled, seeded, and chopped
1 bay leaf
1/2 teaspoon thyme
1/4 cup finely chopped parsley
3 saffron stamens
salt and cayenne
1 cup dry white wine

Scale and gut the fish and rinse well to remove all traces of blood. Prepare the seafood for cooking and rinse well. Cut the fish and the lobster into large pieces. Heat the oil in a large casserole and saute the onions and garlic until wilted. Add the leek and continue sauteeing until wilted. Add the tomatoes, bay leaf, thyme, parsley, saffron, salt, cayenne, 8 cups of water, and wine. Cover and simmer 20 minutes. Add the fish and shellfish and simmer for about another 20 minutes. Remove the fish from the soup and debone. Remove shellfish from soup with a slotted spoon and remove shells. Serve the soup in deep plates or wide bowls. On top of each, float a piece of bread rubbed with garlic and toasted. Serve the fish and shellfish separately or divide pieces among the bowls of soup.

oil in a pan on high heat and saute the onion and hot pepper. Pour in the wine and cook until it is nearly evaporated. Serve the fish topped with the sauteed vegetables and accompanied with new potato salad. Sprinkle with the chopped parsley.

Baked Fish with Potatoes

Serves 4
Preparation time 40 minutes
Baking time 1 hour and 30 minutes

3 lb (1½ kg) cod or grouper
3 lb (1½ kg) potatoes
2 large onions, sliced
14 oz (400 g) finely chopped canned tomatoes
2 cloves garlic
1/4 cup finely chopped parsley
1 cup olive oil
salt and freshly ground pepper
1/2 teaspoon cayenne

Remove scales, innards, gills, and tail from the fish. Slice into thick pieces. Peel and cut the potatoes into thick pieces. Cook in boiling water until medium tender. Heat the oil and saute the onions until wilted and add the garlic, parsley, tomatoes, salt, and pepper. Cover and simmer the sauce for 30 minutes. Add the cayenne. Brush a large oven-proof dish or baking sheet with oil and arrange the potatoes and the fish slices. Pour the sauce on top. Bake the fish at 350°F (180°C) for 1 hour and 30 minutes or until the fish is opaque and flaky, and the potatoes, tender. Serve immediately.

Baked Red Mullet

Serves 4
Preparation time 30 minutes
Cooking time 30 minutes

3 lb (1½ kg) red mullet or snapper
2 tablespoons lemon juice
1/2 cup olive oil
flour as needed
1 hot green pepper, sliced
1 small onion sliced
1/4 cup dry white wine
salt and freshly ground pepper
2 tablespoons chopped parsley

Scale, gut and rinse the fish, leaving the heads and tails intact. Drain well, coat with flour and dip into the oil. Arrange in a baking pan lined with oiled baking paper. Sprinkle with the lemon juice, salt and pepper and cover with oiled baking paper. Bake in a 400°F (200°C) oven for about 15 minutes. Meanwhile heat the rest of the

Fried Red Mullet

Serves 4
Preparation time 20 minutes
Frying time 15 minutes

2½ lb (1 kg 200 gr) red mullet
salt and pepper
flour for coating, olive oil for frying

Scale, gut and rinse the fish, leaving the heads and tails intact. Drain well and season with salt and pepper. Put the fish a few at a time in a plastic bag with flour and shake to coat. Empty into a colander and shake again to remove excess flour. Fry in very hot olive oil, for 5-7 minutes on each side, turning once. Serve immediately garnished with tender lettuce leaves and lemon wedges.

Seabream with Celery and Capers

Serves 4
Preparation time 20 minutes
Baking time 25 minutes

1 large seabream or porgy or 4 small (2½ lb/3 kg)
1/4 cup olive oil
1/4 cup finely chopped onion
1 cup finely chopped celery
1/4 cup capers in brine
2 tablespoons lemon juice
2 tablespoons dry white wine
salt and freshly ground pepper

Put the capers in a bowl with water to cover and set aside for 1-2 hours, changing the water 3-4 times. Drain well. Remove scales, gills, and innards from the fish, leaving head and tail intact. Rinse well and pat dry with absorbent paper. Make several slashes on each side of the fish with a knife so it cooks thoroughly. Heat the oil and saute the onions until wilted. Add the celery and drained capers to the pan and stir with the onions for 5 minutes. Pour in the lemon juice, wine, salt, and pepper and stir. Lightly rub all surfaces of the fish with salt and pepper and brush with olive oil. Stuff the inside of the fish with half the caper-celery mixture. Broil the fish on both sides 5-6 inches (14 cm) from the heat source until well done. Remove the broiled fish to a platter and pour the remaining sauteed mixture on top. Serve immediately.

*We shall now discuss pulses. Whole
broad beans when properly cooked both
in stock and in oil are better with
seasoning or salt than chopped beans.
Chickpeas are, if cooked thoroughly
until soft, good when seasoned
with oil and salt.
Lentils are good when washed and
carefully boiled in fresh water.
Make sure that the first lot of water
is poured away, and a second lot of hot
water added as required,
but not too much, and then boil the
lentils slowly on the hearth.
When they are cooked, add for flavour
a little vinegar... a spoonful of oil,
and a pinch of salt for seasoning.*

P U L S E S

On the Observance of Foods by Anthimus,
Greek physician from Constantinople
at the Frankish court, 6th c. AD
(*translation M. Grant, Prospect Books, 1996*)

P U L S E S

Fava (Broad Bean Puree)

Serves 4
Preparation time 12 hour
Cooking time 2 hours

2 lb (1 kg) dried fava or broad beans
1 small whole onion
1 clove garlic
1 bay leaf
salt and white pepper
1/2 cup olive oil
oil, lemon juice, finely chopped parsley or dill, and
finely chopped onion, for garnish

Cut the black spot off the fava beans and soak in water to cover for 12 hours with 1 tablespoon salt. Drain, remove skins and put in a large pan with water to cover. Add the onion, garlic, and bay leaf; cover, and simmer for about 2 hours. Remove and discard the onion, garlic, and bay leaf. Puree the fava beans and put in a pan with the oil, salt, and white pepper. Stir over low heat until thick. Serve sprinkled with finely chopped dill or parsley, chopped onion, lemon juice and a little olive oil. Following the same procedure, prepare fava with yellow or green dried split peas, omitting the soaking step, as they cook up more readily.

Broad Bean Stew

Serves 4
Preparation time 12 hours
Cooking time 1 hour 30 minutes

1 lb (500 g) dried fava (broad) beans
2 large onions, finely chopped
2 large ripe tomatoes, finely chopped
2/3 cup olive oil
2 tablespoons finely chopped fresh oregano or
1 teaspoon dried
1 hot red pepper, minced
2 teaspoons paprika

1/4 cup finely chopped green onions
salt and freshly ground pepper

Remove the black spots from the broad beans and soak for 12 hours in water to cover with 1 tablespoon salt. Drain, remove skins, and simmer for 15 minutes in water to cover. In another pan, heat the oil and saute the onions. Add the tomatoes and cook for 10 minutes on high heat, stirring occasionally. Add the precooked beans, oregano, hot pepper, salt, and pepper. Cover and simmer until the sauce has cooked down almost to the oil. Serve the stew sprinkled with paprika, finely chopped green onions, and olive oil dribbled on top.

Rigatoni with Chili

Serves 4
Preparation time 15 minutes
Cooking time 30 minutes

10 oz (300 g) rigatoni or penne
1/4 cup olive oil
2 cloves garlic, slivered
1 red bell pepper
1/4 cup water
7 oz (200 g) canned red kidney beans
7 oz (200 g) canned corn
2 tablespoons chili seasoning or
3 tablespoons chili sauce
salt and freshly ground pepper

Heat the oil in a pan and saute the garlic. Put the pepper and water in the blender and puree. Add to the pan along with the beans, corn, chili, salt and pepper. Cover and simmer until the sauce is thick. Cook the pasta in salted boiling water with 2 tablespoons olive oil and drain. Serve on heated plates accompanied by the beans. Serve hot or at room temperature.

RIGATONI WITH CHILI

Tricolor Bean Salad

Serves 6
Preparation time 10 minutes
Cooking time 2 hours 30 minutes

3-4 oz (100 g) small white beans
3-4 oz (100 g) black beans
3-4 oz (100 g) black-eyed beans
3-4 oz (100 g) canned red kidney beans, drained
6 cups (1½ liters) vegetable stock
2-3 large fresh mushrooms, sliced
4 green onions, chopped
1 medium onion, finely chopped

for the dressing
1/3 cup wine vinegar
1/3 cup finely chopped parsley or basil
2 teaspoons prepared mustard
1 small clove garlic, finely minced
1/3 cup olive oil or sesame oil

Precook all the beans (except for the kidney beans), in water to cover for about 1 hour and 15 minutes. Drain and return to the pot with the vegetable stock. Cover and simmer until tender. Drain and empty into a bowl. Add the red kidney beans, mushrooms, and onions and toss gently to mix. Combine the ingredients for the dressing in a well-sealed jar and shake until blended. Pour on the salad, toss and refrigerate 2-3 hours before serving. Garnish the salad with thinly sliced tomato.

Beans with Peppers

Serves 6
Preparation time 12 hours
Cooking time 2 hours

5 oz (150 g) black beans
5 oz (150 g) black-eyed beans
1/2 cup olive oil
1 large onion, sliced
1 each green, red, and yellow bell pepper,
cut into strips
14 oz (400 g) pureed canned tomatoes
4 tablespoons ketchup
1 tablespoon paprika
1 teaspoon chili sauce
1/4 teaspoon cayenne
salt and freshly ground pepper
2 tablespoons margarine
7 oz (200 g) canned corn
3 cups cooked basmati rice

Soak the beans for 12 hours in water to cover. Drain and cook for 1 hour in salted water to cover. Meanwhile, heat the oil in a pan and saute the onions and peppers until wilted. Add the tomatoes, ketchup, spices, salt and pepper. Drain the beans and combine with the sauce in the pan. Cover and simmer until the beans are tender and the sauce has cooked down. Melt the margarine and saute the corn briefly. Serve the beans with the rice and corn on the side.

Bean Salad

Serves 4
Preparation time 30 minutes
Cooking time 1 hour 30 minutes

8 oz (250 g) small white beans
1 small red onion, sliced
2 green onions, finely chopped
1/4 cup chopped green bell pepper
3 tablespoons finely chopped parsley
1/4 cup chopped pickles
5-6 pitted black olives, for garnish
1/4 cup vinegar
1/4 cup olive oil
salt and freshly ground pepper

Put the beans in a large pan with plenty of water and cook for 30 minutes. Drain and return beans to the pan with fresh water to cover. Simmer until tender. Drain and cool slightly. In a deep platter combine the beans with the onions, green pepper, parsley, and pickles. Mix the vinegar, oil, salt and pepper in a well-sealed jar and shake until blended. Pour over the beans, toss, cover with plastic wrap, and refrigerate. Allow to marinate for several hours. Garnish with the black olives.

Black Bean Salad with Rice

Serves 4
Preparation time 15 minutes
Cooking time 1 hour 30 minutes

8 oz (250 g) black or black-eyed beans
1 cup long-grain rice, cooked
1/2 cup finely chopped green onions
10 pimento-stuffed green olives, sliced
1 cup vinaigrette dressing (see basic recipes)
2 tablespoons finely chopped mint

Soak the beans in ample water 12 hours. Drain and put in a large pan with enough water to cover. Cook until tender, about 1 hour and 30 minutes, drain, and allow to cool. Combine the beans with the rice, onions and olives. Pour the dressing on top and adjust seasonings. Allow the salad to marinate 1-2 hours in the refrigerator before serving with cooked greens salad such as chard, amaranth or endive.

Bean and Vegetable Tart

Serves 8
Preparation time 2 hours
Cooking time 35 minutes

15 oz (450 g) medium dried beans, soaked overnight
1 large onion
1 hot green pepper
1 stalk of celery
1 red bell pepper
2 tablespoons olive oil
2 tablespoons grated onion
2 cloves garlic, minced
15 oz (450 g) spinach, chopped, blanched,
and well-drained
1 tablespoon vinegar
1 tablespoons finely chopped basil

salt and freshly ground pepper
1 slice of tomato
several large fresh mushrooms, sliced
1 recipe for pizza dough (see basic recipes)

Put the beans in a pot with water to cover and cook for 1 hour. Drain and cook with fresh water to cover along with the onion, green pepper, and celery until tender. Drain and reserve the cooking liquid. Puree the beans in the food processor adding just enough liquid to make a soft puree. Broil the red bell pepper on the grill for 5 minutes. Devein, deseed, and cut half the pepper into strips lengthwise and finely chop the other half. Heat the oil in saucepan and saute the grated onion and garlic. Add the chopped grilled pepper, blanched spinach, vinegar, basil, salt, and pepper. Remove from the heat and allow to cool. Cover with plastic wrap and refrigerate until ready to use. Prepare the pizza dough according to the recipe. Grease a 10-inch (25-cm) heart-shaped or round tart pan and evenly spread the dough on the bottom and up the sides. Pierce here and there with a fork and let it rise for 15 minutes. Brush with olive oil and bake in a 400°F (200°C) oven for 35 minutes. Cool slightly, spread the bean puree on the dough and cover with the spinach mixture. Garnish with the red pepper strips, tomato round, and sliced mushrooms. Sprinkle with a little olive oil and bake another 15 minutes at the same temperature, until heated through. Serve hot.

Beans Piquant

Serves 4
Preparation time 12 hours
Cooking time 2 hours 30 minutes

1 lb (500 g) medium white beans
6 cups (1½ liters) vegetable stock
1/3 cup olive oil
3 cloves garlic slivered
1 medium onion, finely chopped
1 red bell pepper, chopped
1 lb (500 g) ripe tomatoes, cubed
20 drops Tabasco sauce
4 tablespoons ketchup
1/4 teaspoon cumin
1 teaspoon oregano
1/2 teaspoon ground coriander
salt and freshly ground pepper
finely chopped cilantro or parsley, for garnish

Soak the beans for 12 hours in water to cover. Drain and put in a large pot with the vegetable stock. Cover and simmer to precook, about 1 hour. Drain the beans and reserve 1 cup of the cooking liquid. Heat the oil in another pan, and saute the garlic, onions and peppers. Add the beans, reserved liquid, tomatoes, Tabasco, ketchup, spices, salt, and pepper. Cover and simmer until beans are tender and sauce has cooked down. It may be necessary to add a little water. Place the beans in a bowl, sprinkle with finely chopped cilantro or parsley and serve immediately.

Shell Pasta with Lentil Sauce

Serves 4
Preparation time 15 minutes
Cooking time 1 hour

1/4 cup olive oil
2 cloves garlic, finely minced
1 large onion, grated
1 green bell pepper, finely chopped
1 medium carrot, finely chopped
1 cup lentils
$1^2/_3$ cups vegetable stock
1/2 teaspoon oregano
1/4 teaspoon rosemary
1 teaspoon salt
1/4 teaspoon pepper
14 oz (400 g) shell pasta
1/3 cup finely chopped green onions

Heat the oil on medium heat and saute the garlic, onions, pepper, and carrot until wilted. Add the lentils, stock, oregano, rosemary, salt, and pepper and simmer 30-35 minutes until the lentils are tender and the sauce is thick. Meanwhile, cook the pasta in salted boiling water with 2 tablespoons olive oil. Drain well and arrange on a hot platter. Pour the lentil sauce on top and serve immediately sprinkled with chopped green onions.

Cranberry Bean Stew

Serves 4
Preparation time 30 minutes
Cooking time 1-2 hours

2 lb (1 kg) shelled borlotti (cranberry) beans
(4 lb/2 kg unshelled)

3/4 cup olive oil
1 medium onion, grated
14 oz (400 g) pulped canned tomatoes
1 tablespoon tomato paste
1 tablespoon ketchup
1/2 cup finely chopped parsley
1 small green bell pepper, cubed
salt and freshly ground pepper

Shuck the beans, rinse, and drain in a colander. Heat the oil in a pan on high heat, and saute the onion until wilted. Add the pulped tomatoes, tomato paste, ketchup, parsley, peppers, beans, salt, and pepper, and two cups of water. Cover, lower heat, and simmer until the beans are tender and the sauce has cooked down. Depending on the condition of the beans, it may be necessary to add some water. Serve hot or at room temperature.

Beans with Anchovies

Serves 6
Preparation time 2 hours

1/4 cup olive oil
3 cloves garlic, minced
1/4 cup finely chopped green onions
14 oz (400 g) canned sliced mushrooms
5 anchovy fillets, boned
1/4 cup white vinegar
2 cups (250 g) cooked medium white beans
2 tablespoons lemon juice
salt and freshly ground pepper
oregano, finely chopped green onion

Saute the garlic and onions in the oil. Add the mushrooms and saute until wilted. Stir in the anchovies and vinegar and cook until the sauce cooks down by half. Add the beans, lemon juice, salt and pepper, and toss. Transfer to a serving platter and sprinkle with oregano and finely chopped green onion. Serve immediately.

Fusilli with Beans

Serves 4
Preparation time 12 hours
Cooking time 1 hour 30 minutes

8 oz (250 g) medium white beans
1 liter vegetable stock
1 cup zucchini julienne
1 cup black sliced olives
10 oz (300 g) fusilli
1 cup red pepper sauce (see basic recipes)
2 tablespoons finely chopped parsley
salt and freshly ground pepper

Soak the beans for 12 hours in water to cover. Drain and put in a pan with the stock, salt and pepper. Bring to a boil, cover, and simmer until tender, about 1 hour 30 minutes. Drain and combine with the zucchini and olives. Cook the pasta in boiling salted water with 2 tablespoons olive oil. Drain and combine with the bean mixture in a bowl. Pour the red pepper sauce on top, toss, and serve cold sprinkled with the parsley and freshly ground pepper.

Bean Soup with Pasta

Serves 6
Preparation time 12 hours
Cooking time 2 hours

1 cup medium white beans
1/2 cup olive oil
1 large onion, grated
1 carrot, cubed
1 clove garlic, minced
1/2 cup finely chopped celery
2 cups shredded cabbage
2 cups tomato juice
salt and freshly ground pepper
1 teaspoon thyme
1/4 cup finely chopped parsley
8 cups (2 liters) vegetable stock (see basic recipes)
1/2 cup elbow macaroni

Soak the beans in water to cover for 12 hours. Drain and simmer for 30 minutes in salted water. Heat the oil in a large pan and saute the onions, carrots, and garlic until wilted. Drain the precooked beans and add to the sauteed vegetables along with the remaining ingredients except for the macaroni. Simmer the soup until both beans and vegetables are tender. Add the macaroni and continue cooking 10 minutes. Serve hot.

Rice with Lentils and Vegetables

Serves 4
Preparation time 1 hour
Cooking time 40 minutes

1 medium eggplant, cut in small cubes
1/4 cup olive oil
2 cloves garlic, slivered
1 cup chopped ripe tomatoes
1/4 cup fresh basil leaves
1/2 cup lentils
3 tablespoons margarine
1 medium onion, finely chopped
2 cups vegetable stock
1/2 cup rice
2 cups mixed cubed vegetables
1/3 cup peas
3-4 oz (100 g) broccoli florets

Sprinkle the eggplant with salt and set aside in a colander for 30 minutes. Rinse and squeeze out excess moisture. Heat the oil in a small pan and saute the garlic. Remove with a slotted spoon, add the eggplant, and saute lightly. Add the tomatoes and basil and simmer for 15 minutes until the sauce is thick. Meanwhile, blanch the lentils and drain. Melt the margarine in a large pan and saute the onions until wilted. Add the vegetable stock and bring to a boil. Add the rice, lentils, mixed vegetables, and peas. Cover and simmer for about 20 minutes or until the vegetables and rice are tender. Stir in the eggplant-tomato sauce and broccoli florets. Cook for 5 minutes more and serve hot or at room temperature.

Baked Giant Beans

Serves 6-8
Preparation time 24 hours
Cooking time 1 hour

1 lb (500 g) large white beans
1 stalk of celery with leaves
1 carrot
several black peppercorns
1 cup olive oil
1 cup grated onion
5-6 cloves garlic, thinly sliced
2 lb (1 kg) ripe tomatoes, pulped and strained
salt and pepper, a pinch each of sugar and oregano
1/2 cup finely chopped parsley
2 large ripe tomatoes, thinly sliced in rounds

Soak the beans in water to cover for 24 hours. Drain and put in a pan with ample fresh water. Add the celery, carrot, and peppercorns. Cook the beans until tender and drain. Place in a glass or ceramic baking dish. Heat half the oil on high heat and lightly saute the onions and garlic. Add the tomatoes, salt, pepper, sugar and cook the sauce for 10 minutes. Remove from the heat and stir in the parsley. Pour the sauce over the beans and arrange the sliced tomato rounds on top. Sprinkle with a little salt, pepper, and oregano and dribble the remaining olive oil over the entire surface. Bake in a 350°F (175°C) oven until the beans are tender and the sauce has cooked down almost to the oil, about 1 hour. It may be necessary to add a little water during baking. Serve warm or at room temperature.

Lentils with Vegetables

Serves 4-5
Preparation time 35 minutes
Cooking time 30-50 minutes

10 oz (300 g) lentils
1 medium onion, finely chopped
1 clove garlic, minced
1 zucchini, cut in small cubes
1 leek, white part only, sliced
1/2 green bell pepper, chopped
1 medium carrot, cut in small cubes
2 medium tomatoes, chopped
2 bay leaves
20 peppercorns
1 cup olive oil
1 medium potato, cut in small cubes

Pick over and rinse the lentils. Put in a pan with water to cover on high heat. When they come to a boil, remove from the heat, and drain. Peel and chop the vegetables. Heat 2/3 of the oil on medium heat and saute the onions, garlic, zucchini, leek, pepper, and carrot until wilted. Add the lentils, tomatoes, bay leaves, peppercorns, salt, and enough fresh water to cover. Simmer until both lentils and vegetables are tender, about 25 minutes. Meanwhile, saute the potatoes in the remaining oil, drain, and stir into the cooked lentils. Continue simmering for another 5 minutes. Serve hot accompanied by olives and taramosalata.

Tricolor Lentil Salad

Serves 6
Preparation time 15 minutes
Cooking time 1 hour

3-4 oz (100 g) red lentils
3-4 oz (100 g) yellow lentils
3-4 oz (100 g) green lentils
4 green onions, finely chopped
1 green bell pepper, finely chopped
2 medium tomatoes, finely chopped
2 tablespoons finely chopped dill
2 tablespoons pine nuts (optional)

for the dressing
1/4 cup olive oil
2 tablespoons balsamic vinegar

1 cloves garlic, minced
1/2 teaspoon paprika
1/2 teaspoon chili powder
salt and freshly ground pepper

Put the red and yellow lentils in a pan with water to cover and cook until tender, but still hold their shape, about 8-10 minutes. Cook the green lentils separately for 20-30 minutes, until tender. (Use vegetable stock for tastier results). Drain all the lentils and combine in a bowl along with the chopped vegetables, dill, and pine nuts. Mix lightly. Combine the ingredients for the dressing in a well-sealed jar and shake until blended. Pour on the lentils, toss, and refrigerate for 1 hour before serving.

1 teaspoon ground cumin
2 tablespoons chili sauce or chili ketchup
1½ teaspoon salt
freshly ground pepper

Rinse the lentils and put in a pan with water to cover. Bring to a boil, lower heat, and simmer for about 15 minutes, to precook. Drain and discard the liquid. Heat the oil in a large pan over high heat and saute the onions, celery, garlic, peppers, and mushrooms until wilted. Add the tomato juice, tomatoes, beans, spices, ketchup, salt, pepper, and lentils. Mix lightly, cover, and simmer until the lentils are done and the sauce has cooked down. Serve the lentil chili hot or at room temperature.

Chickpeas with Herbs

Serves 6
Preparation time 12 hour
Cooking time 1 hour

1 lb (500 g) chickpeas
4 cups (1 liter) vegetable stock
1/2 cup olive oil
2 cloves garlic, slivered
1 small onion, chopped
3 leeks, white part only, sliced
1 large carrot, cut into small cubes
2 small stalks celery, chopped
rosemary or thyme
3 tablespoons tomato paste
salt and freshly ground pepper

Soak the chickpeas 12 hours in water to cover with 1 tablespoon salt. Rinse under running water, and drain. Simmer in the vegetable stock for about 30 minutes to precook. In another pan, heat the oil and saute the garlic, onions, and vegetables until wilted. Add the rosemary or thyme, the chickpeas with their cooking liquid, and the tomato paste dissolved in 1/2 cup water. Add plenty of freshly ground pepper and, if needed, a little salt. Cover and simmer until the chickpeas are soft and the sauce has cooked down. Serve hot or at room temperature.

Lentil Chili

Serves 6
Preparation time 40 minutes
Cooking time 1 hour

6 cup water
10 oz (300 g) lentils
1/3 cup olive oil
1 cup finely chopped onion
1 cup finely chopped celery
1 cloves garlic, minced
2 long green sweet peppers, finely chopped
8 oz (250 g) canned sliced mushrooms, drained
14 oz (400 g) tomato juice
28 oz (800 g) canned chopped tomatoes
14 oz (400 g) canned red kidney beans
2 teaspoons chili powder

CHICKPEAS WITH HERBS

Chickpeas in Tomato Sauce

Serves 6
Preparation time 12 hours
Cooking time 1 hour 30 minutes

1 lb (500 g) chickpeas
4 cups (1 liter) vegetable stock (see basic recipes)
1/3 cup olive oil
1 large onion, grated
2 leeks, white part only, sliced into rounds
2 cloves garlic, minced
14 oz (400 g) canned tomatoes with juice
1 tablespoons tomato paste
1 teaspoon oregano
10-12 basil leaves, finely chopped
salt and freshly ground pepper

Soak the chickpeas overnight in water to cover with 1 tablespoon salt. The next day, rinse, drain and cook in the vegetable stock for about 45 minutes, to precook. Meanwhile, heat the oil in a large pan and saute the onions, leeks, and garlic until wilted. Add the tomatoes, tomato paste, oregano, chopped basil, and mix. Stir in the chickpeas with their cooking liquid. Taste, and adjust the seasonings. Cover and simmer until the chickpeas are tender and sauce has cooked down almost to the oil. Serve hot garnished with whole basil leaves.

Chickpeas with Spinach

Serves 4-5
Preparation time 12 hours
Cooking time 35 minutes

1 cup chickpeas
2 large onions, thinly sliced
2 lb (1 kg) fresh spinach, torn into pieces
1/2 cup finely chopped dill
salt and freshly ground pepper
1 cup tomato juice
2/3 cup olive oil
1/4 cup lemon juice

Soak the chickpeas overnight in water to cover with 1 tablespoon salt. The next day, drain and rinse with fresh water. Heat half the oil and saute the onions until wilted. Add the chickpeas and tomato juice; simmer for 30-40 minutes until half-tender. Combine the spinach with the dill and put half in the bottom of a large pan. Place the chickpeas on top. Cover with the remaining spinach, sprinkle with salt and pepper, and pour in the remaining oil. Cover and when it comes to a boil, lower heat, and simmer for 30-35 minutes until the chickpeas and the spinach are cooked but not mushy, and the sauce has cooked down almost to the oil. Serve with freshly squeezed lemon juice. If desired, blanch and drain the spinach before combining with the dill.

Peppers Stuffed with Beans

Serves 6
Preparation time 50 minutes
Cooking time 1 hour 45 minutes

7 oz (200 g) small white beans

7 oz (200 g) dried red beans
4 cups (1 liter) vegetable stock (see basic recipes)
1/4 cup olive oil
1 medium onion, grated
2 cloves garlic, minced
4 leeks, white part only, finely chopped
12 large red or green bell peppers
8 oz (250 g) vegetarian cheese, cubed
1/2 cup finely chopped dill
1/2 cup finely chopped parsley

for the sauce
1/2 cup olive oil
2 cups fresh tomato juice
salt and freshly ground pepper

Soak the beans for 12 hours in water to cover. Drain and cook in the vegetable stock for about 1 hour, until tender. Heat the oil in a large pan and saute the onions, garlic, and leeks. Cover and simmer for 15 minutes, until the leeks are half-cooked. Drain the beans and combine with the sauteed vegetables. Add salt and freshly ground pepper and remove from the heat. Meanwhile, slice the stem-ends off the peppers. Deseed, devein, and fry both peppers and stem-ends lightly in oil. Combine the beans with the cubed cheese, dill, and parsley. Mix lightly and fill the peppers. Arrange the stuffed peppers in an oven-proof pan. Heat the oil for the sauce in a small pan and add the tomato juice, salt, and pepper and simmer for about 10 minutes. Pour 2 tablespoons of sauce into each stuffed pepper. Pour the remaining sauce around the peppers. Cover with foil and bake in a 350°F (175°C) oven for 40-45 minutes. Serve hot.

Chickpea and Eggplant Casserole

Serves 4-6
Preparation time 12 hours
Cooking time 1 hour 30 minutes

14 oz (400 g) large chickpeas
1/4 cup olive oil
1 large onion, sliced
4 cloves garlic, slivered
14 oz (400 g) chopped canned tomatoes
1/2 teaspoon allspice
1 teaspoon paprika
1/2 teaspoon ground coriander
salt and freshly ground pepper
4 large eggplants, in 1/2-inch (1-cm) thick slices

4 large tomatoes, thinly sliced

Soak the chickpeas for 12 hours in water to cover with 1 tablespoon salt. Drain, rinse, and put in a large pan with water to cover. Bring to a boil, skim the surface, and simmer for 30 minutes. Heat the olive oil and saute the onions and garlic until wilted; add to the chickpeas along with the tomatoes, allspice, paprika, coriander, salt, and pepper and continue cooking for 1 hour until the chickpeas are tender and the sauce is thick. Meanwhile, salt the eggplant and set aside for 30 minutes. Rinse, drain, and squeeze out excess water. Saute lightly in olive oil. Arrange half of the slices on the bottom of a medium oven-proof dish. Spread the chickpea mixture on top and cover with the remaining eggplant slices. Arrange the tomato slices over the entire surface of the casserole. Sprinkle with salt, pepper, coriander, and dribble with a thin stream of olive oil. Bake in a 350°F (180°C) oven for about 50 minutes, until the sauce has cooked down. Serve hot or at room temperature.

Rocket or Spinach Salad with Chickpeas

Serves 4
Preparation time 15 minutes

10 oz (300 g) rocket or spinach leaves
2 carrots, coarsely grated
1 small cucumber, julienne
1 cup cooked chickpeas

for the dressing
1/4 cup olive oil
2 tablespoons lemon juice
1 tablespoon vinegar
1 small clove garlic, minced
salt and pepper
10 drops Tabasco sauce, to taste

Thoroughly rinse the rocket or spinach leaves. Trim the leaves by removing the tough stems and veins. Arrange the leaves on a large platter with the grated carrots, cucumbers, and the chickpeas on top. Combine the ingredients for the dressing in a well-sealed jar and shake until blended. Pour over the salad shortly before serving.

Hummus or Chickpea Paste

Serves 4
Preparation time 12 hours
Cooking time 1-2 hours

8 oz (250 g) chickpeas
1/4 cup tahini (sesame seed paste)
1-2 tablespoons lemon juice
1/4 cup olive oil
1-2 cloves garlic, mashed
salt and finely ground pepper
finely chopped parsley, for garnish

Soak the chickpeas for 12 hours in water to cover with 1 tablespoon salt. Rinse, drain, and cook in fresh water to cover until very soft. Drain and press through a fine sieve or puree in a food processor. Beat the tahini with 1-2 tablespoons water. Combine the chickpea puree with the garlic, a little salt, and pepper. Stirring with a fork, add the tahini a little at a time and then the olive oil little by little, beating until smooth and blended. Finally add the lemon juice, to taste. Put the hummus in a shallow bowl and sprinkle with the chopped parsley. Cover with plastic wrap and refrigerate several hours before serving with pickled vegetables or pita (pocket) bread.

Chickpea Patties

Serves 4-5
Preparation time 12 hour
Frying time 30 minutes

1 lb (500 g) chickpeas
1½ cup self-rising flour
1 large onion, grated
1 tablespoon tomato paste dissolved in
1/2 cup water
3 tablespoons finely chopped dill or mint
salt and freshly ground pepper
olive oil for frying

Soak the chickpeas for 12 hours in water to cover with 1 tablespoon salt. Drain the chickpeas and grind in a mortar and pestle or food processor to a coarse puree. Put the puree in a bowl and add the onions, tomato, herbs and 2 tablespoons olive oil. Add enough flour to make a medium-thick mixture which retains its shape, neither too stiff nor too loose. Cover and set aside for 1 hour. Heat the oil in a pan and fry large tablespoons of the mixture, a few at a time, until browned on one side. Turn over and fry until the other side is browned. Remove with a slotted spoon and drain well on absorbent paper. If desired, substitute the tomato paste with 1/2 cup of pureed ripe fresh tomatoes. Serve immediately.

Broccoli Salad with Mushrooms and Chickpeas

Serves 4
Preparation time 30 minutes

24 oz (700 g) broccoli florets
7oz (200 g) fresh mushrooms
2 cups cooked chickpeas
1/4 cup olive oil
3 tablespoons lemon juice
salt and freshly ground pepper
1 teaspoon rosemary

Put the broccoli in a bowl with ample cold water and gently rinse them. Drain and repeat with fresh water. Drain again and blanch in boiling water for 5 minutes. Meanwhile, rinse the mushrooms and pat dry with paper towels. Slice lengthwise. Remove the blanched broccoli with a slotted spoon onto a

platter and arrange the mushrooms and chickpeas on top. Combine the olive oil, lemon juice, rosemary, salt, and pepper in a well-sealed jar and shake to blend. Pour over the salad and serve immediately. This salad is tastier if served while the broccoli is still warm. As the dressing discolors the broccoli, add the dressing just prior to serving.

Sini Manti with Chickpeas

Serves 6-8
Preparation time 12 hours
Cooking time 1 hour

**10 sheets of homemade phyllo, slightly
dried (see basic recipes)
1/2 cup olive oil
1 lb (500 g) chickpeas
1 large onion, finely chopped
salt and freshly ground pepper
1/4 cup olive oil
1/4 cup lemon juice (optional)**

Soak the chickpeas overnight in water to cover with 1 tablespoon

salt. Roll up the phyllo sheets and cut into 1/2-inch (1-cm) strips. Unroll the phyllo strips and arrange on the bottom of a large baking dish. Sprinkle with the olive oil and bake in a 350°F (180°C) oven for 35 minutes, until well-browned. Heat the 1/4 cup olive oil in a pan and saute the onions. Drain the chickpeas, rinse, and mix with the onions in the pan. Add enough water to cover and simmer until tender. Stir in pepper and more salt, to taste. Measure and add water, if needed, to make 5 cups. Pour on top of the baked phyllo-noodles in the baking dish. Return to the hot oven and bake until all the liquid is absorbed and the phyllo has swelled. Serve hot with fresh lemon juice.

Sifnos-Style Chickpeas

Serves 6
Preparation time 12 hours
Cooking time 12 hours

1 lb (500 g) chickpeas
2 large onions, sliced
1 teaspoon peppercorns
1 tablespoon flour
1 teaspoon salt
2 cloves garlic, minced (optional)
lemon juice

Soak the chickpeas overnight in water with 1 tablespoon salt. Drain and put in a ceramic or oven-proof baking dish. Sprinkle with flour and stir to distribute evenly. Soak the onions for 1 hour in cold water and drain. Stir into the chickpeas along with the peppercorns and garlic (if used). Add enough water to cover. Cover the dish, and if desired, seal the edges with a stiff dough made from flour and water. Bake overnight or for 12 hours in a slow oven, 300°F (150°C). Serve hot or at room temperature sprinkled with fresh lemon juice.

Chickpea-Potato Patties

Makes 30-35 patties
Preparation time 12 hours
Frying time 15 minutes

8 oz (250 g) chickpeas
8 oz (250 g) potatoes
3/4 cup onions, grated
1/2 cup dried breadcrumbs
1/3 cup finely chopped fresh parsley or
1 teaspoon dried parsley
1 teaspoon dried marjoram
1 tablespoon chopped dill
flour for dusting
oil for frying

Soak the chickpeas overnight in water with 1 tablespoon salt. The next morning drain and cook until tender. Drain and coarsely puree in the food processor. Cook the potatoes, peel and mash with a fork. Soak the onions in a bowl of water for 1 hour, drain, and squeeze out the excess water. Combine the chickpeas with the potatoes, onions, and remaining ingredients. Refrigerate for 1 hour. Form the mixture into small balls and roll in flour. Briefly dip each one in water and then roll in breadcrumbs. Deep-fry in hot oil until golden brown. Serve hot or cold.

Black-eyed Bean Stew

Serves 4
Preparation time 30 minutes
Cooking time 1 hour 30 minutes

11 oz (350 g) black-eyed beans
1/2 cup grated onion
1/2 cup chopped green onion
1 cup chopped romaine lettuce
1/2 cup finely chopped dill
1/2 cup finely chopped parsley
1/2 cup olive oil
salt and freshly ground pepper

Put the beans in a large pan with ample water and cook for 30 minutes. Drain and return beans to the pan with fresh water to cover. Bring to a boil, add both kinds of onions, cover and simmer for about 15 minutes. Add the lettuce, dill, parsley, oil, salt, and pepper. Continue simmering until the beans are tender, about 15-20 minutes. It may be necessary to add more water during cooking. Serve hot sprinkled with lemon juice.

First I shall recall the gifts
to humankind of fair-haired Demeter.
The finest of all is the barley from the
sea-washed breast of famous Eresus
in Lesbos – if the gods eat barley, this is
where Hermes goes shopping for it.
Take a Thessalian roll, a circling whirl
of dough well-kneaded under hand.
They call it "crumble" in Thessaly.
I also commend a child of durum wheat,
the bread of Tegea that is baked under
ashes. Fair is the loaf that famous
Athens sells to mortals in her market-
place; those from the clay ovens of
vinous Erythrae, white and blooming
with the gentle seasons,
are a joy with dinner.

BREADS / DOUGHS

Archestratus, Fragment 4 in Athenaeus
(From A. Dalby & S. Grainger
"The Classical Cookbook" British Mus. Press, 1996)

Most people would agree that there are few things in the world that smell as delicious as a loaf of bread or a Greek spanakopita fresh from the oven. And whose mouth doesn't water at the sight of a plate of stuffed crepes or homemade gnocchi with pesto or tomato sauce? All of these dishes have one thing in common; they evolved from a mixture of flour and water we call dough-paste (zymi), which over a very long period of time was improved with the addition of other ingredients like yeast, eggs, milk, oil, butter or lard. Dough-paste was undoubtedly one of the most important culinary inventions for it could be stretched, shaped, rolled, stuffed, baked, fried, or boiled to create a large number of products familiar to us today as bread, pita, pizza, pasta, pastry, pie, etc.

THE HISTORY OF DOUGH is as old as civilization itself which began about 10,000 years ago with the discovery of the cultivation and use of the grains, barley and wheat to make bread. This turning point in the history of the Eastern Mediterranean was commemorated in the ancient Greek myth of Demeter, Goddess of Grain, who taught Triptolemos, a young shepherd, the secrets of agriculture. Man's transition from an "uncivilized" meat-eating nomad to a "civilized" grain-eating farmer was celebrated at the ancient festivals of the Eleusinia and the Athenian Thesmoforia, where offerings of bread were made in honor of the Goddess. Thus, bread became the enduring symbol of life and culture in the ancient Mediterranean. Archeologists have estimated that as early as the 6th millenium BC bread was being made, first from barley and later, from wheat. After learning to remove the outer husks (or chaff) of the grain by pounding or parching and grinding the inner-core between two stones, the first flour was made. Mixing this rough flour with water to make grain-paste gave man a food that not only filled his stomach but was nourishing and palatable. Perhaps by accident, it was found that cooking clumps of grain-paste on the hearth or on the sides of clay ovens improved the taste. The ancient Greeks called barley-paste, *pastos* (the word from which paste and pastry evolved). Flat barley bread was known as *maza* while wheaten bread was called *artos*, a word still used in the

B R E A D S / D O U G H S

modern Greek word for bakery – *artopoleio*. A Greek poet from Sicily, Archestratos, who wrote Europe's first gastronomical treatise in the 4th C. BC, "The Life of Luxury," mentioned several kinds of bread. Barley rolls were called *krimnitas* in Thessaly and *chondrinos* elsewhere. These breads were made from barley groats while a better quality wheat bread was made at Tegea and baked under ashes. Athens was famous for the white loaves sold in the Agora (market place), and Archestratos sings the praises of the white bread from the ovens of Erythrea in Evia. The various stages of the bread-making process were depicted in the famous Greek terracotta figurines of the 6th and 5th centuries BC, now housed in European museums of Great Britain (London and Oxford), Berlin, and the Louvre.

IN THE CHRISTIAN ERA bread continued to serve not only as a primary source of nourishment ("give us this day our daily bread") but was also elevated in Christian worship to the ultimate symbol and source of Salvation and Eternal Life. During the Divine Liturgy of the Orthodox Church, a special bread called Prosforon (meaning offering), is the vehicle by which the mystic power of Christ's Sacrifice, Death, and Resurrection is conveyed to the faithful. The "Blessing of the Loaves" by Christ to feed the 5000 men is recalled by the five loaves of bread (the Artoclassia) which are brought by those who celebrate their name-day to the church to be blessed and distributed after the service. Another traditional religious dish called Koliva, made with boiled wheat kernels, sugar, nuts, herbs, and pomegranate seeds, is blessed and offered in memory of a deceased. Koliva is served to all attending the Mnimosino or Memorial service. It is believed that just as the

small amount of fat, wheat has been – as we have seen throughout the ages – the primary source of energy for the peoples of the Mediterranean Basin and elsewhere. Wheat flour made into bread and other "dough products" with or without additional nutrients, is a "complete" food. Flours made by grinding other cereals such as rye, barley, maize, rice, legumes like chickpeas, broad beans as well as chestnuts have also been utilized for thousands of years, but are of less nutritional value. Gluten, the protein complex contained in the endosperm of germ of the wheat, has elastic properties that develop when dough is kneaded, allowing its shape to be retained when rolled out or swelled by the gases released from yeast or other raising agents (baking powder, soda or ammonia). Wheat flour is classified as soft when it contains less gluten than hard (or strong) flour which has a higher gluten content. Soft flour is suitable for pastries and cakes while hard or bread flour is ideal for yeast-risen dough. All purpose or plain flour is a blend of both hard and soft wheat flours. Whole-grain flour retains most of the outer layer of the wheat kernel (bran) where the vitamins, minerals, and fiber are found. Semolina is a granular flour made from gluten-rich durum wheat used in making pasta and noodles. At one time, making bread was a time-consuming process. A sour-dough starter had to be made, or the yeast had to be "proofed" and the temperature of the ingredients carefully

wheat kernel buried in the earth, sprouts and bears fruit again, so does the soul gain Salvation and Everlasting Life.

THE CHEMICAL MAKE-UP OF WHEAT makes it one of the most nourishing of the plants cultivated for food. Rich in protein and starch, vitamins B and E, trace elements and a

monitored. Nowadays active dry yeast mixed directly with the flour and the heated liquid ingredients makes a quick-rising dough that results in a better-textured product. The recipes in this section represent just a few of the infinite ways in which wheat flour is used in the Mediterranean to make bread, pitas, pastries, and pastas.

BREADS/DOUGHS

Savory Carrot Biscuits

Yields 30 pieces
Preparation time 1 hour 30 minutes
Baking time 15 minutes

3 cups self-rising flour
1/2 teaspoon baking soda
1½ teaspoon sugar
4 medium carrots, cooked
2 tablespoons olive oil
2 tablespoons grated onion
1/4 teaspoon pepper
1/2 cup vegetable shortening
1/3 cup olive oil
1/4 cup finely chopped mint

Sift the dry ingredients together into a bowl and make a well in the center. Saute the onion in 2 tablespoons of olive oil, and blend along with the carrots, pepper, shortening, olive oil and mint in a food processor until well-mixed. Pour into the center of the dry ingredients, and with a spoon, gradually incorporate them into the liquid until a uniform dough is formed. Do not overwork the dough or the biscuits will be tough. Break off pieces of dough the size of a walnut and roll into strands the thickness of the small finger. Twist into desired shapes. Line a sheet with baking paper and arrange biscuits 1 inch (2 cm) apart. Bake in a 350˚F (180˚C)

oven for about 15 minutes. Remove from the oven and cool on racks. Store in air-tight containers or cookie tins.

Savory Biscuits with Spinach

Yields 30 pieces
Preparation time 1 hour 30 minutes
Baking time 15 minutes

3 cups self-rising flour
1 teaspoon salt
1/2 teaspoon baking soda
1½ teaspoon sugar
1/2 cup frozen spinach puree or
8 oz (250 g) fresh spinach, cooked and pureed
2 tablespoons olive oil
1 small leek, white part only, grated
2 green onions, finely chopped
1/3 cup soya milk
1/4 cup finely chopped dill
1/4 teaspoon pepper
1/3 cup vegetable shortening
1/3 cup olive oil

Sift the dry ingredients together into a large bowl and make a well in the center. If using fresh spinach, rinse, blanch, and squeeze out excess water. Saute the leek and onions in 2 tablespoons of oil. Add the soya milk and when the mixture comes to a boil, lower the heat and simmer until the vegetables are soft, about 5 minutes. Remove from the heat, cool slightly, and blend along with the spinach, dill, pepper, shortening, and oil until uniform. Empty the mixture into the center of the dry ingredients, gradually incorporating them into the liquid to form a uniform dough. Do not overwork the dough or the biscuits will be tough. Pinch off pieces of dough the size of a walnut and roll strands the thickness of the small finger. Twist into desired shapes. Line a baking sheet with non-stick baking paper and arrange the biscuits 1 inch (2 cm) apart. Bake in a 350˚C(180˚F) oven for about 15 minutes. Cool completely on racks and store in air-tight containers.

Bread with Pesto and Sun-Dried Tomatoes

Yields 2 loaves
Preparation time 2 hours
Baking time 25-30 minutes

5 sun-dried tomatoes
1/2 cup pesto (see basic recipes)
3¹/₂ cups flour
1 tablespoon dried yeast or
1 oz (30 g) fresh yeast
1/2 teaspoon salt
2 tablespoons honey
2 tablespoons olive oil
1 cup warm water (100°F/40°C)

Soak the dried tomatoes in water for 2-3 hours to swell. Meanwhile, prepare the pesto according to basic recipe. Mix the flour with the yeast and salt. Make a well in the center and pour in the honey, oil, and warm water. Stir with a spoon, gradually incorporating the flour from the sides into the liquid. Knead the dough until smooth and pliable. Cover with plastic wrap and allow to rise in a warm place for 1 hour or until doubled in bulk. Squeeze excess liquid from the tomatoes and chop. Divide the dough into two equal parts and roll out into two 10-inch (25-cm) squares. Spread the dough with pesto and scatter the pieces of tomato here and there on top. Roll up the dough and place the loaves on a lightly oiled baking sheet. Cover with a damp towel and allow to rise for 1 hour or until doubled in bulk. Bake in a 400°F (200°C) oven for about 25-30 minutes, until lightly browned. Serve the bread the same day or freeze in plastic wrap until ready to use.

Olive Bread

Yields 2 loaves or 20-30 rolls
Preparation time 2-3 hours
Baking time 20 minutes

3 cups flour, all purpose or whole-grain
1½ cups strong or bread flour
1 tablespoon oregano (optional)
3 tablespoons sugar or honey
3 tablespoons olive oil
2 teaspoons salt
1½ tablespoons dry yeast or
1½ oz (45 g) fresh yeast
1½ cups warm water (100°F/40°C)
1 cup finely chopped Calamata olives

Mix both kinds of flour with the dry yeast and the oregano in a large bowl. If using fresh yeast, dissolve in 1/2 cup warm water until foamy. Open a well in the center and pour in the sugar, oil, water, (and dissolved yeast, if used). Stir, gradually incorporating the flour from the sides of the well into the liquid. Knead the dough until smooth and pliable. Cover with plastic wrap and allow to rise in a warm place until doubled in bulk (about 2 hours). Divide the dough into two equal parts and roll each out into an 8x16-inch (20x40-cm) rectangle. Sprinkle the surface with the chopped olives and roll up tightly from the long edge. Put the loaves on a lightly oiled baking sheet, cover with a damp towel, and allow to rise until doubled in bulk. Or cut the rolls crosswise into 1-inch (3-cm) slices and arrange flat on the baking sheet, cut surfaces up and down. Cover and allow to rise again until doubled in bulk. Before baking, brush tops with a little water and, if desired, sprinkle with sesame seeds. Bake the loaves in a 400°F (200°C) oven for 20-30 minutes (or the rolls for 15-20 minutes). Remove from the oven and allow to cool. If not serving the same day, freeze in airtight bags or containers until ready to use.

Fried Olive Flatbread

Yields 20 pieces
Preparation time 1 hour 30 minutes
Baking time 30-40 minutes

3½ cups all purpose flour
1 tablespoon dry yeast or
1 oz (30 g) fresh yeast
2 tablespoons honey
2 tablespoons olive oil
1 cup warm water 100°F (40°C)
2 cups finely chopped Calamata olives

Mix the flour with the dry yeast in a large bowl. Open a well in the center and pour in the honey, oil, and water. Gradually incorporate the flour from the sides of the well into the liquid and knead until a soft, pliable dough is formed. Add more flour if necessary. Cover the dough with plastic wrap and allow to rise for about 1 hour, or until doubled in bulk. Roll the dough out into a rectangle about the thickness of your small finger and sprinkle the olives on top. Roll up tightly. With a floured knife cut the roll crosswise into 18-20 pieces, 1/2-inch (1-cm) thick. Flatten each piece with the rolling pin about 1/4-inch (1/2-cm) thick. Allow to rise for about 20 minutes and then fry on both sides in hot oil. It is preferable to serve them hot but they are delicious even when cold.

Olive Rolls (Eliotes - Cyprus)

Yields 5 rolls
Preparation time 1 hour 30 minutes
Baking time 40-50 minutes

for the dough
4 cups all purpose flour
2 teaspoons baking powder
1 cup corn oil
1 cup orange soda
sesame seeds

for the filling
4 green onions, finely chopped
4-5 tablespoons olive oil
1½ cups finely chopped black olives
1/2 cup finely chopped cilantro or mint
salt and freshly ground pepper
1/2 teaspoon cinnamon

To prepare the filling, lightly saute the onions in the oil. Stir in the chopped olives and the remaining filling ingredients. Remove from the heat and set aside to cool. Sift the flour with the baking powder into a large bowl. Work the oil into the flour with your fingertips until the mixture resembles coarse bread crumbs. Add the orange soda little by little and knead the dough until smooth and pliable. Allow to rest 30 minutes. Divide the dough into five parts and roll each one out on a floured surface into a thin sheet about 10x14 inches (25x35 cm). Spread each sheet of dough with 1/5th of the mixture. Roll up into long thin rolls. Brush the surface of the rolls with water and sprinkle with sesame seeds. Arrange the rolls on one or two lightly oiled baking sheets and bake in a 350°F (180°C) oven for 40-50 minutes, until lightly browned. Serve hot.

OLIVE BREAD

Gnocchi with Mint Pesto

Serves 4
Preparation time 20 minutes
Cooking time 5 minutes

1 recipe for potato gnocchi (see basic recipes)
1 recipe for pesto sauce (see basic recipes)
1/2 cup fresh mint leaves

Prepare the pesto substituting half the amount of basil with mint. Drop the gnocchi into boiling salted water and cook for about 5 minutes. Pour some of the mint/pesto sauce (2-3 tablespoons) on a serving platter. When the gnocchi rise to the top of the water, remove them with a slotted spoon to the platter, on top of the sauce. Pour the remaining pesto over the gnocchi and serve immediately.

Gnocchi with Tomato Sauce

Serves 4
Preparation time 20 minutes
Cooking time 1 hour

1 recipe for potato gnocchi (see basic recipes)
1/4 cup olive oil
1 clove garlic, minced
1 small onion, grated
2 lb (1 kg) ripe tomatoes, peeled, seeded,
and coarsely chopped
1 teaspoon tomato paste
1 teaspoon rosemary
1 teaspoon sage
1 teaspoon thyme
salt and freshly ground pepper

To prepare the sauce, saute the garlic and onions in the oil until wilted. Add the tomatoes, tomato paste, herbs, salt, and pepper and simmer the sauce for about 1 hour, until cooked down almost to the oil. Pour some sauce on a serving plate. Cook the gnocchi in boiling salted water. When they rise to the top of the water, remove with a slotted spoon to the serving plate on top of the sauce. Pour the remaining sauce on top and serve immediately.

Olive Oil Breadsticks

Yields 45-60 breadsticks
Preparation time 45 minutes
Baking time 30 minutes

2 cups whole-wheat flour
5 cups all purpose flour
1½ teaspoon salt
1½ tablespoons sugar
2 cups olive oil
1¾ cup dry white wine
1 tablespoon baking soda
1 tablespoon ammonia

Mix both kinds of flour with the sugar and salt in a large mixing bowl. Rub the oil into the flour with your fingers (or a pastry cutter) until all of it has been absorbed by the flour. Dissolve the baking soda and ammonia in a small amount of wine and add along with the remaining wine to the flour mixture. Knead until the dough is soft and pulls away from the fingers and the sides of the bowl. It may be necessary to add a little more wine. Cover the dough with plastic wrap and allow to rest for 30 minutes. Form the dough into finger-thick strips 8-10 inches (20-25 cm) long. Arrange the strips 1/2 inch (1 cm) apart on a baking sheet lined with baking paper. Bake in a 400°F (200°C) oven for about 30 minutes. Cool on racks and store in biscuit tins.

Eggplant Rolls

Yields 20 pieces
Preparation time 2 hours
Cooking time 40-50 minutes

1 lb (500 g) phyllo pastry (commercial
or see basic recipes)
2/3 cup olive oil

for the filling
4 lb (2 kg) eggplant
1/3 cup olive oil

1 large onion, grated
1 tablespoon balsamic vinegar
1/2 cup finely chopped parsley or mint
1/2 cup vegetarian cream
2 tablespoons dried breadcrumbs
salt and freshly ground pepper

To prepare the filling, grill or bake the eggplant whole as for eggplant salad according to the recipe on page 56. Peel and chop. Heat the oil in a pan and saute the onions until wilted. Add the chopped eggplant along with the remaining ingredients for the filling and mix. Heat 2/3 cup olive oil. Brush half of each sheet of phyllo with oil and fold the other half on top. Brush again with oil. Place 2-3 tablespoons of filling on the long edge and roll up tightly. Then twist the roll into a coil. Repeat with the other sheets of phyllo and arrange the eggplant rolls on a lightly oiled baking sheet, side by side. Brush rolls with olive oil and bake in a 350°F (180°C) oven for about 50 minutes, until well-browned. Serve hot or at room temperature.

Crepes with Spinach

Yields 16 pieces
Preparation time 50 minutes
Baking time 30-40 minutes

16 crepes (see basic recipes)

for the sauce
1 red bell pepper
1/4 cup water
1/4 cup olive oil
2 tablespoons grated onion
1 small clove of garlic, minced
3 cups tomato juice
1 teaspoon Italian herbs
a pinch of salt and freshly ground pepper

for the filling
2 lb (1 kg) spinach, blanched and drained
1/4 cup olive oil
pinch of salt
1 large onion, finely chopped

1/2 cup finely chopped dill

Prepare the sauce. Puree the red pepper with the water in the blender. Heat the oil and lightly saute the onions and garlic until wilted. Add the tomato juice and red pepper puree, herbs, salt, and pepper and simmer the sauce until slightly thick. Prepare the crepes according to the recipe. Finally, prepare the filling. Heat the oil and saute the onions until wilted. Add the spinach and dill, stirring continuously over the heat for 5-6 minutes. Pour in 1/3 of the sauce and stir to mix. Put 2-3 tablespoons of the spinach mixture on each crepe and roll up. Arrange side by side in a lightly oiled baking dish and pour the remaining sauce on top. The crepes can be frozen at this point. Bake in a 350°F (180°C) oven for 40-45 minutes. Serve hot or at room temperature.

Crepes with Vegetables

Serves 4
Preparation time 1 hour
Baking time 20-25 minutes

1/4 cup olive oil
1 small clove garlic, minced
2 medium onions, sliced
2 medium carrots, julienne
1 each green, red, and orange bell pepper, julienne
2 medium zucchini, julienne
2 tablespoons ketchup
2 tablespoons chopped fresh cilantro or
1/2 teaspoon ground coriander
salt and freshly ground pepper
8 crepes (see basic recipes)
7 oz (200 g) day-old bread, grated
2 tablespoons olive oil
1 cup bechamel sauce (see basic recipes)
1/8 teaspoon nutmeg

Heat the oil in a large pan and saute the garlic and onions, until wilted. Add the carrots, peppers, and zucchini and stir over the heat until wilted. Add the ketchup, spices, salt, pepper, and simmer for 15-20 minutes, until the vegetables are tender and the sauce has cooked down almost to the oil. Prepare the crepes according to the recipe. Put 2-3 tablespoons of the vegetable mixture on each crepe and roll up. Place the crepes side by side in a lightly oiled baking dish. Heat the oil in a small pan and fry the breadcrumbs in the oil until golden brown. Prepare the bechamel according to the recipe and stir in the nutmeg. Pour the bechamel over the crepes and sprinkle with the browned breadcrumbs. Bake in a 400°F (200°C) oven for 10-15 minutes and serve immediately.

Crepes with Mushroom Sauce

Serves 6
Preparation time 1 hour
Cooking time 30 minutes

for the mushroom sauce
1/4 cup olive oil
2 cloves garlic, slivered
1 lb (500 g) oyster mushrooms
8 oz (250 g) fresh white mushrooms
1/4 cup Dijon mustard

1 oz (35 g) dried porcini mushrooms
1/3 cup warm water
1/4 cup white dry wine
1/4 cup soya sauce
salt and freshly ground pepper
1 tablespoons cornstarch dissolved in
2 tablespoons water
18 crepes (see basic recipes)

Prepare the sauce. Rinse both kinds of mushroom, pat dry, and chop into small pieces. Soak the porcinis in warm water for 15 minutes and drain, reserving the liquid. Strain the liquid through a paper filter or cheesecloth. Heat the oil in a pan over medium heat and saute the garlic until wilted. Add the mushrooms, reserved liquid, mustard, wine, soya sauce, salt, and pepper. Cover, and simmer for about 30 minutes or until the mushrooms are tender. Stir in the dissolved cornstarch and cook until the sauce is clear and thick. Prepare the crepe batter according to the recipe and make small 3-inch (7-8-cm) crepes. Spread each crepe with mushroom sauce, stacking three on each plate with remaining sauce on top. Serve the crepes accompanied by a fresh green salad.

the olive oil in a pan over medium heat and saute the garlic and onion until wilted. Add the tomatoes and cook for 5 minutes. Drain over a bowl and return the liquid to the pan, reserving the sauteed vegetables. Add the sugar, pepper, chili powder, and salt to the pan. Cover and simmer until the sauce has cooked down almost to the oil. Set aside to serve separately with the baked phyllo roll. Lay a sheet of phyllo out on the worktop with the long edge towards you and brush with olive oil. Lay the remaining sheets on top of the first, one by one, brushing each with olive oil. Spoon the blanched leeks along the long edge of the stack of phyllo leaving a 2-inch (5-cm) margin on either side. Spread the spinach on top of the leeks, then the grated carrots and the zucchini, sprinkling a little salt and pepper between the layers. Finally, spread the reserved sauteed vegetables on top. Turn in the side edges and roll up. Transfer to a baking sheet lined with non-stick baking paper. Make 7 slashes through the top phyllo layers dividing it into 8 equal sections. Brush with olive oil and sprinkle with sesame seeds. Bake in a 400°F (200°C) oven for 30 minutes or until well-browned on top. Allow to cool for 5 minutes before cutting the roll into 8 separate pieces. Serve immediately with the reserved sauce.

Zucchini Yeast Fritters

Yields 60 fritters
Preparation time 2 hours
Cooking time 30 minutes

1 cup lukewarm water (110°F) (40°C)
2 oz (60 g) yeast
1 lb (500 g) zucchini, grated
1 lb (500 g) flour
1/2 cup finely chopped dill
salt and pepper
1/4 cup olive oil
more water as needed
oil for frying

Dissolve the yeast in the lukewarm water in a large bowl. Add the remaining ingredients and beat for 1 minute at high speed. If the batter is too thick, add a little more water. Cover the bowl with plastic wrap and allow the batter to rise in a warm place until doubled in bulk. Punch it down and scoop out pieces with a spoon. To prevent the dough from sticking to the spoon, dip it each time into a glass of water. Drop the batter into the hot oil, 380°F (190°C) and fry until all sides are golden brown. Do not overheat the oil so that the fritters will brown slowly and evenly. Serve immediately.

Vegetable-Stuffed Phyllo Roll

Serves 4
Preparation time 1 hour
Baking time 40 minutes

7 oz (200 g) zucchini, grated
7 oz (200 g) leeks, white part only, chopped, blanched and drained
7 oz (200 g) spinach, chopped, blanched and drained
7 oz (200 g) carrots, grated, blanched and drained
salt and freshly ground pepper
9 sheets of phyllo
1/4 cup corn oil

for the sauce
2 cloves garlic, minced
1 medium onion, chopped
1/4 cup olive oil
14 oz (400 g) chopped ripe tomatoes
1/4 teaspoon sugar
1/4 teaspoon pepper
1/4 teaspoon chili powder

Sprinkle the zucchini with a little salt and drain in a colander for 30 minutes. Squeeze out excess water with your hands. Heat

Little Olive Pizzas

Yields 12 small pizzas
Preparation time 20 minutes
Baking time 30 minutes

12 puff pastry rounds (to fit bottom and sides
of muffin cup)
3 tablespoons olive oil
2 large onions, thinly sliced
2 cloves garlic, minced
14 oz (400 g) white mushrooms, sliced
10 black olives, pitted and sliced
1 cup grated vegetarian cheese
1/4 cup finely chopped parsley
1 teaspoon oregano
3-4 ripe tomatoes, thinly sliced into rounds
salt and freshly ground pepper

Brush the cups of a muffin pan with oil and place one pastry round in each, pleating the sides to make them fit. Heat the oil in a pan over high heat and saute the onions, garlic, and mushrooms until wilted. Remove from the heat, cool slightly and stir in the olives, grated cheese, parsley, salt, and pepper. Spoon 2-3 heaping tablespoons of the mixture into each pastry cup and place a tomato slice on top of each. Brush each slice with olive oil and sprinkle with a pinch of oregano, salt, and pepper. Bake the pizzas for 20-30 minutes in a 425°F (220°C) oven, until the pastry is golden brown. Serve hot or at room temperature.

Leek Crescents

Yields 48 mini crescents
Preparation time 1 hour
Cooking time 30 minutes

for the pastry dough
1 oz (30 g) fresh yeast
1 cup warm water (110°F/40°C)
3-4 cups all purpose flour
2 tablespoons olive oil
1 tablespoon sugar
1 teaspoon salt
8 oz (250 g) margarine

for the filling
5-6 green onions, finely chopped
4 leeks, white and light green leaves, finely chopped
1/4 cup olive oil
salt and freshly ground pepper
1/4 cup finely chopped dill or parsley

Prepare the filling. Put the onions and leeks in a pan with the oil and 1/2 cup water. Cover and simmer until cooked down almost to the oil. Add the salt, pepper, and dill or parsley. Mix and set aside. Dissolve the yeast in lukewarm water and stir in a little flour. Allow to set about 10 minutes until foamy. Put the remaining flour in a large bowl and make a well in the center. Pour in the salt, sugar, and oil. Add the yeast mixture and gradually incorporate the flour from the sides of the well a little at a time to form a dough. Knead until it is soft and elastic and pulls away from the fingers. Divide the dough into 6 equal parts and roll out each one to a thickness of about 1/8 inch (3 mm) round sheet. Cut each round into quarters and then into eighths. Place a teaspoonful of filling at the large end of each triangle and roll up into crescents. Arrange on a baking sheet lined with baking paper, spacing well apart to allow enough room for expansion. Cover with a damp towel and allow to rise until doubled in bulk. Cut the margarine into small pieces and scatter here and there between and on top of the crescents. Bake in a 350°F (175°C) oven for about 30 minutes until lightly browned. Remove from the oven and serve either hot or at room temperature.

1/4 cup olive paste (see basic recipes)
1/4 cup pesto (see basic recipes)
2 tablespoons olive oil
1/2 cup grated vegetarian cheese
14 oz (400 g) canned artichoke hearts, quartered

Combine the peppers, mushrooms, vinegar, garlic, salt, pepper, and a pinch of oregano in a bowl. Cover and refrigerate for 2 hours. Drain the vegetables and saute in the oil until wilted. Meanwhile, prepare the pizza dough according to the recipe except for the oregano. Oil a 14-inch (35-cm) pizza pan and pat the dough onto the bottom and up the sides. Spread the olive paste evenly on the surface up to 1 inch (2 cm) from the edges. Arrange the sauted vegetables on top and scatter the artichokes here and there. Mix the pesto with 2 tablespoons of olive oil and pour on top. Sprinkle with the cheese and Italian herbs. Allow the pizza to rise for 30 minutes in a warm place. Bake in a 425°F (220°C) oven for 20-25 minutes. Serve immediately.

Pizza ala Grecque

Serves 4
Preparation time 1 hour
Baking time 30 minutes

1 recipe pizza dough (see basic recipes)
1/4 cup ketchup
1 small onion, sliced
1 small green bell pepper, julienne
3 cloves garlic, thinly sliced
5 white mushrooms, thinly sliced
10 large black olives, pitted and quartered
1 large tomato, cut into thin slices
1 tablespoon capers
1/2 teaspoon oregano
1/4 cup olive oil
salt and freshly ground pepper

Saute the onions and garlic in 2 tablespoons of the olive oil until wilted. Liberally oil a 12-inch (30-cm) pizza pan and spread the prepared pizza dough on the bottom and sides. Spread the ketchup evenly on the surface up to 1 inch (2 cm) from the edges. Arrange the remaining ingredients on top ending with the tomatoes. Sprinkle the entire surface with the oregano, freshly ground pepper, and the remaining olive oil. Allow to rise for 30 minutes in a warm place. Bake in a 400°F (200°C) oven for 30 minutes. Serve immediately.

Mediterranean Pizza

Serves 8
Preparation time 25 minutes
Baking time 25 minutes

1 recipe pizza dough (see basic recipes)
1 teaspoon dried Italian herbs
(basil, oregano, rosemary, garlic, thyme)

for the topping
1 each green, red, and yellow bell pepper, julienne
7 oz (200 g) oyster mushrooms, chopped
2 tablespoons balsamic vinegar
2 cloves garlic, minced
salt, pepper, and a pinch of oregano
2 tablespoons olive oil

Mixed Vegetable Pizza

Serves 4
Preparation time 1 hour 30 minutes
Baking time 25-30 minutes

1 long thin eggplant, sliced
1 medium zucchini, thinly sliced
1 medium onion sliced
1 each green, yellow, and red bell pepper, sliced into rings
5 large white mushrooms, sliced (optional)
1 large tomato, peeled, seeded, and finely chopped
1 clove garlic, minced
1½ teaspoon pizza herbs
1/4 cup olive oil
1 recipe pizza dough (see basic recipes)
1/4 cup ketchup
1/2 cup shredded day-old white bread
2 tablespoons olive oil
1/2 cup shredded vegetarian cheese (optional)
salt and freshly ground pepper

Place the sliced eggplant and zucchini in separate colanders, sprinkle with salt, and allow to drain for 1 hour. Rinse and gently squeeze out excess water. Heat the oil in a large frying pan and fry the eggplant, zucchini, and the next 6 ingredients until wilted. Spread the prepared pizza dough in an oiled 14-inch (35-cm) pizza pan. Spread the ketchup on the surface up to 1 inch (2 cm) from the edges. In a small pan, heat 2 tablespoons of olive oil and saute the bread crumbs. Sprinkle the crumbs and half the cheese on top of the ketchup. Arrange the prepared vegetables on top, sprinkle with the herbs, salt, and pepper and allow the pizza to rise for 30 minutes in a warm place. Bake in a 350°F (180°C) oven for about 25 minutes or until edges are browned. Sprinkle with the remaining cheese and bake another 3-5 minutes until cheese is melted. Serve hot.

Beggar's Pouches with Pumpkin

Yields 27 pieces
Preparation time 1 hour
Baking time 40-45 minutes

1/4 cup olive oil
1 medium onion, finely chopped
1 clove garlic, minced
1 lb (500 g) pumpkin or yellow squash, cut into pieces
1/2 teaspoon fresh rosemary
2 tablespoons rice or semolina
1 cup grated vegetarian cheese

2-3 tablespoons vegetarian cream
salt and freshly ground pepper
9 sheets of phyllo
1/3 cup olive oil for brushing

Heat 1/4 cup of olive oil and saute the onions and garlic until wilted. Add the squash, rosemary, salt, pepper, and 2-3 tablespoons water. Cover and simmer until the squash is soft and cooked down almost to the oil. Mash with a fork and stir in the semolina or rice, cheese, and cream. Lay three phyllo sheets out on the worktop, one on top of the other, each layer brushed with olive oil. Repeat two more times with the remaining 6 sheets of phyllo. Cut each pile of phyllo into a total of nine 5-inch (13-cm) squares. You will end up with 27 squares containing three layers of phyllo each. Place 2 tablespoons of the pumpkin mixture on each square and gather the edges up over the filling to form little pouches. Twist to close and arrange on a greased baking sheet. Brush each one with a little oil and bake in a 350°F (175°C) oven for 40-45 minutes. Serve hot or at room temperature.

parsley, salt and pepper, toss in the hot oil and remove from the heat. Put the rice into the food processor or blender to break up into small pieces. Stir into the greens mixture. Oil and line a large baking sheet with half the phyllo sheets, brushing each with a little oil. Spread the greens mixture on top, and cover with the remaining phyllo sheets, brushing each with oil. Roll up the excess phyllo hanging over the edges around the sides of the pan. Score the pitta into serving pieces and brush the surface with the remaining oil. Bake in a 400°F (200°C) oven for 15 minutes. Remove from the oven and pour the soda water on top. Return to the hot over and bake for about another 45 minutes, or until the surface is browned and crisp. Serve hot or at room temperature.

Monastery Greens Pitta

Serves 20
Preparation time 1 hour
Cooking time 1 hour

2 lb (1 kg) assorted field greens (rocket, nettles, mustard greens, chard, poppies, amaranth, etc.)
1/3 cup olive oil
3/4 cup grated onion
1 cup finely chopped green onions
2 leeks, white part only, finely chopped
1 cup finely chopped fennel weed
1/2 cup finely chopped parsley
2 tablespoons rice or semolina
salt and freshly ground pepper
1 lb (500 g) phyllo, homemade or commercial
3/4 cup olive oil

Trim, rinse, and blanch the greens. Drain well in a colander and squeeze out excess water with your hands. Heat the oil and lightly saute the onions and leeks. Add the drained greens, fennel, parsley, semolina, salt, and pepper. Toss in the hot oil and remove from the heat. Oil a 16-inch (40-cm) baking pan and lay 4 sheets of phyllo on the bottom, brushing each one with oil. Spread half the filling evenly on the surface, sprinkle with freshly ground pepper, and lay 2 sheets of phyllo on top. Spread the remaining filling on top and cover with the remaining 4 sheets of phyllo, brushing each one with oil. Roll up the excess phyllo hanging over the edges neatly around the sides. Score the pita into serving pieces and brush with the remaining oil. Sprinkle with a little water and bake in a 400°F (200°C) oven for about 1 hour or until surface is golden brown. Serve hot or at room temperature. To keep the phyllo crisp, do not cover left-over pita.

Greek Pitta with Greens

Serves 20
Preparation time 1 hour
Cooking time 1 hour

1 lb (500 g) fresh spinach leaves
1 lb (500 g) assorted fresh field greens (nettles, mustard greens, amaranth, chard, rocket, etc.)
1/3 cup olive oil
3/4 cup grated onion
8 green onions, finely chopped
1 leek, white part only, finely chopped
1/2 cup finely chopped dill
1/2 cup finely chopped parsley
3 tablespoons rice
salt and pepper
1 lb (500 g) phyllo, home-made or commercial
2/3 cup olive oil
3/4 cup soda water

Trim and rinse the spinach and greens. Chop, sprinkle with salt, and rub until wilted. Drain well, and squeeze out excess water with your hands. Heat the oil in a pan and lightly saute both kinds of onions and leek. Add the spinach, greens, dill,

MONASTERY GREENS PITTA

and squeeze out the excess water with your hands. Heat the oil and saute the leeks and onions until wilted. Add the drained greens and toss with the hot onion mixture. Add the dill or fennel, salt, and pepper. Divide the mixture into the 18 prepared tarts. Heat the cream. Dissolve the cornstarch in 2 tablespoons of water and stir into the hot cream. Stir over medium heat until thick. Remove from the heat and add the nutmeg and a pinch of salt and pepper. Spread 1 tablespoon of cream sauce on the surface of each tart. Bake the tarts in a 400°F (200°C) oven for 35-40 minutes, until the surface is lightly browned. Serve hot or cold.

Garlic Flatbread with Tomatoes

Serves 8
Preparation time 1-2 hours
Baking time 25 minutes

1/4 cup olive oil
1/2 teaspoon garlic powder
1 teaspoon Italian herbs
6 sun-dried tomatoes
2 cups all purpose flour
1¹/₂ teaspoons dried yeast
1/2 teaspoon salt
1 tablespoons honey
1 tablespoon margarine, melted
1/2 cup lukewarm water (110°F/40°C)
10 cloves garlic, slivered

Shake the oil, garlic powder, and herbs in a well-sealed jar until well-blended. Set aside for several hours. Chop the sun-dried tomatoes, and soak in warm water for 1-2 hours. Mix the flour with the yeast and the salt in a large bowl. Make a well in the center and pour in the honey and margarine. Add the water and mix, slowly incorporating the flour from the sides of the well into the liquid to form a soft pliable dough. Knead the dough until smooth and elastic. Cover with plastic wrap and allow to rise in warm place for about 1 hour, or until doubled in bulk. Meanwhile, drain the tomatoes, squeezing out the excess water with your hands, and lightly saute in a little oil. Roll out the dough and pat into a 12-inch (30-cm) round pizza pan. Cover and allow to rise again for 20-25 minutes. Brush the surface with half the herbed oil and scatter the slivered garlic and the sauteed tomatoes on top. Dribble with the remaining herbed oil. Bake the bread in a 400°F (200°C) oven for about 25 minutes, until lightly browned.

Spinach Tarts

Yields 18 pieces
Preparation time 1 hour
Baking time 35-40 minutes

10 phyllo sheets
1 lb (500 g) spinach or assorted field greens
1/4 cup olive oil
2 leeks, tender white and light green part only, finely chopped
1/2 cup finely chopped green onions
1/2 cup finely chopped dill or
1/2 cup finely chopped fennel weed
1/2 cup finely chopped parsley
salt and freshly ground pepper
1¹/₂ tablespoons cornstarch
1¹/₂ cup vegetarian cream
1/8 teaspoon ground nutmeg

Lay 5 phyllo sheets at a time on the worktop, one on top of the other, brushing each with olive oil. Cut into 9 squares. Repeat with the remaining 5 phyllo sheets. Oil 18 muffin cups, line with the phyllo squares, and trim around edges with a pair of scissors. Trim, rinse, and blanch the spinach or greens. Drain

Tomato Flatbread

Serves 8
Preparation time 1-2 hours
Baking time 25 minutes

2 cups all purpose flour
1½ teaspoons dried yeast
1/2 teaspoon salt
1 teaspoon Italian herbs
1 tablespoon honey
1 tablespoon margarine, melted
1/2 cup warm water (110°F /40°C)
1/4 cup olive oil
4 cloves garlic, slivered
2 lb (1 kg) tomatoes, peeled, seeded,
and coarsely chopped
1 tablespoon tomato paste
2 tablespoons ketchup
salt and freshly ground pepper
1 teaspoon oregano
1 teaspoon thyme

Mix the flour with the yeast, salt, and herbs. Make a well in the center and add the honey, margarine, and water. Mix with a spoon and then knead until a soft elastic dough is formed. Cover with plastic wrap and allow to rise in a warm place for 1 hour until doubled in bulk. Meanwhile, heat the oil and lightly saute the garlic. Add the tomatoes, tomato paste, ketchup, salt, and pepper and simmer the sauce for 15 minutes until slightly thickened. Roll out the dough and pat into a 12-inch (30-cm) pizza pan. Spread the sauce evenly on the surface of the dough up to 1-inch (2-cm) of the sides. Sprinkle the oregano and thyme on top. Bake the bread in a 400°F (200°C) oven for 25 minutes, until edges are browned.

Bell Pepper and Onion Pitta

Serves 8-10
Preparation time 40 minutes
Baking time 1 hour

10 sheets of phyllo, homemade or commercial
1/2 cup olive oil

for the filling
1 each large red, yellow and green bell pepper,
cut into strips
2 large onions, sliced
1/2 cup finely chopped green onions
1/4 cup olive oil
1/2 cup finely chopped parsley
1/4 teaspoon cayenne
1 tablespoon dried breadcrumbs
salt and freshly ground pepper

Trim the phyllo sheets into 15-inch (38-cm) rounds. Line a 14-inch (35-cm) round baking pan or ovenproof glass dish with half the sheets, brushing each with olive oil, and allowing the edges of the phyllo to ruffle around the edge of the pan. Prepare the filling. Heat the oil and saute the peppers and onions until wilted. Remove from the heat, add the parsley, breadcrumbs, cayenne, salt, and pepper. Spread the filling on the bottom of the prepared baking pan and lay the remaining phyllo sheets on top, brushing each one with oil, and allowing the edges to ruffle. Score into serving pieces and bake in a 350°F (180°C) oven for about 1 hour, until the phyllo is golden brown. Serve immediately.

Zucchini Pitta

Yields 20-30 pieces
Preparation time 2 hours
Baking time 1 hour

1 recipe phyllo dough (see basic recipes) or
1 lb (500 g) commercial phyllo
3 lb (1½ kg) zucchini
1 lb (500 g) endive, chard, or amaranth,
blanched, drained, and squeezed dry
2 tablespoons fine semolina or dried bread crumbs
3 tablespoons olive oil
1/2 cup vegetarian cream
1/2 teaspoon freshly ground pepper
1/2 cup finely chopped mint or dill
3/4 cup olive oil

Prepare and divide the phyllo dough into 12 balls. Cover with a damp towel and allow to rest 1 hour. Meanwhile, prepare the filling. Grate the zucchini coarsely, sprinkle with a little salt and allow to drain in a colander for 2 hours. Squeeze out excess water. Combine drained zucchini with the remaining ingredients except for the olive oil. Heat the oil in a small pan over low heat until warm. On a floured surface, flatten and roll out the balls of phyllo into thin sheets about 18-inches (45-cm) in diameter. Oil a large round 16-inch (40-cm) pitta pan and lay five phyllo sheets on the bottom, brushing each one liberally with the warm oil. Spread half the filling on them, place two more oiled phyllo sheets over the filling, and spread the remaining filling on top. Cover the pitta with the remaining five sheets of phyllo, again brushing each one with the warm oil. Gather and roll up the edges of the phyllo hanging over the sides inward to form a rim. Score into serving pieces and brush the surface with the remaining oil. Sprinkle with a little water and bake in a 350°F (180°C) oven for about 1 hour, until the phyllo is golden brown. Commercially prepared phyllo absorbs much less oil than the home-made, so brush each sheet lightly. At the end, beat the remaining oil with 4 tablespoons each of flour and water and brush the surface of the pitta with the mixture. Bake in a 350°F (180°C) oven for about 1 hour until golden brown. Serve hot or at room temperature.

Cauliflower Tarts

Yields 12 tarts
Preparation time 20 minutes
Baking time 30 minutes

12 puff pastry rounds to fit bottom and sides of
standard muffin cups
4 tablespoons margarine
1 small onion, finely chopped
2 cloves garlic, minced
7 oz (200 g) canned sliced mushrooms, drained
1 small cauliflower, (2½ cups florets)
1 tablespoon flour
1 large tomato, finely chopped or
1 cup canned chopped tomato
2 tablespoons ketchup
1/2 teaspoon thyme
1/2 teaspoon oregano
1/4 cup finely chopped parsley
salt and freshly ground pepper
1½ cup vegetarian cream
2 hot peppers, finely minced (optional)

Melt the margarine in a pan and saute the onions and garlic. Add the mushrooms and stir until lightly browned, about 3-4 minutes. Add the cauliflower florets and continue stirring over the heat for another 2 minutes. Sprinkle the surface with the flour, cooking and stirring for about 1 minute. Add the tomatoes, ketchup, thyme, oregano, parsley, salt, and pepper. Cover, lower the heat and simmer for 10 minutes, until the mixture thickens. Grease 12 standard muffin cups and line with the puff pastry rounds. Put 2-3 heaping tablespoons of the filling in each cup and dribble 2 tablespoons of cream on top of each. Sprinkle, if desired, with the minced hot pepper. Bake the tarts in a 400°F (200°C) oven for about 30 minutes, or until lightly browned. Alternatively, to prepare a large tart, line a 10-inch (25-cm) tart dish with a sheet of puff pastry and spread the mushroom-cauliflower mixture on it. Bake for 35-40 minutes.

Artichoke Tarts

Yields 24 tartlets
Preparation time 40 minutes
Cooking time 45 minutes

10 phyllo sheets
1/3 cup olive oil for brushing phyllo
29 oz (800 g) canned artichoke hearts
3 tablespoons olive oil
1/2 cup finely chopped carrot
1/2 cup finely chopped mushrooms
1/2 cup finely chopped onions
1 small clove garlic, minced
1 medium eggplant, cut in small cubes
1 cup tomato juice
1 tablespoon ketchup
1/4 cup finely chopped mint or fennel weed
salt and freshly ground pepper
2 cups bechamel sauce, (see basic recipes)

Lay 5 phyllo sheets out on worktop, one on top of the other, brushing each one with olive oil. Repeat with the other 5 phyllo sheets. Using a 4-inch (10-cm) cook cutter, cut 24 rounds large enough to cover the sides and bottoms of two mini-muffin pans. Strain the artichokes and cut in pieces. Place 2 pieces in each tartlet. Heat the oil in a pan and saute the carrots, mushrooms, onions, garlic, and eggplant until soft. Add the tomato juice, ketchup, mint or fennel, salt, and pepper. Simmer until sauce has cooked down almost to the oil. Fill the 24 tartlets 3/4 full with the mixture. Prepare the bechamel and put one tablespoonful on top of each tartlet. The tartlets may be frozen at this point. Bake in a 350°F (180°C) oven for about 45 minutes, or until the bechamel is lightly browned. Garnish each tartlet with a sprig of mint or fennel. Serve hot or at room temperature.

Piroshki with Potatoes

Yields 40 pieces
Preparation time 1 hour and 30 minutes
Cooking time 8- 10 minutes

for the filling
1 lb (500 g) potatoes, peeled
1 large onion, finely chopped
1/4 cup olive oil
3 tablespoons finely chopped parsley, dill, or mint
salt and freshly ground pepper

for the dough
1 cup lukewarm water (110°F/40°C)
1 tablespoon dried yeast or
1 oz (30 g) fresh yeast
1 teaspoon salt
1 teaspoon sugar
1/4 cup olive oil
2-3 cups all purpose flour

Dissolve the yeast in the warm water, stir in 2-3 tablespoons flour and set aside until foamy. Put 2 cups of flour in a bowl and open a well in the center. Add the salt, sugar, oil, and dissolved yeast. Mix slowly incorporating the flour from around the sides of the well, adding more flour, if necessary, to form a soft pliable dough. Allow to rise in a warm place until doubled in bulk. Meanwhile, prepare the filling. Cook the potatoes and mash. Heat the oil and saute the onions until lightly browned. Add the mashed potatoes, salt, pepper, and herbs. Roll out the dough 1/2 inch (1 cm) thick and cut 4-inch (10-cm) rounds with a cookie cutter. Place a teaspoonful of filling in the center, fold in half and pinch the open edge shut with your fingers. Allow the piroshki to rise for 15-20 minutes and fry in hot oil until lightly browned. Serve immediately.

Mussel Croquettes

Yields 20 pieces
Preparation time 1 hour 30 minutes
Frying time 15 minutes

1 lb (500 g) shelled mussels
1 cup batter for frying (see basic recipes)
2 tablespoons ketchup
2 tablespoons finely chopped dill
salt and freshly ground pepper
oil for frying

Prepare the batter and combine with the ketchup, dill, salt, pepper, and mussels. Heat the oil in a heavy-bottomed frying pan. Drop large spoonfuls of batter with 3 mussels at a time into the hot oil and fry over medium heat until golden brown on both sides. Serve hot accompanied by Thousand Island dressing (see basic recipes).

Fish Roe Cakes

Yields 30 pieces
Preparation time 30 minutes
Frying time 15 minutes

1½ lb (750 g) day-old sliced bread, crusts removed
7 oz (200 g) taramas
2-3 cloves garlic, finely minced
1 large onion, finely chopped
1/4 cup mint, finely chopped
1/4 cup parsley, finely chopped
freshly ground pepper

Soak the bread in water and squeeze out excess with your hands. Place soaked bread in a large bowl with the remaining ingredients and knead to mix. Make small round cakes, press to flatten, and fry in hot oil until golden brown on both sides.

Mussel-Potato Cakes

Yields 30 pieces
Preparation time 30 minutes
Frying time 15 minutes

1 lb (500 g) shelled mussels
7 oz (200 g) potatoes
1 medium onion, grated
1 cup dried bread crumbs
1/3 cup finely chopped dill
salt and freshly ground pepper
oil for frying

Rinse the mussels, put them in a pan and stir over medium heat for 5 minutes to release some of their liquid. Do not overcook or they will shrink and toughen. Drain, cool slightly, and mash in the food processor. Peel the potatoes and cook until soft. Mash with a fork and combine with the mussels, onion, dill, salt, and pepper. Add enough bread crumbs to form a stiff mixture. Refrigerate for 1 hour. Make small flat cakes, coat with flour, and deep-fry in hot oil. Serve hot or cold with cocktail sauce.

Tomato Fritters Santorini

Serves 4
Preparation time 1 hour 30 minutes
Frying time 15 minutes

2 lb (1 kg) fresh ripe tomatoes
1 lb (500 g) onions, grated
1/2 cup finely chopped mint or parsley
2 tablespoons finely chopped fresh oregano or
1 teaspoon dried oregano
1¹/₂ cup self-rising flour
salt and freshly ground pepper

Finely chop the tomatoes, place them in a colander, sprinkle with salt and allow to drain 1-2 hours. Sprinkle the onions with salt, rub lightly and rinse. Squeeze out excess water. Combine the onions with the drained tomatoes in a bowl along with the mint or parsley, oregano and enough flour to make a stiff batter. Add the pepper. Do not add salt as the salt treated onions will provide enough. Heat ample oil in a heavy-bottomed frying pan and fry tablespoonfuls of batter until golden brown on both sides. Serve immediately accompanied by a salad of fresh garden greens.

Zucchini Rissoles

Yields 30 pieces
Preparation time 1 hour
Frying time 10-15 minutes

2 lb (1 kg) zucchini, coarsely grated
1 large ripe tomato, coarsely grated
7 oz (200 g) vegetarian cheese, grated
1/2 cup finely chopped dill
1/2 cup finely chopped parsley
flour and dried breadcrumbs
salt and freshly ground pepper

Sprinkle the grated zucchini with a little salt and allow to drain in a colander for 1 hour. Squeeze out excess water with your hands. Mix with the tomato, cheese, herbs, salt, and pepper. Combine equal amounts of flour and breadcrumbs and stir in as much as needed until the mixture holds its shape. Roll tablespoonfuls of the mixture in breadcrumbs. Heat ample oil in a heavy-bottomed pan and fry the rissoles until lightly browned on all sides. Serve hot or at room temperature.

Greens Fritters

Serves 4
Preparation time 20 minutes
Frying time 15 minutes

1 lb (500 g) assorted greens (spinach, nettles, amaranth, chard)
2/3 cup self-rising flour
1/4 cup corn starch
1/2 cup finely grated onion
1/4 cup finely chopped green onions
2/3 cup soya milk or water
1/4 cup finely chopped fennel leaves
1/4 cup finely chopped mint
salt and freshly ground pepper

Pick over and thoroughly rinse the greens. Trim, removing all thick stems which should be discarded. Finely chop the greens and combine with the other ingredients, adding enough flour to form a smooth thick batter. Heat ample oil in a heavy-bottomed pan and fry tablespoonfuls of the batter until fritters are golden brown on all sides. Serve hot or at room temperature.

with cornstarch. At this point they may be frozen. Fry the rolls 3-5 minutes in hot deep oil until golden brown. Serve hot or at room temperature.

Arab Pocket Bread

Yields 12 large or 30 small breads
Preparation time 2 hours 30 minutes
Baking time 10 minutes

2 oz (60 g) fresh yeast or
1 tablespoons dried yeast
3 tablespoons sugar
2 cups lukewarm water (110°F/40°C)
1/4 teaspoon salt
1/4 cup corn oil
6 cups strong flour
1/2 cup cornstarch for rolling out

Dissolve the yeast and sugar in the lukewarm water in a large bowl. Stir in the salt and corn oil. Add the flour a little at a time stirring with a spoon and then mixing with your hands to form a stiff dough. Turn dough out onto a work surface sprinkled with cornstarch and with your hands dipped in cornstarch, knead for 10 minutes, until the dough is soft and pliable. Place the dough in an oiled bowl, cover and allow to rise in a warm place until doubled in bulk. Punch down and shape into a ball, cover, and allow to rise a second time for another 30 minutes. Divide into 12 medium balls or 30 walnut-sized balls. Roll out on a surface dusted with cornstarch, the large ones into 8-inch (20-cm) circles and the small ones into 4-inch (10-cm) circles. Line 2-3 baking sheets with baking paper, and sprinkle with a little cornstarch. Arrange the flatbreads on top, cover with a towel and allow to rise for 30 minutes. Bake in a 450°F (230°C) oven for 5-7 minutes. As the bread dries out quickly, it should be eaten the same day. Otherwise, freeze in airtight plastic bags until ready to use for up to 3 months.

Phyllo Rolls with Vegetables

Yields 12 rolls
Preparation time 30 minutes
Frying time 3-5 minutes

2 tablespoons corn oil
1 clove garlic, minced
2 teaspoon grated fresh ginger
2 large oyster mushrooms, julienne
2 green onions, chopped
1/2 cup shredded white cabbage
1/2 cup bean sprouts (optional)
1/2 cup finely chopped leeks, white part only
salt and freshly ground pepper
1 tablespoon cornstarch dissolved in
2 tablespoons water
4 phyllo sheets, cut widthwise into 3 strips each

Heat the corn oil in a pan and saute the garlic and ginger. Add the mushrooms, onions, cabbage, sprouts, and leek. Stir for 5 minutes over medium heat until wilted. Add the dissolved cornstarch, salt, and pepper and stir the mixture over low heat until thickened. Brush the phyllo strips with oil and fold in half. Place 1 tablespoonful of the filling on the bottom of each one, turn in the sides over the filling, and roll up. Moisten the edge with a little water to seal. Set the rolls aside on a surface dusted

Stuffed Pocket Bread

Yields 4 large Arab pocket breads
Preparation time 40 minutes

4 large Arab pocket breads (previous recipe)
1 cup pepper sauce (see basic recipes)
7 oz (200 g) oyster mushrooms, grilled
1 medium onion, finely chopped
4 dill pickles, sliced
4 pickled peppers
fried potatoes

Prepare the pocket breads and pepper sauce according to the recipes. Grill the mushrooms and fry the potatoes shortly before serving. Fill the breads with some mushrooms, fried potatoes, onion, pickles, and peppers. Spoon some pepper sauce on each. Heat in a 400°F (200°C) oven for 8 minutes and serve immediately.

Fried Vegetable Patties

Yields 30 patties
Preparation time 30 minutes
Frying time 3-5 minutes

1 lb (500 g) potatoes, peeled
4 medium carrots
5 medium zucchini
1/3 cup peas
1/4 teaspoon cumin
1/2 teaspoon curry powder
1/4 cup all purpose flour, oil for frying
salt and freshly ground pepper

Cook the potatoes and carrots in salted water until soft. Drain and cook the zucchini and peas in the same cooking liquid. Combine the cooked vegetables in a colander and drain well. When cool mash them with a fork. Add the spices, salt, pepper, and as much flour as needed to make a stiff mixture which holds its shape. Wet your hands, form the mixture into patties, coat with flour and fry in hot oil on both sides. Drain on absorbent paper. Serve hot or at room temperature.

Barley Rusks with Tomatoes

Serves 6
Preparation time 30 minutes

12 barley rusks
2 cloves garlic, minced
1/2 cup olive oil
2 tablespoons finely chopped parsley
1 each yellow, red, and green bell pepper
2 tablespoons balsamic vinegar
salt and freshly ground pepper
3 medium ripe tomatoes, seeded and finely chopped
1/3 cup finely chopped basil or mint
1/2 teaspoon oregano
1 tablespoon olive oil

Cut the bell peppers in half lengthwise, devein and deseed. Grill until the skin is slightly burnt. Peel and cut into strips. Combine with the parsley in a bowl, add 1 tablespoon of the olive oil, vinegar, salt, and pepper. Cover with plastic wrap and refrigerate. Combine the tomatoes, basil, oregano, salt, freshly ground pepper and 1 tablespoon of the olive oil in a large bowl. Slightly wet the rusks. Combine the minced garlic with the remaining olive oil and brush the rusks. Cover half the rusks with the pepper mixture and the other half with the herbed tomato mixture. Serve immediately.

Fava Croquettes

Yields 20 croquettes
Preparation time 1 hour
Frying time 20 minutes

2 cups yellow split peas
4 cups (1 liter) vegetable stock
1/2 teaspoon paprika
1/2 teaspoon chili powder
1/4 teaspoon soda
1/4 teaspoon salt
1/2 cup finely chopped dill
1 cup finely chopped tomato
1 cup finely chopped green bell pepper
1 small onion, grated
1/4 cup dried breadcrumbs
flour for dusting, oil for frying

Cook the split peas in the stock until all the liquid has been absorbed and they are very soft. Combine the cooked peas with the paprika, chili powder, soda, and salt. Add the dill, tomatoes, bell peppers, onion, breadcrumbs and mix well. Form the mixture into bite-sized balls and refrigerate for 30 minutes. Roll in four, flatten slightly, and deep-fry in hot oil. Serve immediately.

Greek Onion Pitta

Yields 8- 10 pieces
Preparation time 2 hours
Baking time 1 hour

1 lb (500 g) phyllo sheets
2/3 cup olive oil

for the filling
2 lb (1 kg) onions, sliced lengthwise
1/2 cup finely chopped mint
2 large tomatoes, peeled and seeded
3 tablespoons rice or breadcrumbs
1/2 cup vegetarian cream (optional)
10 oz (300 g) vegetarian cheese, shredded (optional)

Put the onion slices in a pan with a little water and simmer for 15 minutes. Drain well and combine with the remaining ingredients. Cut the phyllo sheets into 15-inch (38-cm) rounds. Line a 14-inch (35-cm) baking pan or an oven-proof dish with half the sheets, brushing each one with olive oil and allowing edges to ruffle around the pan. Spread the filling on the bottom of the prepared pan and cover with the remaining phyllo sheets, again oiling each one and allowing the edges to ruffle. Score the pitta into 8-10 pieces with a sharp knife and bake in a 400°F (200°C) oven for about 1 hour. Serve immediately. To maintain its crispness, do not cover.

Anchovy Pizza

Serves 8
Preparation time 1 hour
Baking time 40 minutes

2 cups strong or bread flour
1½ teaspoons dry yeast
1/2 teaspoon salt
1/4 teaspoon each oregano and dried basil
1 tablespoon honey
1 tablespoon margarine, melted
1/2 cup lukewarm water 110°F (40°C)
3 tablespoons olive oil
3 lb (1½ kg) onions, sliced lengthwise
1/4 teaspoon garlic powder
1/2 teaspoon each oregano, thyme, rosemary
salt and freshly ground pepper
18 anchovy fillets
10 whole Calamata olives, pitted
10 green stuffed olives, sliced

Combine the flour with the dry yeast, salt, oregano, and basil. Make a well in the middle and pour in the honey, water, and margarine. Gradually incorporate the flour from the sides of the well into the liquid with a spoon, and continue kneading with your hands until a soft, pliable dough is formed. Or put all the ingredients in a mixer bowl and knead with the hook for 8 minutes. Cover with plastic wrap and allow to rise in a warm place for 1 hour until doubled in bulk. Meanwhile, combine the oil, onions, garlic powder, and herbs in a pan, cover and simmer until the onions are nearly transparent. Pat the dough into the bottom of an oiled 12-inch (30-cm) pizza pan and spread the onion mixture evenly on the surface of the dough up to 1-inch (2-cm) of the sides. Scatter the anchovies and olives here and there on top of the onions. Allow to rise for 30 minutes. Bake in a 400°F (200°C) oven for 40 minutes, until the edges are browned. Serve immediately.

ANCHOVY PIZZA

Appetizer Assortment for Buffet

30 mini Arab pocket breads
1/3 cup olive oil
1 teaspoon Italian herbs
1/4 teaspoon garlic powder
1/4 teaspoon freshly ground pepper
fried eggplant or zucchini rounds
cooked scallops
cooked, marinated octopus
fried squid rings
fried onion rings
large white mushrooms, sliced
rocket leaves
pesto sauce (see basic recipes)
olive paste (see basic recipes)
pine nut salad (see basic recipes)
eggplant salad (see basic recipes)
pimento salad (see basic recipes)
fish roe salad (see basic recipes)

cherry tomatoes and cucumber slices
flat leaf parsley

Mix the olive oil, herbs, and garlic powder in a bowl. Brush some on each bread and fry briefly in a non-stick pan. Arrange on a large platter and spread each with the sauce or salad of your choice, combined with the various other ingredients as: pesto sauce with octopus, olive paste with mushrooms and rocket, fish roe salad with scallops and parsley, pimento sauce with fried eggplant or zucchini, pine nut salad with fried squid or onion rings, and eggplant salad with chopped tomato and green peppers. Garnish the appetizer tray with lemon slices and rocket leaves.

Greek Flatbread (Laganes)

Yields 4 breads
Preparation time 12 hours
Baking time 20 minutes

2 cups lukewarm water (110°F/40°C)
1 heaping tablespoon dry yeast or
2 oz (60 g) fresh yeast
2 tablespoons sugar
6-7 cups strong or all purpose flour
2 teaspoons salt
2 tablespoons olive oil
3 tablespoons sesame seeds

Dissolve the yeast and sugar in the lukewarm water and set aside for 8-10 minutes until foamy. Add 2 cups of flour and mix with kneading hook until the batter is smooth. Add the oil, salt, and flour, in small amounts, kneading until the dough gathers on the kneading hook. Continue kneading for 8 minutes until dough is smooth and elastic. Remove from the mixer and divide into 4 balls. Brush each one with a little oil, cover and allow to rise in a warm place until doubled in bulk. Roll out each ball on a floured surface into 4 flat rounds, 6-7 inches (16-18 cm) in diameter. Arrange on lightly greased baking sheets. Brush again with a little oil, cover, and allow to rise until doubled in bulk. Make depressions in the surface of the risen dough with your fingers. Cover and allow to rise another 10 minutes. Brush with a little water and sprinkle with sesame seeds. Bake the laganes in a 400°F (200°C) oven for about 15-20 minutes. As this type of flatbread dries out quickly, it should be eaten the same day. Otherwise, freeze in airtight plastic bags until ready to use for up to 3 months.

Pimento Bread

Yields 2 loaves
Preparation time 1 hour and 30 minutes
Baking time 25-30 minutes

3¹/₂ cups strong or bread flour
1 tablespoon dried yeast or
1 oz (30 g) fresh yeast
1 teaspoon salt
1 teaspoon ground dried ginger
2 tablespoons honey
2 tablespoons olive oil
1 cup lukewarm water (110°F/40°C)

for the filling
5 canned pimentos or red bell peppers, chopped
10 green olives, chopped
2 tablespoons sesame seeds

Mix the flour with the dry yeast, salt, and ginger in a large bowl. If using fresh yeast, dissolve in the warm water, add several spoonfuls of flour and set aside until foamy, for about 10 minutes. Make a well in the center of the flour, add the honey, oil, water or the dissolved fresh yeast, and mix with a spoon, until ingredients are combined. Knead until the dough is smooth and elastic. Cover with plastic wrap and allow to rise in a warm place for 1 hour or until doubled in bulk. Divide into two parts and roll out into two 10-inch (25-cm) squares. Sprinkle the chopped peppers and olives on top and roll up tightly. Put rolls on a lightly oiled baking sheet, cover with a cotton towel and allow to rise in a warm place for 1 hour or until doubled in bulk. Score the tops crosswise with a sharp knife, brush with a water and sprinkle with the sesame seeds. Bake the loaves in a 400°F (200°C) oven for 25-30 minutes, until lightly browned. Serve the same day or wrap in plastic wrap and freeze.

During the last war, the only survival
rations carried by Japanese soldiers
consisted of a bag of soya flour.
Soya can be eaten in a variety
of ways, fresh, dried, plain, sprouting,
ground, fermented, as curd, in soup, as
a dessert or a drink.
It is a curious fact that outside
of Asia there has been so little interest in
so versatile a plant.
Until the 20th century,
Western countries have ignored it, while
rice has been extremely popular – even
though it has nothing like the same
nutritional balance to offer.

S O Y A   D I S H E S

M. Toussaint-Samat, *History of Food*,
trans. A. Bell, Blackwell Publishers, 1992

The soy(a)bean is an Asiatic legume known as *glycine soja* or *max* which is believed to be indigenous to Central and Northeast China where it has been used as food and medicine for over 5000 years. Its cultivation did not spread to Southern Asia until the 17th century and it was unknown in Europe and North America prior to the 19th century. One of the most inexpensive sources of high quality vegetable protein and oil known, 90% or the world supply of soybeans today comes from the USA, Brazil, China, and Argentina.

Compared to other legumes, the soybean contains very little starch in proportion to its protein and oil content, making it an ideal food for humans including diabetics. Depending on the type, ground soybean mash yields 17-25% oil and 30-63% soya flour. Dried soya flour contains 45-50% protein, making it an ideal fodder for fattening animals. Further processing of soya flour results in a 97% protein meat-analog sometimes referred to as TVP – textured vegetable protein – which has the appearance and many of the same characteristics as ground meat. The chemical make-up of soya protein is of particular interest to nutritionists because it contains all the amino acids – the basic molecular units of all proteins – necessary to the human organism. Not only are these amino acids present in balanced amounts suitable for human metabolism, soya also contains iron, calcium, zinc, niacin, thiamin (B_1), riboflavin (B_2), and isoflavones (a natural plant estrogen).

SOYA DISHES

The usefulness of soya flour does not end there. Mixed with water, a white dispersion is derived called soya milk. Also high in protein content, this "milk" is used by people who are sensitive or allergic to cow's milk. From this extract, a cheese-like curd is made, which, when compressed, produces the favorite vegetarian cheese substitute – tofu – and other vegetarian cheeses.

The oil extracted from soybeans is used as cooking oil as well as to make margarine and other vegetable cooking fats. Soya oil contains large amounts of poly-unsaturated fats, linoleic fatty acid 48-54%, oleic fatty acid 21-30% and linolenic acid 10-13%. Soya oil also contains saturated fats, palmitic acid 10-13%, and steric acid 3,5-4,5%. While poly-unsaturated linoleic acid makes soya oil a valuable addition to the human diet, its linolenic content reduces its desirability in the kitchen. This is due to the instability of this fatty acid which, when it oxidizes, imparts an unpleasant odor of rancidity to the oil that not only detracts from its culinary value but may also be harmful. Soya oil is also the source of the emulsifier and stabilizing agent, lechithin, widely used in food processing and the manufacture of cosmetics.

Fans of soya products are many, most of them proponents of vegetarian or macrobiotic diets, who see the soybean as the ultimate food. The soybean is a rare source of genistein and daidzein, two anti-oxidants believed to protect the body against the ravages of cancer, and aging. Although soya was for many years known as "the food of the poor," today it is utilized on a world scale due not only to its nutritional value, but also to its positive role in the biochemistry of the human organism. Thus, its consumption assures the maintenance of the cardiovascular system, the reduction of cholesterol, as well as the balance of blood sugar, and the

prevention of osteoporosis.

The recipes in this section utilize soya as a ground meat substitute. Elsewhere in this book, soya milk, vegetarian (non-diary) cream and cheese are utilized wherever the analogous dairy products would be called for.

SOYA DISHES

Eggplant Stuffed with Soya

Serves 4
Preparation time 1 hour 30 minutes
Cooking time 1 hour

4-5 medium eggplants
1 recipe for soya mince sauce (see recipe page 212)
1/2 cup finely chopped parsley
3 tablespoons vegetarian cream
1¹/₂ cup bechamel sauce (see basic recipes)
1 cup grated vegetarian cheese
10 thin slices tomato
salt and freshly ground pepper

Cut each eggplant in half lengthwise. Score the pulp lengthwise 2-3 times without breaking the outer skin. Sprinkle with salt and drain the eggplant for 1-2 hours. Rinse and squeeze out excess water. Fry in olive oil until lightly browned. Drain on paper towels and arrange in an oven-proof glass casserole. Prepare the soya mince sauce according to the recipe. Stir in the cream and parsley. Make a depression in the center of each eggplant with the back of a spoon and place 2-3 tablespoons of the filling in each one. Spread some bechamel sauce over the filling. Place a slice of tomato on top of each and sprinkle with a little salt and freshly ground pepper. Bake in a 350°F (180°C) oven for about 1 hour until the bechamel is lightly browned. Serve immediately.

Spaghetti with Mushroom Sauce

Serves 4
Preparation time 20 minutes
Cooking time 30 minutes

1/4 cup margarine
7 oz (200 g) oyster mushrooms, cut into strips
1 oz (35 g) dried porcini mushrooms,
1/2 cup dry white wine

1 tablespoon flour
1 tablespoon extra margarine
2/3 cup soya milk
1/3 cup vegetarian cream
1 teaspoon prepared mustard
2 tablespoons finely chopped parsley
salt and freshly ground pepper
10 oz (300 g) spaghetti

Melt the margarine in a pan and saute the oyster mushrooms. Add the wine and the porcini mushrooms, cover, and simmer for 15 minutes, until the porcinis have swelled. Heat the extra margarine in a saucepan and stir in the flour for 1 minute. Pour in the soya milk and cook until the sauce begins to thicken. Stir in the cream and mustard. Pour the sauce into the mushrooms and stir over low heat until the mixture is thick and creamy. Cook the spaghetti in salted water with 2 tablespoons olive oil. Drain and transfer to a heated platter. Pour the mushroom sauce on top and sprinkle with the chopped parsley and freshly ground pepper. Serve immediately

Macaroni Bolognese

Serves 4
Preparation time 15 minutes
Cooking time 30 minutes

14 oz (400 g) elbow macaroni, ziti, or penne
1 recipe for soya mince sauce (see page 212)
1 cup grated vegetarian cheese
10 oz (300 g) oyster mushrooms

Prepare the soya mince sauce according to the recipe. Brush the mushrooms with a little olive oil and grill. Cut into thin strips and combine with the soya mince sauce. Cook until heated through before serving on top of pasta. Cook the pasta al dente in salted water with 2 tablespoons of olive oil and drain. Serve on hot plates topped with sauce and grated cheese.

MACARONI BOLOGNESE

Fried Soya Rissoles

Yields 25-30 pieces
Preparation time 30 minutes
Cooking time 20 minutes

1 medium potato, grated
2 medium carrots, grated
1 large onion, finely chopped
2 cloves garlic, minced
2 cups prepared soya mince (see basic recipes)
1/4 cup finely chopped parsley
1/4 cup finely chopped mint
7 oz (200 g) stale breadcrumbs, soaked and squeezed
1/4 cup tomato paste
3 tablespoons soya sauce
1/4 cup olive oil
2 teaspoons baking powder
3 tablespoons cornstarch
salt and pepper

Blend the potato, carrot, onion, and garlic together in a food processor until uniformly minced. Transfer to a bowl, add the prepared soya mince along with the remaining ingredients. Knead well and refrigerate the mixture for 30 minutes. Form small balls, roll in flour, and fry in hot oil, turning often until all sides are browned. Alternatively, prepare the rissoles substituting the mint and parsley with 1 teaspoon cumin and 1/8 teaspoon ground clove. Shape into oblong rissoles, coat with flour, and fry as above. Prepare a tomato sauce (see basic recipes) and pour over fried rissoles. Serve with basmati rice or mashed potatoes.

Greek Pita with Soya Mince

Yields 20 pieces
Preparation time 1 hour
Baking time 50 minutes

1/2 cup olive oil
2 large onions, finely chopped
14 oz (400 g) canned mushrooms, drained,
and finely minced in food processor
2 tablespoons tomato paste
2 tablespoons ketchup
2 tablespoons balsamic vinegar
1 cup prepared soya mince (see basic recipes)
1/2 cup finely chopped dill or mint
1/2 cup vegetarian cream
1/4 teaspoon allspice
salt and freshly ground pepper
2 sheets commercial puff pastry or 1 lb (450 g)
phyllo sheets or
1 recipe homemade phyllo (see basic recipes)

1/2 cup olive oil for brushing the pastry

Heat the oil in a large pan over high heat and saute the onions until wilted. Add the mushrooms and saute lightly, stirring for 5 minutes. Add the soya mince and continue stirring 6-8 minutes. Dissolve the tomato paste in 1/4 cup water and stir in the ketchup and vinegar. Add and mix with the ingredients in the pan. Cover and simmer for 5 minutes. Stir in the dill, cream, allspice, salt, pepper, and remove from the heat. Lay one sheet of puff pastry in an oven-proof baking pan and brush with a little oil. If using phyllo, lay half the sheets in the pan, brushing each one with oil. Spread the filling on top and cover with the second sheet of puff pastry (or the remaining phyllo sheets, each brushed with oil). Score the pitta with a sharp knife into serving pieces and brush with oil. Bake in a 350°F (180°C) oven for about 50 minutes, until the surface is well-browned. Serve hot.

Velvet Mushroom Soup

Serves 4
Preparation time 15 minutes
Cooking time 30 minutes

10 oz (300 g) white fresh mushrooms, sliced
2 oz (70 g) dried porcini mushrooms
2 tablespoons olive oil
3 tablespoons margarine
1 small onion, grated
1 tablespoon flour
1 cup soya milk
2 cups vegetable stock (see basic recipes)
1 tablespoon finely chopped parsley
1/2 teaspoon powdered coriander
1/4 cup vegetarian cream
salt and freshly ground pepper

Heat the oil with half the margarine in a large pan and saute the onions. Add 2/3 of the fresh mushrooms and porcini mushrooms. Cover and simmer for about 10 minutes, until the porcini have swelled. Dissolve the flour in 3 tablespoons of the vegetable stock and pour into the mushrooms along with the remaining vegetable stock and soya milk. Add the parsley, coriander, salt, and pepper. Simmer for 15 minutes and allow the soup to cool slightly before pouring into the food processor. Blend until smooth. Heat the remaining margarine in a saucepan over medium heat and saute the rest of the mushrooms for 3-4 minutes. Stir into the soup along with the cream. Sprinkle with the finely chopped parsley and serve immediately.

Baked Penne with Soya Mince

Serves 4
Preparation time 1 hour
Cooking time 40-50 minutes

1/2 cup olive oil
1 large onion, finely chopped
2 cloves garlic, minced
1 medium carrot, finely chopped
1 stalk celery, finely chopped
10 oz (300 g) fresh mushrooms, sliced
2 cups prepared soya mince (see basic recipes)
14 oz (400 g) tomato juice
1/4 cup tomato paste
1 teaspoon vinegar
1 teaspoon oregano
salt and freshly ground pepper
10 oz (300 g) penne
1 cup vegetarian cream
1 cup grated vegetarian cheese

Heat the oil in a pan and saute the onions, garlic, carrot, and celery, stirring until the vegetables are wilted. Add the mushrooms and continue cooking for 2 minutes. Add the prepared soya mince and continue stirring on medium heat for another 5 minutes. Stir in the tomato juice, tomato paste, vinegar, oregano, salt, and pepper. Mix well, lower the heat, cover, and simmer for 15 minutes until the sauce is thick. Meanwhile, cook the pasta al dente in salted water with 2 tablespoons olive oil and drain well. Toss the pasta with the soya mince sauce and pour into a lightly oiled 2-quart (2-liter) oven-proof baking dish. Dribble the cream on top, sprinkle with the grated cheese and bake in a 350°F (175°C) oven for about 15 minutes, until the top is lightly browned. Serve immediately.

Soya Mince Sauce

Yields 3 cups sauce
Preparation time 12 hours
Cooking time 30-40 minutes

2 cups prepared soya mince (see basic recipes) or
commercial re-hydrated soya mince substitute
1/2 cup olive oil
1 large onion, grated
2 cloves garlic, minced
1 teaspoon chili powder
1/8 teaspoon cinnamon
1/8 teaspoon ground clove
1/4 teaspoon allspice
3 tablespoons ketchup
3 tablespoons soya sauce
2 tablespoons balsamic vinegar
14 oz (400 g) canned tomatoes, pureed
salt and freshly ground pepper

Heat the oil in a pan and saute the onion and garlic until wilted.

Stir in the prepared soya mince along with the remaining ingredients. Cover and simmer until the soya mince is soft and the sauce has cooked down almost to the oil. Taste and adjust the seasonings. Use the sauce as a substitute for ground meat sauce with cooked pastas or rice, to make moussaka, pastitsio, to stuff cannelloni, vine leaves, and other vegetables such as tomatoes, peppers, and zucchini.

Macaroni Loaf with Soya Mince

Serves 6
Preparation time 2 hours
Cooking time 1 hour

1 recipe for soya mince sauce (see previous recipe)
10 oz (300 g) pastitsio macaroni or ziti
2 tablespoons margarine, in pieces
salt and freshly ground pepper
7 sheets of phyllo dough
2 cups bechamel sauce (see basic recipes)

for the spinach mixture
1 lb (500 g) fresh spinach, trimmed
2 tablespoons olive oil
3 medium leeks, white part only, finely chopped
1/4 cup soya milk
salt and freshly ground pepper

Prepare the soya mince sauce according to the previous recipe. Prepare 2 cups of bechamel sauce and combine 2/3 cup of it with the soya mince sauce. Cook the pasta al dente in salted water with 2 tablespoons olive oil. Drain and stir in the margarine, salt, pepper, and 2/3 cup bechamel sauce. Rinse the spinach, blanch, drain, and squeeze out excess water. Heat the oil in a pan over medium heat and saute the leeks. Add the soya milk, cover, and simmer until the sauce is reduced. Stir in the drained spinach, salt, pepper, the remaining 2/3 cup bechamel sauce. Brush a deep loaf pan with corn oil and line with the phyllo sheets, brushing each one with a little olive oil. Make sure the excess phyllo hangs evenly over the sides of the pan. Spread the spinach mixture evenly on the bottom. Arrange half the cooked pasta lengthwise in straight lines on top of the spinach. Spread the soya mixture over it and arrange the remaining pasta on top. Lift the excess phyllo up from both sides and fold over the macaroni mixture. Brush with oil, tucking in the edges all around. Bake the macaroni loaf in a 400°F (200°C) oven for about 1 hour. Remove from the oven and allow to cool 15 minutes before turning out upside down onto a platter. Slice and serve immediately.

Stuffed Cannelloni

Serves 4-5
Preparation time 1 hour
Cooking time 40 minutes

1 lb (500 g) cannelloni
1 recipe for soya mince sauce (see recipe page 212)
14 oz (400 g) canned sliced mushrooms
salt and freshly ground pepper
2 cups grated vegetarian cheese
2 cups vegetarian cream
1/4 teaspoon ground nutmeg
1 tablespoon finely chopped parsley

Cook the pasta in salted water with 2 tablespoons olive oil. Drain well and lay out on a cotton towel. Prepare the soya mince sauce according to the recipe. Remove from the heat and cool slightly. Stir in the mushrooms, half the cheese and half a cup of cream. Fill the cooked cannelloni with the soya mixture and arrange side by side in a lightly oiled oven-proof baking dish. Stir the nutmeg, salt, and pepper into the remaining cream and pour on top of the cannelloni. Sprinkle with the remaining cheese and bake in a 400°F (200°C) oven for 35-40 minutes. Sprinkle with the parsley and serve immediately.

Spinach, Catalan Style

Serves 4
Preparation time 30 minutes
Cooking time 15 minutes

1 lb (500 g) fresh spinach
3 tablespoons margarine
2 green onions, finely chopped
3 tablespoons golden raisins
1/4 cup pine nuts
1/4 cup vegetarian cream
salt and white pepper

Rinse and trim the spinach, removing thick stems, if necessary. Blanch the spinach and drain well. Melt the margarine in a heavy-bottomed pan and saute the pine nuts. Remove from the pan with a slotted spoon, add the onions and saute for 5 minutes. Add the spinach and cook for another 5 minutes, stirring constantly. Pour in the cream along with the raisins, pine nuts, salt and freshly ground pepper. Cook, stirring the mixture until it is heated through. Serve the spinach hot or at room temperature to accompany soya burgers.

Grilled Soya Mince Burgers

Yields 10-12 patties
Preparation time 30 minutes
Cooking time 20 minutes

2 cups prepared soya mince (see basic recipes)
3/4 cup grated onion
1 medium potato, cooked
1 small tomato, grated
1 clove garlic, minced
1 teaspoon oregano
1 teaspoon thyme
3 tablespoons soya sauce
1/4 cup olive oil
3-4 oz (100 g) day-old bread, soaked
and lightly squeezed
salt and freshly ground pepper

Combine all the ingredients in a bowl and knead until the mixture is light and uniform. Form into burgers, coat with flour and fry in olive oil until well-browned on both sides. Or brush both sides with olive oil and grill under the broiler. Serve with mashed potatoes, Catalan spinach, and the tomato sauce of your choice (see basic recipes).

Eggplant Rolls Stuffed with Soya Mince

Serves 5-6
Preparation time 1 hour
Baking time 1 hour

4 lb (2 kg) long thin eggplant
1 recipe for soya mince sauce (see page 212)
1/2 cup finely chopped parsley or dill
2 tablespoons dried breadcrumbs
1/2 cup grated vegetarian cheese
salt and freshly ground pepper
1 recipe tomato-garlic sauce (see basic recipes)

Rinse the eggplant and slice lengthwise into strips 1/4 inch (1/2 cm) thick. Sprinkle with salt and drain for 1 hour. Rinse and squeeze out excess water. Fry lightly in olive oil, drain and cool on absorbent paper. Prepare the soya mince sauce according to the recipe. Stir in the parsley, breadcrumbs, and cheese. Put a tablespoonful of the mixture at one end of each eggplant strip and roll up. Arrange side by side in an oven-proof glass baking dish. Pour the tomato sauce on top and sprinkle with a little pepper. The dish may be frozen at this stage. Bake in a 400°F (200°C) oven for about 1 hour. Serve immediately.

Creamed Potatoes

Serves 4
Preparation time 20 minutes
Baking time 30 minutes

3 lb (1½ kg) potatoes, thinly sliced
1/4 cup margarine
2 tablespoons flour
1½ cups soya milk, scalded
1 cup water
2 teaspoons prepared mustard
1/8 teaspoon ground nutmeg
salt and freshly ground pepper
1/4 cup finely chopped parsley

Cook the potatoes in salted water for 15 minutes, until half-cooked. Melt the margarine over medium heat and stir in the flour for 1 minute. Stirring vigorously, pour in the soya milk and water. Cook, stirring until the sauce is slightly thick and remove from the heat. Mix the mustard, nutmeg, salt, and pepper with 2-3 tablespoons of the sauce, return the mixture to the pan and mix with the rest of sauce. Add the potatoes and gently mix until coated. Transfer the potato mixture to an oven-proof baking dish and bake in a 400°F (200°C) oven for 30 minutes, until the surface is lightly browned. Sprinkle with the parsley and freshly ground pepper. Serve immediately.

BASIC RECIPES

Easy Puff Pastry

Yields 1 lb (500 g) of dough
Preparation time 2 hours

2	cups (8 oz/250 g) flour
1	teaspoon salt
1	cup (8 oz/250 g) cold margarine, shaved
1/2	cup cold water

Sift the flour and salt into a large bowl. Cut the margarine into the flour with a pastry blender until the mixture resembles coarse crumbs. Add just enough water to hold the crumbs together and gently work the dough until it pulls away from the sides of the bowl. Gather the dough into a large ball and wrap in plastic wrap. Refrigerate for about 45 minutes or place in the freezer for half the time. Place the cold dough on a cool surface lightly dusted with flour and gently flatten it with the rolling pin. Sprinkle the surface of the dough with flour and roll out to a rectangle about 5x15 inches (13-x38 cm). Lift and fold the short ends to meet in the center and fold in half along that center line. Turn dough a 1/4 of a circle (90°) around, bringing the folded edges to the sides with one open end towards you. Roll out again into a rectangle and repeat the folding procedure. Wrap the dough in plastic wrap and refrigerate for 30 minutes. Repeat the entire procedure one more time. The dough keeps for 2-3 days in the refrigerator and for 6 months in the freezer.

Pizza Dough

Yields one 14-inch (35-cm) pizza
Preparation time 2 hours

2-2½	cups all purpose flour
3/4	cup hot water
1	envelope (1/4 oz/7 g) dry yeast
1	tablespoon sugar
1	tablespoon olive oil
1/2	teaspoon salt
2	teaspoons oregano (optional)

Combine the yeast with the flour and oregano, if used. Dissolve the sugar and salt in the water, pour into the flour mixture along with the oil and mix. Knead until the dough is soft and elastic. Roll the dough into a 14-inch (35-cm) round and pat into the bottom of a pizza pan. Allow the dough to rise for 10 minutes before arranging the pizza toppings on it.

Phyllo Dough

Yields about 1 lb (500 g) dough
Preparation time 1½-2 hours

1 lb	(500 g) all purpose flour
2	tablespoons olive oil
1	tablespoon vinegar
2	teaspoons salt
2	teaspoons baking powder
1	cup lukewarm water
	cornstarch for rolling out

Sift the flour into a large bowl with the salt and baking powder. Make a well in the center and pour in the oil, vinegar, and water. Using your hands, gradually draw the flour from around the sides into the center and continue blending until mixed. Gather the dough into a ball and gently knead adding enough water (if needed) until the dough is soft and smooth. Divide the dough into small balls, according to the number of phyllo sheets needed and the size of the pan. Place the balls side by side in a floured pan and cover with a plastic wrap and a damp towel. Allow to rest for 1-2 hours. On a floured surface, flatten each ball with a long thin rolling pin and roll out into very thin sheets. To roll the dough extra thin, roll each sheet around the rolling pin, pressing lightly while rolling backwards and forwards. To prevent sticking, frequently sprinkle a little corn or wheat starch on the sheet as your work. To save time, flatten three balls of dough, brush each generously with olive oil, and lay one on top of the other. Roll them out into one large round sheet. When baked, the layers will separate. You may also roll out five layers at a time, using it for the bottom of the pitta. Roll out the top multiple-layered phyllo into a sheet a bit larger than the baking pan and "pleat" it to fit the top of the pitta. This is the way "village" (horiatiki) pittas are made in the country (see photo on page 193).

Soya Mince (Ground Meat Substitute)

Yields 2 cups, about 1 lb (500 g) mince
Preparation time 12 hours

1	cup dried textured soya protein
4	cups water or vegetable stock
1	teaspoon salt
1/4	teaspoon pepper

Soak the soya protein in a bowl with the water or the stock, salt, and pepper overnight to swell. The next day, strain in a sieve and squeeze out the excess water. Use in the recipe of your choice as a substitute for ground meat. A tastier product results if soya is soaked in vegetable stock.

Thousand Island Dressing

Yields 1 cup dressing
Preparation time 10 minutes

2/3	cup eggless mayonnaise
2	tablespoons chili sauce
1	teaspoon grated onion
1	teaspoon prepared mustard
1	tablespoon ketchup
1	tablespoon finely chopped pickles
2	tablespoons finely chopped stuffed green olives

Blend the ingredients in a food processor for 2 minutes until smooth. Serve the dressing with seafood or on green salads. The dressing keeps for 2 weeks in the refrigerator.

Vinaigrette Dressing

Yields 3/4 cup dressing
Preparation time 10 minutes

1/2	cup olive oil
1/4	cup wine vinegar
1/2	teaspoon salt and freshly ground pepper
1	small clove garlic, minced
1	teaspoon prepared mustard or
1	teaspoon Italian Herbs
5	drops Tabasco sauce

Shake the ingredients in a well-sealed jar until blended. Use on salads. The dressing keeps for 2 weeks in the refrigerator.

Balsamic Dressing

Yields 3/4 cup dressing
Preparation time 10 minutes

1/4	cup balsamic vinegar
1/2	cup olive oil
2	tablespoons basil, parsley, or mint, finely chopped
	salt and freshly ground pepper

Shake the ingredients in a well-sealed jar until blended. Use on salads and grilled vegetables. The dressing keeps for 1 week in the refrigerator.

Bechamel Sauce

Yields 1 cup sauce
Preparation time 15 minutes

1	cup soy milk or 1½ cups vegetarian cream
2	tablespoons margarine
2	tablespoons cornstarch or flour
1/8	teaspoon ground nutmeg
	salt and white pepper

Scald the soy milk just to the boiling point. Heat the margarine in a saucepan over medium hea, add the cornstarch or flour and cook for 1 minute, stirring continuously. Pour in the scalded milk and continue stirring until the sauce thickens. Remove from the heat and stir in the nutmeg, salt, and pepper. If it is too thick, stir in several tablespoons of soy milk to obtain the desired consistency. At this stage, the bechamel may be refrigerated. Nutmeg may be substituted by other aromatics such as thyme, tarragon, or allspice. For a garlic-flavored sauce, saute 1 slivered garlic clove in the margarine. Remove and discard before adding the flour.

Olive Paste (Pasta Di Oliva)
Poor Man's Caviar

Yields 1 cup paste
Preparation time 30 minutes

3	cups pitted black olives, sliced
3	tablespoons olive oil (optional)
2	tablespoons balsamic or wine vinegar
1-2	cloves garlic, minced

Process the ingredients in the blender or food processor for several seconds until the mixture is smooth and well-blended. Use as a dip or spread with crackers, breadsticks, crudites, on sandwiches, or as a sauce for cooked pasta. Alternatively, blend 1/4 cup ground cashews along with the other ingredients.

Pesto

Yields 1 cup sauce
Preparation time 20 minutes

3	cups fresh basil leaves
1-2	cloves garlic
1 oz	(30 g) pine nuts
	salt and freshly ground pepper
2	tablespoons lemon juice or balsamic vinegar
1/4	cup olive oil

Pulse the garlic, pine nuts, salt, pepper, and lemon juice (or vinegar) in the blender or food processor until the mixture is smooth. With the motor running, add the basil leaves and finally, add the olive oil in a thin steady stream until it has all been absorbed and the mixture is thick and uniform. Serve pesto with cooked pasta or seafood. Blanch the basil leaves for a smoother textured pesto.

Mushroom Sauce

Yields 2½ cups sauce
Preparation time 10 minutes
Cooking time 10 minutes

2	tablespoons margarine
1	clove garlic, minced
2	tablespoons onion, finely grated
7 oz	(200 g) canned sliced mushrooms, drained
2	tablespoons flour
1½	cups soy milk, scalded
2	tablespoons finely chopped parsley
	salt and freshly ground pepper

Melt the margarine in a saucepan and saute the garlic and onions until wilted. Add the mushrooms and saute until lightly browned. Sprinkle with flour and stir for 1 minute. Stir in the scalded milk, salt, and pepper. Continuously stirring, simmer the sauce for 5-10 minutes until thick. Sprinkle with the parsley and serve on cooked pasta, fried potatoes, or rice.

Vegetable Stock

Yields 6-8 cups stock
Preparation time 15 minutes
Cooking time 30-35 minutes

1	large onion, sliced lengthwise
1	large carrot, thinly sliced
1	leek, white part only, chopped
5	sprigs of flat-leaf parsley
1	small stalk celery, chopped
3	cloves garlic (optional)
2	bay leaves (optional)
3	sprigs of fresh thyme or
1/2	teaspoon dried thyme
1	small bell pepper (optional)
6	cups water
2	teaspoons salt,
10	peppercorns
1½	cups dry white wine (optional)

Combine all the ingredients except for the wine and peppercorns in a large pan. Bring to a boil, lower the heat, cover, and simmer for 10-20 minutes. Add the wine and peppercorns and continue simmering for another 15 minutes. Cool and strain the stock through a fine sieve. Refrigerate up to 3-4 days. Or freeze in small amounts in plastic containers or plastic bags for up to 2 months for use as needed. Alternatively, cook 1 chopped sour green apple with the vegetables.

Tomato-Onion Sauce

Yields 1½ cups sauce
Preparation time 25 minutes

3	tablespoons olive oil

```
1       small onion, grated
1       clove garlic, minced
1       cup tomato juice
2       tablespoons dry red wine
1       teaspoon sugar
        salt and freshly ground pepper
1       small red pepper, finely chopped
2       tablespoons finely chopped parsley or basil
```

Heat the oil in a saucepan and saute the onions and garlic until wilted. Add the wine along with the remaining ingredients and simmer the sauce until slightly thick. Serve with cooked pasta, fried potatoes, or cooked soya rissoles.

Tomato-Garlic Sauce

Yields 1½ cup sauce
Preparation time 35 minutes

```
3       tablespoons olive oil
2       cloves garlic, slivered
1       small hot pepper, quartered (optional)
2       cups pureed tomato pulp, fresh or canned
1-2     tablespoons ketchup
        salt and freshly ground pepper
```

Heat the oil in a saucepan and saute the garlic and hot pepper, if used, for 1 minute. Remove with a slotted spoon, drain over the pan, and discard. Stir the tomatoes, ketchup, salt, and pepper into the flavored oil. Cover and simmer for 30 minutes. Strain through a fine sieve to obtain a smooth, uniform sauce.

Sesame Sauce

Yields 1 cup
Preparation time 10 minutes

```
2       tablespoons Dijon mustard
3       tablespoons honey
2       tablespoons balsamic vinegar
1/3     cup sesame oil
1/3     cup sesame seeds, toasted
2       cloves garlic, minced
1/2     teaspoon powdered ginger
        salt and freshly ground pepper
```

Process all the ingredients together in the blender until smooth and uniform. The sauce is excellent with grilled vegetables and seafood. Or you may add 1/2 cup of red wine and use it to marinate vegetables or seafood before grilling.

Pimiento Sauce

Yields 1½ cups sauce
Preparation time 45-50 minutes

```
2       large canned red chillies or pimientos
1       hot red pepper
3       small ripe tomatoes
2       cloves garlic
1       small onion
1/3     cup olive oil
1       tablespoon finely chopped cilantro or parsley
2       tablespoons vinegar
        salt and freshly ground pepper
```

Drain and chop the pimientos, tomatoes, garlic, and onion. Puree in the food processor. Heat the oil in a saucepan, add the puree, and simmer until the sauce begins to thicken. Add the remaining ingredients, salt, and pepper. Continually stirring, cook until it comes to a boil. Remove from the heat. Serve cold as an appetizer dip or hot with cooked pasta or seafood.

Marinated Olives

Serves 4
Preparation time 12 hours

```
8 oz    (240 g) black Greek olives (Calamata)
2       tablespoons olive oil
2       cloves garlic, slivered
2       tablespoons vinegar
1       teaspoon oregano
1       teaspoon thyme
```

Heat the oil in a frying pan and saute the garlic. Remove with a slotted spoon, drain over the pan, and discard. Add the olives and stir in the hot garlic flavored oil for 1-2 minutes. Pour in the vinegar and sprinkle with the herbs. Stir and remove from the heat. Let them cool and marinate for 12 hours before serving. A delicious appetizer for ouzo. Use also in salads or to accompany pasta dishes.

Roasted Pepper Sauce

Yields 4 cups sauce
Preparation time 20 minutes
Cooking time 40-60 minutes

```
2 lb    (1 kg) fresh pimiento or red bell peppers
2 lb    (1 kg) ripe tomatoes
1       cup olive oil
6-8     cloves garlic, minced
1/4     cup finely chopped parsley
1/4     teaspoon cayenne or hot red pepper flakes
        salt and freshly ground pepper
```

Roast the peppers and cool in a bowl covered with a plastic wrap. Peel off the skin, and remove the stem, deseed, and devein. Chop finely. Peel the tomatoes and cut in half. Make several cris-cross slashes and squeeze out the seeds with your hands, and chop finely. Put them in a pan with oil, garlic, and parsley and simmer, stirring occasionally until thick. Add the chopped peppers, salt, pepper, and cayenne (or red pepper flakes) to your liking. Continue cooking until the sauce has cooked down almost to the oil. Alternatively, blanch the peppers, drain well, and chop coarsely. Put them in a baking dish with the tomatoes, oil, garlic, cayenne, and a little salt. Bake in a 300°F (150°C) oven for about 3 hours, until all the liquid evaporates and only the oil remains. Keep refrigerated to use as needed, for up to 2 months. Before serving the sauce, add some vinegar (to your liking). Serve the pepper sauce with toast or crackers as an appetizer. To create another tasty appetizer dip, combine equal amounts of pepper sauce and grilled eggplant pulp.

Taramosalata (Fish Roe Dip)

Serves 6-8
Preparation time 10 minutes

```
7 oz    (200 g) stale crustless bread
7 oz    (200 g) taramas, salted fish roe
2       tablespoons onion, finely minced
3/4     cup virgin olive oil combined with
3/4     cup corn oil
1/4     cup lemon juice
3       green onions, finely chopped
```

Soak the bread and squeeze out the excess water with your hands. Put the fish roe, grated onion, and 1/3 of the oil mixture into the blender or food processor and process several seconds until smooth. With the motor on, add the bread in small amounts. Then add the remaining oil in a thin, steady stream. Finally, add the lemon juice, a little at a time, and continue processing for a few seconds, until the mixture is thick and pale pink. Transfer the taramosalata to a small dish, sprinkle with the chopped green onion, and garnish with small black olives. It may be kept in the refrigerator for up to 7 days. Alternatively, mix the taramosalata with 3-4 tablespoons of blanched ground almonds or walnuts.

Potato-Garlic Sauce, Island Style

Yields 2 cups
Preparation time 20 minutes

5-6	cloves garlic, minced
3/4	teaspoon salt
2	medium potatoes (7oz/200 g), cooked
2 oz	(60 g) grated stale bread, without crusts
1/4	cup vinegar
1/3	cup water
1/2	cup olive oil

Process the ingredients in a food processor at medium speed for 2 minutes, or until smooth and uniform. If the mixture is too thick, add a little water and blend for a few more seconds. Serve the garlic sauce with fried cod or galeos (dogfish), fried, grilled, or roasted vegetables such as zucchini, eggplant, peppers, mushrooms as well as with cooked green beans, beets, broccoli, or other vegetables.

Cocktail Sauce

Yields 1¼ cup
Preparation time 5 minutes

1	cup commercial eggless mayonnaise
2	tablespoons chili sauce or ketchup
1	teaspoon Worcestershire sauce
1	teaspoon horseradish
1	teaspoon lemon juice
	pinch of salt and pepper

Combine the ingredients in a bowl and stir gently until well-mixed. Refrigerate until ready to use.

Sun-Dried Tomatoes

To make sun-dried tomatoes at home, choose firm ripe tomatoes. Rinse and wipe dry. Cut in half and lay out on a board, one next to the other with the cut sides up. Sprinkle cut surfaces completely with coarse salt and expose to the sun. Protect from rain or damp. The drying process takes 15-20 days, depending on the weather, during which the tomatoes will shrink and wrinkle. Thread on a heavy string and hang up in the sun with a bowl underneath (to catch any remaining juice) until they are completely dried. The drying step can be speeded up initially by placing the tomatoes in a very slow oven for 15-20 minutes and then stringing them. When they are completely dried, enclose in cheesecloth or muslin bags and hang in a cool, dark, well-ventilated place. To re-hydrate the tomatoes, first rinse under running water. Place in warm water to cover for several hours until they swell. Then rinse and drain well. Sun-dried tomatoes may be used in sauces for pasta, salads, vegetable stews, and in bread. Coated with flour, dipped in a thin batter, and fried in hot olive oil, dried tomatoes make a delicious appetizer.

Crepes

Yields 26 crepes (8 in/20 cm)
Preparation time 1 hour

2	cups all-purpose flour
1/2	teaspoon salt
1	teaspoon sugar
4	tablespoons corn oil
2½	cups ice cold soda water (club soda)

Put all the ingredients in a blender or food processor and beat for 1 minute to make a thin, smooth batter. Do not over-beat. Refrigerate the batter for 30 minutes. Brush the bottom of an 8-in (20-cm) non-stick frying pan with oil, heat, and pour in 2 tablespoons of batter. Tip the pan in a circular motion to evenly spread the batter. When the crepe is lightly browned on one side, turn over with a spatula and cook on the other side. Or use a crepe-maker. Pile the cooked crepes on a plate with baking paper in between. Seal cooked crepes in an air-tight bag and freeze until ready to use.

Potato Gnocchi

Serves 4
Preparation time 1 hour
Cooking time 5 minutes

1lb	(500 g) baking potatoes
3/4	cup flour
1/2	teaspoon salt
1/4	teaspoon white pepper

Scrub the potatoes, and cook in their jackets in salted water for 40 minutes, or until easily pierced with a fork. Drain, cool slightly, and peel. Press through a sieve and mix in a bowl with the salt and pepper. Work with your hands, adding enough flour to make a smooth dough which comes away easily from your fingers. The amount of flour needed depends on the moistness of the potatoes. The less flour used, the lighter the gnocchi will be. Take care not to overwork the dough. Roll the dough into several 1-inch (2-cm) thick-rolls. With a floured knife, cut each roll into 1/2-inch (1-cm) rounds and flatten slightly with your fingers. Press the tines of a floured fork lightly against the surface of each gnocchi. Keep the rolls you are not working with covered with plastic wrap in the refrigerator. Arrange the finished gnocchi side by side on a sheet lined with baking paper and cover with plastic wrap. Refrigerate for up to 3 hours. Drop the gnocchi into a large pan of boiling salted water with 2 tablespoons of olive oil and cook until they rise to the surface, about 2-3 minutes. Remove with a slotted spoon and place in an oiled serving dish. Serve as is with the sauce of your choice or brown under the broiler for a couple of minutes.

Tahini Sauce

Yields 1½ cup sauce
Preparation time 10 minutes

1-2	cloves garlic, minced
1/3	cup tahini (sesame seed paste)
1½	cup water
2-3	tablespoons lemon juice
1/4	teaspoon salt and freshly ground white pepper

Pound the garlic with the salt in a wooden mortar and gradually blend in the tahini. Add the water, a little at a time, working it into the sauce until the desired consistency is reached. Add as much lemon juice as desired, and a pinch of white pepper. Adjust the salt to your liking. Use as a dip, a dressing on salads, or as a sauce for grilled and cooked vegetables. It keeps up to a month in an airtight container in the refrigerator. Alternatively, process all the ingredients with half the water in a blender until smooth. Add extra water, as needed.

Pine Nut & Eggplant Salad

Serves 4-6
Preparation time 30 minutes

1	cup pine nuts
2 lb	(1 kg) eggplant
1/4	teaspoon salt
2	cloves garlic, minced
1/4	cup olive oil or tahini
1/4	cup vinegar or lemon juice
	freshly ground pepper

finely chopped parsley for garnish

Pulse the pine nuts in the blender to form a smooth paste. Rinse and wipe the eggplants dry and wrap each separately in aluminum foil. Grill over charcoal or under the broiler until the skins are burnt and the pulp is soft. Turn often so they cook on all sides. Plunge into cold water and peel immediately to prevent discoloration of the pulp. Drain in a colander and cut crosswise into pieces. Blend in a processor with the garlic, salt, pepper, and ground pine nuts. With the motor on, add the oil a drop at a time in the beginning, and then in a thin, steady stream. If using tahini, add a little at a time. Then, slowly add the vinegar or lemon juice, a little at a time to avoid curdling. Transfer the mixture into a bowl, cover with plastic wrap, and refrigerate. Alternatively, substitute the garlic with 2 tablespoons finely grated onion. For a spicier taste, add several drops of Tabasco sauce. Sprinkle with the parsley before serving.

Pepper Salad

Serves 4
Preparation time 2 hours 30 minutes

3	large red bell peppers, coarsely chopped
3	large green bell peppers, coarsely chopped
1/4	cup olive oil
5	cloves garlic, minced
2	tablespoons vinegar
1 lb	(500 g) tomatoes, peeled, seeded, and cut into small cubes
2	tablespoons ketchup
1/4	teaspoon cayenne and a pinch of salt
	finely chopped parsley

Heat the oil in a frying pan and saute the peppers. Remove from the heat and stir in the remaining ingredients. Refrigerate for 2 hours and serve cold sprinkled with finely chopped parsley.

Avocado Sauce

Yields 1 cup sauce
Preparation time 10 minutes

2	large ripe avocados
1/4	cup lemon juice
2-3	cloves garlic, minced
1	hot green pepper
2-3	tablespoons finely chopped cilantro or parsley
1/4	cup vegetarian cream (optional) or
2	tablespoons olive oil
	salt and freshly ground pepper

Peel and pit the avocados, chop coarsely, and sprinkle immediately with the lemon juice. Blend in a food processor with the remaining ingredients (except for the cream) until smooth. Add enough cream according to desired consistency, less for dip, more for sauce. If not using cream, add olive oil.

Greek Pitta Bread

Yields 6 pittas
Preparation time 2 hours
Cooking time 5-7 minutes

1½	cups all purpose flour
1	teaspoon salt
1	teaspoon dry yeast
2	teaspoons sugar
2	tablespoons olive oil
1/2	cup hot water (100°F/40°C)
	cornmeal for dusting

Combine the flour in a mixer bowl with the salt, yeast, and sugar. Add the oil and water and knead gently until dough pulls away from the sides of the bowl. Allow to rise until doubled in bulk and punch down.

Divide into 6 portions and roll out into 8-in (20-cm) rounds, 1/4-inch (0,5 cm) thick. Dust both sides with cornmeal and allow to rise for 10 minutes. Press parallel lines into the pittas with the tines of a large fork, taking care not to cut through to the bottom. Brush a non-stick frying pan with oil and place on high heat. Fry the pittas for 3 minutes on each side, until they begin to brown. Immediately put the fried pittas into a plastic bag. When they are cool, seal the bag and freeze until ready to use. The pittas can be kept for up to 2 months.

Batter for Frying

Yields 2 cups
Preparation time 1 hour

1	cup all purpose flour
	salt and pepper, to taste
1	tablespoons olive oil
1	cup beer or soda water (club soda)

Sift the flour, salt, and pepper into a bowl. Make a well in the center and add the oil and beer or soda water. Alternatively, dissolve a tiny piece (the size of a chickpea) of fresh yeast in 1 cup of tap water. Gradually mix with the flour until a smooth, thin batter is formed. For a thicker batter, add more flour. Allow the batter to rest for 1 hour before using or it will not stick to the fish or vegetables dipped in it. Alternatively, process all the ingredients in a blender for 1 minute until smooth. Do not overbeat.

Garlic Sauce with Bread and Nuts

Yields 2 cups
Preparation time 15 minutes

7 oz	(200 g) stale crustless bread
1/2	cup chopped walnuts, pinenuts, hazelnuts, or almonds
3-4	cloves garlic, minced
2-3	tablespoons vinegar
	salt and freshly ground pepper
1/4	cup olive oil

Soak the bread in water and squeeze lightly with your hands. Pound the garlic in a wooden mortar with 1/4 teaspoon salt and the nuts. Transfer to a food processor, add the bread and blend the mixture, adding water as needed to form a smooth thick sauce. With the motor on, add the oil in a thin, steady stream. Add vinegar, salt, and pepper, to taste. Serve with fried and cooked vegetables or seafood.

Garlic Sauce

Yields 4 cups
Preparation time 10 minutes

4	tablespoons extra virgin olive oil
2-3	cloves garlic, minced
4	tablespoons flour
1/2	teaspoon salt
5-6	tablespoons vinegar
4	cups hot water

Heat the oil in a saucepan and lightly saute the garlic. Stir in the flour and cook until lightly browned. Stirring vigorously, add the vinegar and immediately afterwards, the hot water. Stirring continuously, cook until the sauce is smooth and creamy. Add salt to taste. Serve the sauce with fried vegetables or fish.

Sauteed Vegetables

Serves 4
Preparation time 15-20 minutes

1 lb	(500 g) fresh or frozen vegetables such as

carrots, peas, zucchini, artichokes, asparagus, green beans, corn, and mushrooms.

3-4	tablespoons margarine
2	tablespoons lemon juice
	salt and freshly ground pepper
2	tablespoons finely chopped parsley, dill, or mint

Peel and rinse the vegetables. Cut the larger ones into pieces. Put them in a pan with the margarine and a small amount of water. Cover and simmer on low heat until all the water has evaporated, the vegetables are tender, and coated with a thin film of fat. Remove from the heat, pour the lemon juice on top, and sprinkle with salt, pepper, and the herb of your choice. Serve hot with fish and seafood.

Fish Stock

Yields 4 cups
Preparation time 30 minutes
Cooking time 45-50 minutes

1 lb	(500 g) bones or backs of sole or flatfish, fins and tails cut off

1	medium onion, sliced
1	stalk celery, in pieces
1	carrot, peeled, cut into pieces
1	small leek, peeled, cut into pieces
1	clove garlic (optional)
1	cup dry white wine
1	tablespoon lemon juice
6	sprigs of parsley
1	bay leaf
6	whole peppercorns

Put the fish bones, onion, celery, carrot, leek, garlic, and a little salt into a large pan with 4 cups (1 liter) of water and bring to a boil over low heat. Skim off the scum that forms on the surface. Add the remaining ingredients, cover, and simmer for 40 minutes. Remove from the heat, and strain through a colander lined with cheesecloth. Allow the stock to cool. It keeps in the refrigerator for up to 3 days. After that, keep in the freezer to use as needed. Put 1 cup of stock into each of 4 heavy-duty freezer bags or plastic containers, tie or cover securely. Before freezing, allow to gel in the refrigerator. The stock may be kept in the freezer for up to 2 months.

USEFUL INFORMATION for the accurate measurement of ingredients

Measuring systems used in cooking vary from country to country. The basic systems in use around the world are the following:

1. Imperial: Used mainly in England and Australia, in this system, dry ingredients are measured in Imperial ounces (oz) and liquid, in fluid ounces (fl.oz).

2. Metric: Used in the European Union (EU), dry ingredients are measured in grams (g) (1000 g=1 kilo) and liquids in cubic centimeters (ml).

3. American: Most ingredients, whether dry or liquid are measured in the standard measuring cup based on a volume of 240 ml. The weight of one cup of different ingredients varies, i.e:

1 cup of ingredient	weighs (approx)	oz	g
Bread crumbs, dry	"	3,5	100
Butter or margarine	"	8	225
Cheese, freshly grated	"	4	115
Chocolate chips	"	6	170
Cocoa	"	4	115
Cream, heavy (35%)	"	8	225
Cream whipped	"	4,5	125
Flour, all - purpose	"	4,5	125
Honey	"	12	350
Milk, fresh whole	"	8,5	240
Nutmeats, ground or grated	"	5-6	140-170
Olive Oil	"	8	225
Rice, uncooked	"	8	225
Sugar, granulated	"	7-8	200-225
Sugar, powdered	"	6	170

Conversion formula: oz to g, multiply oz by 28.35; g to oz, multiply g by .035

Listed below are some approximate equivalents of grated or chopped ingredients frequently used:

1 cup whipping cream	yields	2-2½ c. whipped cream
1 lb fresh crabmeat	"	3 cups
5 large eggs	"	1 cup
8 egg white	"	1 cup
1 large onion	"	1c. chopped onion
1 small onion	"	1/4c. chopped onion
1 bunch (8) green onion	"	1c. chopped
8 oz (500 g) macaroni	"	4c. cooked
1 large selery stalk	"	1/2c. sliced or chopped
3 carrots (1/2 lb)	"	1½ sliced or shredded
1 cup rice	"	3c. cooked

The recipes in this book are given in (°F) and Celcius (°C). The oven should be preheated to the temperature specified, unless specified otherwise. If you have a convection type oven, temperature should be set 65°F (20°C) degrees less than given. When baking or roasting, food should be placed low in the oven so the surface is in the middle of the oven. Place the pan higher when the surface has to brown quickly.

Measuring equivalents

measures	symbol	metric system	symbol
1 teaspoon	tsp	5 cub.centimeters	ml
1 tablespoon	tbsp	15 cub.centimeters	ml
1 fluid ounce	fl. oz	30 cub.centimeters	ml
1 cup	c	0,24 litre	l
1 pint	pt	0,47 litre	l
1 quart	qt	0,95 litre	l
1 ounce	oz	28,35 grams	g
1 pound	lb	0,45 kilogram	kg

Oven temperature chart

	electric		gas range
	°F	°C	regulator
very slow oven	225	110	1/4
	250	120	1 /2
slow	275	140	1
	300	150	2
moderately hot	325	160	3
	350	180	4
	375	190	5
hot	400	200	6
	425	220	7
very hot	450	230	8
	475	250	9

GLOSSARY*

Amaranth: Large pointed green leaf vegetable similar to beet greens.

Balsamic vinegar: Slightly sweet tasting vinegar with origins dating back to 11th c. Italy. The flavor and price vary according to how it's made. The traditional and most expensive is produced from the wines of either Modena or Reggio Emilia provinces of Northern Italy and aged and mellowed in a varied series of wooden casks. The less expensive commercial type is a blend of high quality wine vinegar, young traditional balsamic vinegar, and caramel.

Barley rusks: Thick slices of twice-baked bread made from wheat and barley flour. Also known as hard-tack or paximadia (Greece).

Basmati rice: An aromatic long-grain rice from India.

Bouillabaisse: Ancient Mediterranean fishermen's stew or soup made with several kinds of fish, shellfish, and wine.

Blanching or parboiling: A method of par-cooking foods by plunging them briefly into boiling water to soften or remove strong flavors, salt, or bitterness.

Braise: Method of cooking with very little liquid in a closed vessel.

Bream: Family of Mediterranean fish including red snapper, gilt-head or sea bream. See introduction to fish chapter, page 116.

Bric: Salmon roe. Little round pink flavorful eggs resembling tiny glass beads. An attractive, delicious garnish for seafood appetizers and other dishes.

Bulgur: Cracked wheat which has been soaked, cooked, and dried before the bran is removed. Widely used in the Mediterranean as a substitute for rice.

Calamata olives: Black Greek pointed olives preserved in brine. Meaty in texture yet fruity in taste, they are considered to be the finest quality eating olives. Available at gourmet markets.

Capers: Flower buds or tender seed pods of the caper bush pickled in brine or vinegar. In some Greek islands tender sprigs and leaves of the caper bush are also pickled or dried in a well-ventilated place and used in salads. These must be soaked in water and blanched 3 times to remove the bitterness before using. Pickled caper buds should be rinsed under running tap water to remove excess salt.

Celeriac: A variety of celery with a thick root also known as knob celery or celery root. Regular thick-stalked celery can be substituted where celeriac is called for, but the flavor is much less mild.

Chard: Green leafy vegetable similar to spinach. There are two types, green leafy Swiss chard and ruby chard similar to beet greens. Rarely eaten raw.

Cioppino: An Italian dish of seafood and fish stewed with vegetables.

Coriander: Native herb plant of the parsley family. Ground dried seeds are used in many areas of the Mediterranean. Fresh green leaves are cilantro or Chinese parsley.

Couscous: Flour of millet or fine semolina steamed and served with meat and fish stews on the North African coast and elsewhere in the Mediterranean.

Cranberry beans: Red and beige mottled beans. Also known as borlotti beans.

Croquette: Small pieces of chopped fish, seafood, or vegetables bound with a sauce or batter, rolled in breadcrumbs, and fried.

Crudites: Vegetables, freshly cut into strips or bite-sized pieces and served raw with dips or sauces.

Diet, Mediterranean: See The Elemental Mediterranean: Olive, Oil, and Light, pages 6-7.

Fennel: Thick bulb vegetables with a licorice flavor.

Also called finocchio or Florence fennel. Its thin leaves resemble dill in appearance. Wild fennel grows all over the coastal areas of the Aegean and Eastern Mediterranean where it is widely used as an herb and a vegetable, eaten raw or cooked.

Fritters: Vegetables or other foods dipped in batter and fried.

Giouvetsi: A Greek clay or ceramic vessel used to cook food slowly directly on the fire or in the oven. The dishes take their name from it.

Greens, field: Fresh green leaf vegetables wild or cultivated are eaten raw or cooked everywhere in the Mediterranean. Included but not limited to amaranth, broccoli rabe, chard, collard, dandelions, escarole, endive, flowering kale, nettle, mustard, romaine (green leaf) lettuce, radicchio, rocket, spinach, sorrel, and watercress.

Herbs, aromatic: The cuisine of the Northern Mediterranean coast and the Aegean archipelago is characterized by its use of indigenous wild and cultivated herbs - basil, bay leaf, celery, chervil, cilantro, dillweed, fennel weed, marjoram, flat leaf parsley, spearmint, rosemary, oregano, saffron, sage, savory, tarragon, thyme. Likewise ground aniseed, coriander, cumin, and mustard are also popular in many areas. The cuisine of the Eastern and Southern Mediterranean makes more used of spice.

Julienne: Food cut into tiny matchstick-size pieces.

Lathouri: Small dried pulse also known as vetch or Santorini Island fava. Difficult to find outside the Mediterranean. Usually substituted by yellow split peas.

Macaroni: Hollow-type pasta of various thicknesses and lengths. Greek pastitsio macaroni is made into 10-inch (250cm) "tubes" of pasta which are cooked whole for the dish of the same name. Buy from a Greek supplier or substitute Italian ziti.

Minced: Very finely chopped.

Nuts: the most common nuts of the Mediterranean Region are almonds, hazelnuts (filberts), pistachios, pine nuts, and walnuts.

Oinomelo: Mixture of honey and wine used as a marinade in this book.

Olive oil: Juice of the olive fruit. Use natural cold-pressed (or first-pressed) extra virgin olive oil (less than .01% acidity) for salads, cooked vegetables, and instead of butter, margarine, or other fats (except for sweets and desserts). "Light" oils are often refined and lose their natural healthful properties. The color of olive oil ranges from a pale gold color to greenish-gold hue. Save expensive "boutique" olive oil for salads or addition at the end of cooking. The less expensive brands can be used for general cooking and frying. See also introduction to this book, The Elemental Mediterranean.

Orzo: A type of small pasta shaped like barley grains or melon seeds. Can be used instead of rice or bulgur.

Ouzo: A Greek anise or licorice-flavored alcoholic aperitif. A popular summer drink in the Aegean drunk either "on-the-rocks," or with ice-cold water. Similar to Italian grappa. Is also used in cooking.

Pasta: A Greek word that originally meant paste, now referring to dried dough made from hard wheat. The various types are best-known by their Italian names: fusilli (corkscrew), rigatoni (ribbed tubes), canneloni (large hollow tubes for stuffing), penne (medium tubes cut at an angle), farfalle (bowknots). Flat ribbons of various widths and lengths include lasgane, fettucine, tagliatelli, while string types are spaghetti, vermicelli. See also macaroni, tubular pasta.

Phyllo: Thin pliable fresh sheets of pastry (meaning leaf) made from flour and water. One of the world's most versatile edible culinary materials. Used in a variety of ways in Greek and other Mediterranean cuisines: as a wrapping, for baklava and other sweets, pies (pitas). It can be made by hand (see recipe in this book) or bought commercially. Use

#4 and #5 is suitable for appetizers, baklava, and bite-sized desserts. #7 and #10 are thicker, used for pouches, folding and wrapping, strudel, and Mediterranean country or rustic style dishes. Phyllo is pronounced "FEE-low."

Pilaf: A popular rice dish prepared from long-grain rice so grains remain separate, not soft and glutinous.

Pit(t)a: A Greek word referring to two entirely different dough products. (1) Round or oval flat-breads also known as Arab pocket bread or (2) any one of a number of flat (usually round) sweet or savory pies made in Greece with sheets of phyllo pastry.

Puree: Method of blending or sieving the pulp of ripe or cooked foods into a smooth thick viscous liquid. Purees are often used to thicken sauces or soups.

Rissoles: Finely chopped ingredients bound with breadcrumbs, flour, or other starch, rolled into sausage-shapes, and fried.

Risotto: The Italian way of cooking short to medium-grain rice (Arborio) with stock and chopped vegetables, meat, or poultry.

Saffron: Stigmas from the "crocus sativas" flowers, indigenous to the Aegean and other areas of the Mediterranean. Prized for thousands of years as a yellow dye, it has been used at least since the Byzantine (medieval) period in cookery. Natural Greek red saffron is cultivated in Greek Macedonia near the town of Krokos (Greek word for saffron crocus). 80% of the crop is exported to Spain, France, and Italy where it is more widely used in cooking than in Greece.

Saganaki: A 2-handled shallow frying pan used to quickly fry or braise small portions of food - cheese, seafood, etc. These dishes take their name from it.

Saute: In this cookbook, saute refers to the method of quickly stir-cooking or frying onions or other chopped vegetables in oil or margarine until wilted but not browned.

Semolina: A coarse-milled flour of hard or Durham wheat. Similar to North American "cream of wheat": which can be substituted.

Taramas: Salt-preserved fish roe (tiny eggs) from cod, gray mullet, carp, herring, or other fish. The quality of taramas ranges from the full-flavored light beige roe, the most expensive, to the cheaper but less tasty pink. Some taramas is naturally light pink. The bright pink-colored type is artificially tinted. Many cooks combine the beige type for flavor with a small amount of pink roe which improves the appearance of taramosalata and other dishes made with taramas.

Tahini/tahine: Sesame seed paste used in many Greek and Middle Eastern dishes, such as hummus. In this book, it is used as a substitute for olive oil in some recipes.

Timbale: A dish cooked in a special round mold or bowl lined with potatoes, sliced vegetables, or pasta.

Truffles: Edible white or black fungi grown underground near oak trees. Prized for their special flavor.

TVP - Textured Vegetable Protein: The commercial name for the dried ground meat substitute made from concentrated soya protein, soya isolates, and wheat gluten. It contains no fat or cholesterol. It must be re-hydrated in order to use (see basic recipes).

Vegetarian cheese or cream: In this book, this term refers to those non-dairy products available on the market.

Zest: The grated rind of orange or lemon.

*NOTE: The majority of ingredients for the recipes in this cookbook are available in most supermarkets and groceries everywhere. Those more specific items can be found in food stores specializing in Greek, Italian, and Middle Eastern products.